FIRST BOOK OF
MODERN ELECTRONICS
FUN PROJECTS

FIRST BOOK OF MODERN ELECTRONICS FUN PROJECTS

EDITED BY ART SALSBERG

Howard W. Sams & Co.
A Division of Macmillan, Inc.
4300 West 62nd Street, Indianapolis, IN 46268 USA

Dedication
To the memory of my father, Sol Salsberg,
whose electronics and writing skills inspired me.

International Standard Book Number: 0-672-22503-4
Library of Congress Catalog Card Number: 86-62440

Acquired: *Greg Michael*
Editor: *C. Herbert Feltner*
Interior Design: *T. R. Emrick*
Cover Art: *Lawrence Simmons*
Composition: *Shepard Poorman Communications Corp.,*
Indianapolis

Trademarks
X-ACTO is a registered trademark of the Hunt Manufacturing Co.
E-Z Circuit is a trademark of Bishop Graphics.
Dynaquad probably is a trademark of Dynaco.

Printed in the United States of America

CONTENTS

PREFACE

This book presents electronic construction projects that are either unique or can save a builder considerable money when compared to the price of commercial products.

The construction projects presented here are based on material featured in *Modern Electronics* magazine (76 N. Broadway, Hicksville, NY 11801), and represent the ones that generated the most reader enthusiasm. In many instances they have been refined, as well as occasional glitches being corrected. Sources of parts, printed-circuit boards, and even complete parts kits are noted in each project's Parts List whenever available to simplify gathering of material to build the construction projects from plans published here.

The book is divided into eight sections

- "Introduction to Electronic Projects," which recaps what tools are needed, construction approaches to take, how to make printed-circuit boards without using etching chemicals, etc.
- "Home Electronics," which are useful products for use around the house or apartment to make life more pleasant and efficient.
- "Audio/Video Electronics," which will heighten your listening and viewing fun.
- "Security Electronics," which include plans for making devices to protect your life and your possessions.
- "Telephone Electronics," which shows you how to make unusual use of an instrument that's in everyone's home.

- "Computers," which features complementary electronic products for this electronic marvel.
- "Test Equipment," which gives you the means to experiment with electronic circuits and to extend your servicing ability beyond what you think is possible with limited funds.
- "Electronic Designing," which illustrates how to create your very own circuitry.

Of course, all the "how it works" and "how to build" information is packed into each project. All of them have been built and tested by experienced electronics people who, happily, share their electronics adventures with you. You'll have a lot of fun building and using their creations, as well as increasing your technical competence in a rewarding area. So go for it!

I would like to express my appreciation and admiration to the creative authors who dreamed up these wonderful electronic circuits, built the models that were then tested by *Modern Electronics* editors, and wrote the details that are served up for your reading and building pleasure in the following pages. My special thanks, too, to *Modern Electronics'* staff, without whom these construction projects would not have been produced, and to my wife, Rhoda, who assisted me in assembling the material contained in this book.

ART SALSBERG

Introduction to Electronic Projects

chapter 1

The tools and concepts needed to set up for home electronics construction work

Getting Started in Building Electronic Projects

ART SALSBERG

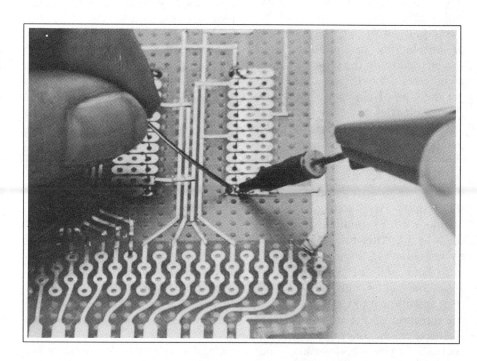

Anyone who embarks on building electronic devices—whether they are projects built from plans in books or magazines, from kit instructions, or from one's own circuit designs—quickly learns that it cannot be done with bare hands. One must use some appropriate tools and devices to do the job effectively.

Happily, it takes only a very modest amount of money to set the foundation for constructing most electronic devices that are not designed to meet military specifications. The basic tools are simple and are widely available from electronics retailers and electronics mail-order companies. They are as follows:

- Soldering iron kit.
- Multimeter.
- Integrated circuit (IC) extractor.
- Hand tools
    diagonal cutting pliers
    long-nose pliers
    set of nut drivers
    blade and Phillips
      screwdrivers
    wire stripper.

Even if you have none of the foregoing in your toolbox, you can buy the whole lot for less than $25 if you limit yourself to the least expensive ones on the market. If you're a serious electronics construction enthusiast, you'd want better-quality tools, of course, which would be more costly. Moreover, there are more devices and instruments you can buy to expand your construction horizons and make your work more efficient. Nonetheless, you can get started with a very low investment.

Soldering Gear

A soldering iron and rosin-core solder are the key tools needed for electronic construction. Together, they make possible electrically sound connections between various circuit points.

For modern electronic circuit work you should use only a low-power iron, say, 25 watts, not the 150-watt types used for work on vacuum-tubed TV sets. Excessive heat can quickly destroy a transistor or integrated circuit, so anything you do to diminish the amount of heat transferred to such devices while joining their leads with solder is beneficial.

In addition to using a low-wattage soldering iron, the amount of time that the iron's heated tip is applied to a device should be as short as possible. Two seconds is about maximum. Furthermore, a heat sink or clip is a useful soldering aid. Attached between the soldering iron point and the device, the heat sink will transfer heat away from the device's body while you're soldering or unsoldering (a long-nose plier can be used to do the same task, but a clip frees a hand). Make sure you get the type of clip that solder and flux won't stick to.

Judging which soldering-iron temperature is best and how long or short a time period you should apply the hot tip is an art. You learn by doing some soldering and observing the results. Heat copper foil and component lead simultaneously with the iron tip. After bringing them up to temperature (about 2 seconds), push the end of small-diameter rosin-core solder into the junction area and allow it to melt and flow in the direction of the iron tip. When the solder is smooth and well formed, remove both solder and iron and allow the joint to cool without being disturbed. A good companion book to project building is *Electronic Prototype Construction* (21895), Howard W. Sams & Co.

Choosing a Soldering Iron

As with most equipment, there are cheap versions and high-quality ver-

sions of soldering irons. If you're at all serious about electronic construction, it pays to invest in the latter. The cheap irons come with permanent tips, for example, which limits your soldering effectiveness.

It's best to get a soldering iron with replaceable tips because different solder jobs are handled best with tips designed especially for them. Solder work might be more efficient with, say, a micro-size tip, a long-taper chisel tip, or a conical-tapered tip, and so on. Further, for desoldering work there are special tips that can desolder all pins of an IC simultaneously, which is necessary in this instance to remove the entire device (Fig. 1.1).

In addition to having a soldering iron that can accommodate different tips, it's nice to be able to switch heating elements, too. This way, you can use, perhaps, a 25-watt element for soldering those heat-sensitive solid-state devices, switching to, say, a 45-watt element to make it easier to solder heavy-gauge wires to a connector point. These elements are sold separately and are simply screwed in to the soldering iron's body in place of another element.

Upgrading Further

The pencil-type soldering irons described are the most comfortable ones to use, as compared to the "gun"-style ones. There are different pencil-like shapes and balances,

so try your hand on them before you buy if you can.

If you can justify spending more money, it's nice to have a temperature-controlled soldering station. These are "smart" soldering-iron systems that use a closed-loop control circuit to continuously monitor tip temperature and keep it at the temperature you set it. Typically, this might be selectable from 400 to 800 degrees F, with wattage on demand from about 18 to 70 watts. These systems come with an iron holder and sponge, too. Some have temperature meters, while more costly ones have digital readouts. Most systems are grounded for safe MOS and CMOS work—these devices are very sensitive to static discharge. If you do a lot of soldering work, the soldering-iron system is well worth the extra cost.

There are cordless, battery-powered soldering irons that are handy to use because you're not tied to a line cord. They're made by Wahl Clipper and come with a convenient battery-charger stand. The iron even has a little light bulb that illuminates the work area. The iron recharges fully inside of an hour and has a fast-charge provision should you lose power in the middle of an incomplete solder joint. Also, there are lots of different tips available for this unit, as well as a miniature printed-circuit board drill attachment that can save you considerable bother when a hole is needed in a board. Watch out for CMOS device applications, though,

Fig. 1.1. A typical low-wattage soldering iron. (Courtesy OK Industries, Inc.)

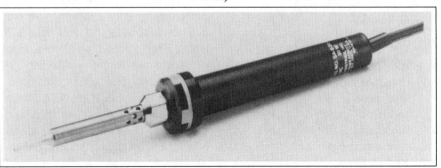

since the iron isn't grounded. The iron is heavier and bulkier than regular soldering irons, but, again, is very handy.

The Extras

As cited earlier, there are some extra devices to make soldering work more convenient to do. Among them is the solder-aid rod, measuring about 6 inches (152 mm) long with steel ends. One end is usually a reamer to clean out printed-circuit-board holes, while the other end is generally a fork to move wires and pins around without risking burning a finger. Some rods are designed with an angle to get into difficult spots, while others have a steel brush at one end to brush away solder balls that could form from solder drippings. Be sure that the ones you buy have a chrome finish so that solder won't stick to it. The rods cost about $2 each.

If you don't buy a soldering-iron kit or system, you'll need a soldering-iron holder or stand so that you can place down a hot soldering iron without worrying about starting a fire. Soldering-iron holders have an open-metal design and generally come with a built-in sponge to clean the iron's tip from time to time to remove oxidation that builds up.

Solder tips are made of copper due to the material's fine heat conductivity. The tips should come plated with iron, though, because tin from the solder itself will damage pure copper (which is why the device is called an ''iron'' not a ''copper''). Iron is not as good a conductor of heat as copper and it oxidizes easily. To minimize oxidation, therefore, you should always ''tin'' the iron with a coating of solder chosen for electronic work, which is a mix of tin and lead with a rosin-flux core. The rosin removes oxidation and other contaminants that prevent good joining of metals

such as transistor leads to a pc-board's copper pads.

There are a few other items that will come in handy if you do much soldering work on pc boards. One is a pc-board holder that can be adjusted to position a board for comfortable work. Panavise popularized this, adding the pc board holder device to a vise whose body was designed to be secured to a surface by means of suction. Lamps with magnifiers offer the assembler fine viewing of a printed circuit board's work area. This will minimize eye strain when soldering in small areas for long time periods.

Another very useful product for anyone doing a lot of work with pc boards is a repair kit. Even the most experienced sometimes overheat a foil pattern and ruin it. A company named Pace in Maryland sells its CirKits for just such situations to repair or replace pc land areas—a land area is where you make the device-to-pc board connection. The kits have plated-through hole replacements and a wide selection of pad diameters. Similarly, another company, Automated Production Equipment, offers what it calls track repair, which includes plated-through holes with swagging eyelets.

Bishop Graphics has all manner of foil and pad replacements that are simply laid on the board and held by adhesive on the back side. Dry transfers are produced by Datak Products, which, like a host of other companies, also makes a photo-etch kit so that you can make pc boards directly from published foil patterns such as those in this book.

The foregoing printed-circuit-

board products are sold by many local electronics stores, including Radio Shack across the country and Dick Smith Electronics in California (Redwood City, Berkeley, San Jose, and Los Angeles). Should you have a simple break, the easiest way to repair it is to string a piece of 18- or 20-gauge stranded wire from one land to another, bypassing the damaged foil altogether.

Desoldering

As important as soldering is for electronic construction work, desoldering is also important. Desoldering is often a frustrating experience because you've already done your soldering work and then discover that you soldered the wrong unit into place, mixed up the leads, or have to replace a defective component.

It's often impossible to desolder a device without the proper desoldering tools especially when you're desoldering a part that has many pins, such as an IC. This chore becomes even more difficult with repair work on manufacturer-assembled equipment, where wave soldering plants electronic parts onto copper lands or pads (Fig. 1.2).

To minimize desolder efforts and prevent heat damage, it's wise to solder in an IC socket to a board then plug the IC into the socket. To remove a defective IC, simply pry out the old one and plug in a new one.

To unsolder leads from a transistor isn't an overwhelming job, but you must be careful that you do not destroy the solid-state device, which you might discover is really not defective. Just remember to use your

Fig. 1.2. A desoldering tool with air-pressure plunger. (Courtesy Wahl Clipper Industrial Products)

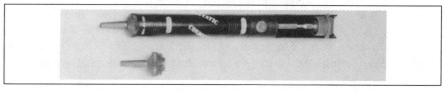

heat-transfer clip and to avoid applying heat too long to the connection point.

Too often, however, you'll find that you must get rid of some solder before you can enjoy a successful part removal. Here are a few ways to do this, using cleverly designed workshop helpers. A popular "tool" for this purpose is the solder wick.

A solder wick is simply braided metal with high heat conductivity that absorbs melted solder. Just heat the wick when it's in contact with the solder that you want to remove and watch the solder flow into the wick. For your convenience, the wick, which generally costs less than $2, comes in different widths. Try to get the type that has some rosin flux integrated so that there won't be any damage due to residues left over.

A more exotic tool for this application that's a bit more costly is the desoldering pump. These solder-sucking devices use air to draw in molten solder. With some you press a button; with others you push a plunger. Whatever method, you're using vacuum power to remove molten solder. Prices for these devices range from $5 to $20. You can melt the solder with an iron and use a rubberized bulb with a Teflon tip that costs only about $2. Professional electric desoldering systems, in contrast, cost many hundreds of dollars.

If you're working with CMOS devices, be sure that your pump has anti-static provisions.

To unsolder an IC you'll need the appropriate desoldering tip. This is a rectangular solder tip that fits over all the pins of the device you're unsoldering so that solder is melted from all leads at the same time for easier removal of the device. You must use such a tip rather than work with a standard soldering tip because as soon as you melt solder on one pin and turn to the next, the former would harden. The most popular desoldering tip used is

made for the standard dual-in-line IC package or DIP.

Even with the foregoing, pulling an IC out of the circuit board is not always an easy chore. To do this without pain (and possible damage to the device) you often need an IC extractor. This might be a spring-loaded dual in-line tool that's applied to the chip topside at the same time you're desoldering pins on the bottom side of the pc board. Pressing a button on the extractor exerts an upward pressure on the device so that when solder holding its pins is melted, the device is pulled up and out. If you wish, you can buy a cheaper puller for this purpose that resembles a tweezer and use your own muscle power.

Other Basic Needs

Every electronics constructor should own a multimeter to measure resistance and voltage. Although you can buy inexpensive analog meters for under $10, they're not highly accurate or sensitive, but can do the basic job for you in many instances.

Your best buy would be a digital multimeter (DMM), however, which has a high input impedance that would not greatly disturb a circuit when measuring voltage. Selling prices start at about $30 for "off-brand" units. Higher accuracy, better construction and name-brand warranty pushes the price much higher, naturally (Fig. 1.3).

For some projects you'll need a signal generator, an oscilloscope, or a frequency counter, depending on what you're building. It doesn't pay to buy these instruments if you anticipate that the particular project you're building will be a once or twice in a lifetime assembly. You can usually borrow one from a friend or have the friend check the finished project for you. But if you are deep into building all manner of

Fig. 1.3. Handheld digital multimeters, such as the one shown here, are very popular today to measure volts, amperes, and ohms. (Courtesy Beckman Industrial Corp)

projects, you'll have to give serious consideration to purchasing more advanced equipment.

In time, maybe sooner than you think, you'll likely want to get a logic probe or monitor and a pulse generator so that you can "see" what's going on in a digital circuit, design your own circuit, or troubleshoot a circuit that isn't performing properly.

For experimenting with your own circuit designs, you'll also require a power supply and prototype boards where devices can be popped into holes and wired on the back.

At the Gate

With the foregoing at hand, you're ready to begin electronic construction. You will note that many projects in this book require printed-circuit boards. Some finished boards are available from a source that's noted in the parts list. After purchasing these, all you have to do is plug in the parts as illustrated in the project and do the necessary soldering.

Some projects require that you fabricate the printed circuit. The blank boards for the circuit you're replicating and etching chemicals are available from a wide variety of local and mail-order sources, as cited earlier. Instructions often come with boards, but if you're unfamiliar with transferring foil patterns as shown in projects that will follow, double check this. Foil pattern versions of the circuits for projects in this book are the precise size required, so don't reduce or enlarge them if you photocopy from a printed page.

One side of a printed-circuit board is fully covered with a layer of copper, called the foil side. The foil pattern is applied to this side, then the copper outside this pattern is etched away. The other side, where the components are mounted, is called the component side. Note that there are different board thicknesses available and different board materials. Typically, pc board thickness ranges from $1/64$ to $1/8$ inch; the price increases with the thickness. Base material is generally paper-base phenolic; fiberglass-base boards are stronger and cost more. You'll have to drill holes for component leads to go through once the foil pattern has been etched, of course. Drill holes are shown on the foil patterns in this book.

Alternatively, you can fabricate a circuit on perforated boards, doing the required wiring on the reverse side while mounting the parts on the other side. Some projects presented in this book use this method.

For the latter, you can hand wire a circuit, soldering the proper connection points, or you can use wire-wrap procedures. In order to use wire wrapping, you have to have wire-wrap boards with wrap posts, DIP wire-wrap sockets, a roll of special thin wire-wrap wire, and a wire-wrap tool. Using a wire-wrap hand tool for this purpose, the wire (which is an insulated, solid type, with ends that have to be bared) is wrapped tightly around the metal posts. A minimal wire-wrap set with tool, wire, 14-pin and 16-pin DIP sockets, and a board costs about $22. Wire wrapping is an art that takes practice to make good, neat connections. Using this method obviates most solder work since the tightly wound coils of wire make fine electrical contact with the metal posts.

Automatic, battery-powered wrap tools are available to make the wire-wrap job a simple task. Wire is fed automatically and cut off whenever the user wishes to do so. Additionally, the tool eliminates the need to precut and prestrip wire. In use, one simply places the tool's tip over a post and simply presses a trigger. The tool costs about $55 in light-duty form. If you do a lot of wire-wrap work, it's a good investment.

Finally, you will probably want to place the entire circuit board in some sort of enclosure. To aid you, there are chassis punches available to make selected holes in the case and nibbling tools for cutting sheet metal. All this is generally available at your local electronics store. If you wish, you may dress up an enclosure so that it looks like a commercially made product, using silk screening, paint, or other decorative means.

Buying Parts

The construction projects presented in this book are generally accompanied by a parts list that lists components shown in the project's schematic. When a supplier of a kit of parts is available, the supplier is listed.

When a kit of parts is offered, you can order the kit or gather the parts by yourself through suppliers, or use the parts that you already have. In the event that a project does not list a parts supplier, you'll have to buy them from other sources.

There are a variety of electronics parts sources available to you locally and nationally. The latter is through mail-order houses, of course. Many of the more popular electronic devices and other parts can be secured through Radio Shack or other retail stores in your area. If you are an electronics professional, you may have access to parts distributors for this purpose, simplifying your search.

Among the many mail-order companies that can serve your parts needs are the following:

All Electronics Corp., P.O. BOX 20406, Los Angeles, CA 90006 (1-800-826-5432).

Digi-Key Corp., P.O. BOX 677, Thief River Falls, MN 56701 (1 800-344-4539).

JDR Microdevices, 1224 S. Bascom Ave., San Jose, CA 95128 (1 800-535-5000).

Jameco Electronics, 1355 Shoreway Road, Belmont, CA 94002 (415-592-8097)

MCM Electronics, 858 East Congress Park Drive, Centerville, OH 45459 (1-800-543-4330).

All of these require a minimum order of $10 plus shipping charges, Digi-Key excepted. Digi-Key has a $2 service charge for orders below $10. Radio Shack has a special-order service for which it claims that most semiconductor orders can be filled through a central warehouse system with no minimum order or postage charge.

In many instances, parts cannot be obtained from a single source.

This is bothersome, but searching out a few different sources, though a bit time-consuming, is part of the electronics hobby adventure.

Conclusion

Most of the electronic construction projects presented in this book are easy to build and should provide you with many hours of building pleasure that are capped by completed products that are not usually available in manufactured form.

There are a smattering of complex projects that will challenge the more advanced builder.

If you are unfamiliar with electronics and have some difficulty understanding terms, schematics, and so on, basic books are available at your library and publisher to help you and bolster your confidence in tackling these projects. Further, most projects describe how the circuits work, so that they constitute a practical learning course unto themselves.

Should you need some hand hold-ing while assembling the projects here, try your local amateur radio club to get some assistance, or your local electronics parts dealer is usually pleased to help out. As a final note, try to set aside a separate work area for your electronics construction work. A kitchen table is a last resort, though it has been used successfully by many builders . . . . Happy building!

The "Easy Circuit" Way to Make Circuit Boards

HAROLD WRIGHT

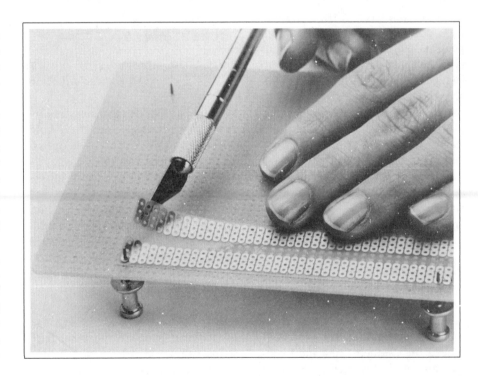

There are a variety of ways to produce printed circuits singly. Typically, photochemical techniques are used on copper-laminated boards. This method enables a builder to accurately replicate printed-circuit foil patterns such as those printed along with construction projects. To many people this is an odious task, requiring photographic methods, dealing with messy chemicals, drilling component-lead pad holes, and careful monitoring time.

An interesting alternate method, our subject, avoids all this, substituting instead the laying down of pressure-sensitive, copper-clad tape on predrilled boards. This E-Z Circuit™ system by Bishop Graphics. Inc., Westlake Village, CA, is examined here.

The Materials

Pressure-sensitive materials used with E-Z Circuit come in the form of copper patterns that are laminated to a thin layer of epoxy-fiberglass substrate. The underside of the substrate is coated with a special adhesive that is protected by a release liner. The adhesive is formulated to provide both good shelf life (as long as the release liner hasn't been disturbed) and good adhesion when the liner is removed and the pattern is placed on an appropriate circuit-board substrate. Patterns can be interconnected with copper tapes of various widths. The tapes have no substrate; instead, the adhesive is applied directly to one side and is protected by a peel-away release liner.

Adhesion of the patterns and tapes increases with time up to about 48 hours after the liner is removed and the materials are placed on the circuit board material. After 48 hours of curing, adhesion is approximately twice as good as it was after one hour. A pattern or tape can be removed and repositioned up to 24 hours after it has been applied to a circuit board. However, patterns removed after about 24 hours are generally no longer reusable, since their adhesion will have diminished to near zero.

Pressure-sensitive patterns and tapes will bond to most epoxy-glass circuit-board materials. However, they will not bond to Teflon or untreated polyolefin boards. So keep this in mind when you're planning to translate a circuit's conductor pattern to a working board design.

Many types of pressure-sensitive patterns are available (see Fig. 2.1), including pads for ICs and transistors, donuts for terminating a copper-conductor run, and various types ranging in width from 1/64 to 1/4 inch (0.40 to 6.35 mm). You'll also find circuit board edge connector patterns for plug-in boards, multiple parallel tapes on a single substrate, power distribution strips, and many others. If you need a special purpose pattern that isn't available you can make your own by cutting them from a sheet of cut-and-peel copper, which also has the special adhesive on one side.

Perhaps the most versatile pattern in use today is the DIP strip popularly used for dual in-line package (hence the DIP acronym) integrated circuits. Such strips contain two continuous rows of pads spaced on 1/10 inch (2.54 mm) centers and with 3/10 inch (7.62 mm) spacing between the rows. Each pad can have two, three or four holes.

DIP strips can be cut to the lengths needed for use with 8-, 14-, 16-, 18-, and 20-pin DIP ICs, as well as for DIP-type bridge rectifier assemblies and optocouplers that require only four pads. They are equally useful for mounting DIP

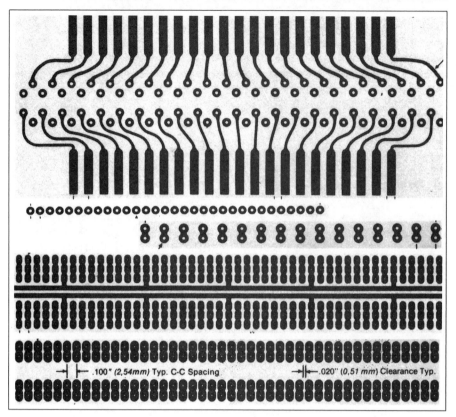

Fig. 2.1. Many types of pressure-sensitive patterns are available, as demonstrated by the small sampling shown here.

switches and DIP-type resistor arrays. The double- and triple-hole strips can be very useful where two or three components must meet. Also, these strips can be used as termination points where a row of resistors and/or capacitors must mate with wires leaving the board.

For 24- to 40-pin ICs, there are strips available with the 6/10 inch (15.24 mm) row spacing required for these devices. However, if you don't anticipate heavy use for these strips and prefer to save the expense of stocking them, the narrower DIP strips can be cut down the center and manually spaced when you do need them.

Even if you're committed to point-to-point wiring, the pads alone will greatly simplify the task of obtaining good, reliable connections to IC and socket pins. While it costs more to use self-adhering patterns than to go strictly the point-to-point wiring route, it costs less than going

the make-it-yourself printed-circuit board route. As compared to wire-wrapping circuits, it's easier to trace when troubleshooting and much simpler to make last-minute changes in the circuit.

Planning the Layout

The procedure for planning the copper tape-and-pattern layout of a given circuit is much the same as that for a printed-circuit layout. If you're laying out a project of your own design, it's a good idea to first assemble the circuit on a solderless socket board and check out its operation to be certain it performs as you want it to.

The next step is to redraw the schematic diagram with the ICs and transistors shown as they appear on the conductor side of the board, assuming this is available. Keep in mind that pinout diagrams are invariably top views for ICs and usually bottom views for transistors. Keep in mind when the IC is on the board and is examined from the *conductor* side, its image will be reversed.

Since many circuits are multiple-device ICs nowadays, we'll use one such as our design example. In the schematic diagram, the triangles that represent the single sections of a quad op amp (Fig. 2.2) are placed to give the simplest, easiest-to-follow circuit. When the circuit is converted to this new format as shown, it may not look simple at all from the circuit board component layout point of view. The schematic layout in Fig. 2.2 has been planned for maximum simplicity, while Fig. 2.3 shows a conductor layout for the circuit.

When working out the first crude layout of a circuit's conductor pattern, one of the limitations of the tape system may be encountered—insufficient space to run a trace between two pads. Although this is a common practice in photochemically produced pc boards, where the pads are made very narrow, you won't normally be able to do this with pressure-sensitive materials. However, if there's an unused pin on an IC that doesn't have to be grounded or tied to B+ (as in the case with all CMOS and some non-CMOS devices), the pad for that pin can be trimmed away to leave a space wide enough for two narrow tape runs, as shown in Fig. 2.4. If you should do this, make sure to cut away the corresponding pin from the socket or IC so that it doesn't protrude through the hole and contact the tape.

Tape runs down the center between the rows of pads spaced $3/10$ inch (7.62 mm) apart are generally limited to three or four, using the narrower tapes. Patterns with $6/10$ inch (15.24 mm) spacing between rows of pads have more space and, thus, accommodate a greater number of end runs. Keep these points in mind as the layout develops.

Note in Fig. 2.3 that many tape runs don't terminate in donut pads. This occurs when several tape runs end side by side and are spaced $1/10$ inch (2.54 mm) apart. Since only very small donut pads could be used in such a case, soldering is much simpler if you puncture the end runs with a darning needle through the underlying holes. Note also in Fig. 2.3 that considerable use has been made of two hole pads snipped from a DIP pattern.

Although Fig. 2.3 is a view from the conductor side, the components are shown in the positions they would normally occupy on the other side of the board. This has been done here to aid in relating Fig. 2.2 to Fig. 2.3. Normal practice when showing component placement gives a component-side view of the board assembly. If such a diagram is needed, it can be derived from the conductor-side pattern simply by laying the latter wrong side up on a piece of glass, shining a light through, and tracing the pattern onto a sheet of paper. Then all you need do is add the components to the tracing.

When you use pressure-sensitive materials, you can frequently avoid

Fig. 2.2. An example of a typical circuit used in modern electronics. Schematic diagram shown is very different from conductor pattern.

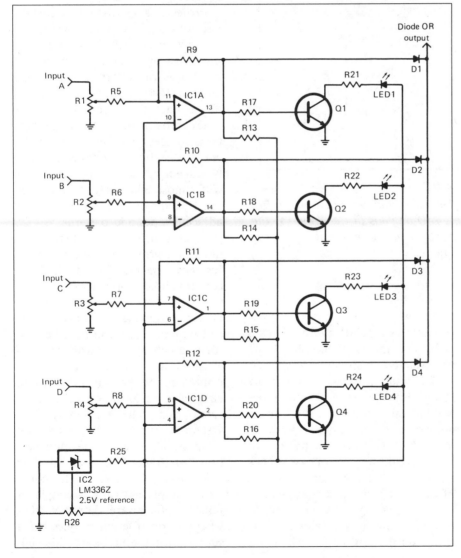

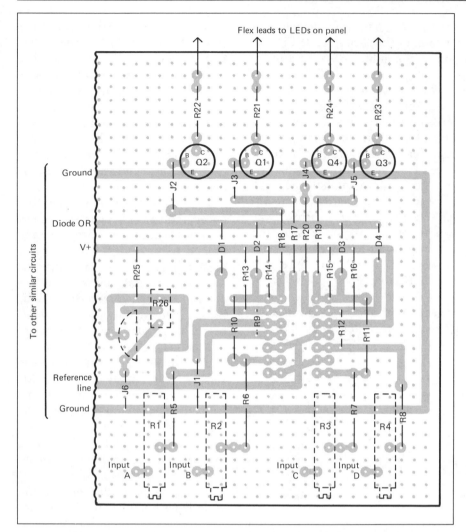

Fig. 2.3. This is the conductor pattern for the partial circuit shown in Fig. 2.2. Note that IC1 plugs into the double row of pads in the center of the drawing, between resistors R9 and R12. This is not a practical circuit for you to build.

also film substrates with grids available from the copper pattern manufacturers and their distributors.

Working on a dotted grid will make it easy to determine if there will be room on the final board for the various components and how much space will be needed between each. For example, a standard 1/4-watt resistor will require five holes spaced 1/10 inch (2.54 mm) apart (one hole for each lead and three holes for the resistor body). If the same resistor is mounted on end, you may need no more than 2/10 inch (5.1 mm) of space. For other components, simply measure their bodies, taking into account lead requirements, and size your layout accordingly.

Projects using this system are easiest to wire if you use perforated board with 1/10 inch (2.54 mm) spacing between holes. Attempts to place a set of patterns and tapes on a nonperforated board blank can be disastrous, since you must drill holes through the holes in the patterns. Unless you use exactly the correct size bit and get the bit exactly on-center, the patterns and tapes will almost invariably "climb" the bit, perhaps even taking with them adjacent tapes and patterns.

When your layout is satisfactorily drawn on grid paper, simply transfer it to the perf board blank by counting holes horizontally and vertically. You will find that your tape layout is equivalent to a printed-circuit pattern. It can, in fact, be used for photochemical pc work at a later time should the need arise. Also printed-circuit layouts provided in electronics magazines can be duplicated using the tape-and-pattern system. If runs are shown between IC pins, however, some modification of the etching-and-drilling guide may be necessary. This could be as simple as using a couple of jumpers. Be aware, however, that where a construction project has a supplier for the pc board, it's sim-

the need for jumper wires. Pressure-sensitive insulating tape is available in various widths. When snipped to size and applied over existing conductors, you can bridge the conductors with copper tape to obtain insulated and mechanically stable crossovers (Fig. 2.5) without having to resort to traditional wire-in jumpers. This technique will usually suffice, except in high-frequency circuits and especially with wider tapes. (Where the tapes cross, a tiny capacitor is formed and at high frequencies could cause unwanted coupling between traces.) If in doubt, use a standard wire jumper

on the *component* side of the board. Beneficially, if a wide positive supply tape crosses a wide ground bus tape, a small r-f bypass effect is obtained. Figure 2.5 shows an insulated crossover.

The final drawing of the scale layout for the patterns and tapes will be easier to draw if the work is done on grid paper, preferably with 1/10 inch (2.54 mm) spacing. It will be easier still if you work two times actual size. A large scale equivalent of standard perforated board can be made by placing ink dots every 2/10 inch (5.1 mm) horizontally and vertically on the grid paper. There are

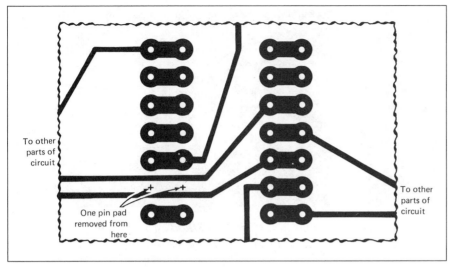

Fig. 2.4. How to route one or more conductors between IC pins. Use this technique only if unused IC pins do not have to be tied to B+ or grounded.

pler, less time-consuming and usually less expensive to purchase the ready-made board, especially if it's very complex.

Another method of board construction uses cut-and-peel copper sheets. Applying a copper sheet to a board blank allows you to draw the conductor pattern directly on the copper and to use an X-ACTO® knife to cut away unwanted copper. This method, however, should be confined to simpler circuits, such as a power supply, and be used in conjunction with standard prefabricated patterns.

Tape runs must follow straight lines and various angles—but no curves! Don't attempt to bend a tape into an arc, no matter how narrow the tape or shallow the arc. This isn't really a handicap, because most routing required can be produced with a series of wide angles at the expense of a few extra solder joints. While 90° patterns are available, they do add an extra joint and increase cost.

Getting It onto the Board

If you prepared a 1:1 or 2:1 drawing of the required pattern, assembly will go very quickly. The drawing should have a frame around it to define the size and shape of the final board (and that takes into account the needs of mounting hardware). Get the DIP patterns in place first. Count the number of holes from a reference corner in both directions in your diagram to determine where to place the first pattern, aligned with the same hole on the board.

To aid in registering patterns, insert a bulletin-board push pin into the reference hole from the component side of the board. If you don't have a board-holding jig or vise, push three or more pins through holes near the corners of the board to keep it level on your work surface.

If a 14-pin pattern is to be positioned, cut off 14 sections in one piece from the DIP strip and peel off the release liner. Figure 2.6 shows one method for getting the release liner started. The liner can also be started from a corner by using a fingernail to pry it up. Figure 2.7 shows how to use the push pin to achieve accurate alignment between patterns and board holes. Alignment is sometimes more easily accomplished with a pair of large darning needles.

Use a fine pointed tweezer to handle the pattern and avoid finger contact with the adhesive side. Slide the pattern's outermost hole over the pin (or spear the hole on one

Fig. 2.5. Insulated crossover, shown to right of IC pad, obviates need for a physical wire jumper in many cases.

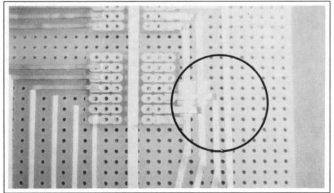

Fig. 2.6. Shown here is one way to get the release liner started. Use sharp-pointed tweezers for handling patterns.

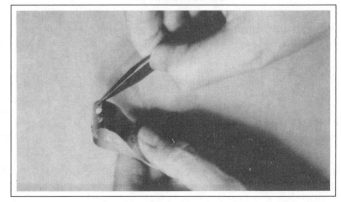

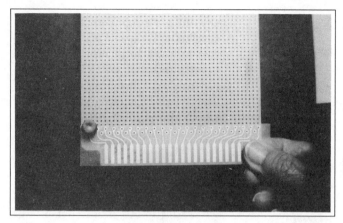

Fig. 2.7. How to use registration pins to obtain correct alignment between perf board and E-Z Circuit pattern holes.

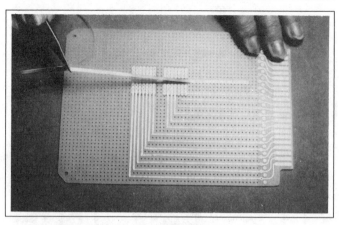

Fig. 2.8. Correct method of laying out tape. Use tweezers to avoid unnecessary handling of tape copper and adhesive.

darning needle) and line it up so that the row of holes is in exact registration with the row on the board. A darning needle can be used at the other end of the pattern to further aid in registering the pattern. If the pad is a bit out of line, it can be levered into position with the darning needle.

When the pattern is properly aligned, press it firmly onto the board's surface. Hold the pad down alongside the needle with a fingernail and remove the needle and push-pin. Firmly press the pattern down over its entire surface. However, try to avoid touching the raw copper traces on the pattern and the copper tapes when you use them with your fingers. Place a piece of paper or plastic film over them before you use your fingers to press the patterns and tapes into place.

With all IC and transistor patterns in place, the circuit's conductor pattern can be completed by following your drawing to interconnect the various points with copper tape. Where there's room, terminate the tape ends with donut pads.

A word of caution: When a roll of copper tape is first used, it has a tendency to unravel. If it does this, the tape is almost impossible to roll up again. If you succeed in getting it rolled up again, it will invariably be kinked and wrinkled in places.

When this occurs, the release liner is likely to work loose, allowing the adhesive to dry out and rendering those portions of the tape useless. To prevent any of this from happening, it's a good idea to gently press newly opened tape packs onto the adhesive side of a piece of wide masking tape to keep it wound.

Figure 2.8 shows a short length of tape being positioned on a circuit board. Figure 2.9 shows a short length of tape positioned to connect with a DIP pad being trimmed to

the correct length with an X-AC-TO® knife.

There are two methods for making connections between two tapes. The manufacturer recommends butting together the two tapes and then flow-soldering the ends at the joint. If the ends of the tapes don't butt exactly and the cuts aren't precise, you'll have difficulty getting the solder to "take" across the joint. Even a hairline separation between the two butt ends will defeat soldering. Solder will build up on both sides of the joint

Fig. 2.9. Shown here is a short length of adhesive-backed copper tape being positioned to connect to a DIP pad. The terminating end of the tape is best trimmed cleanly and squarely with an X-ACTO® knife or other very sharp cutting tool.

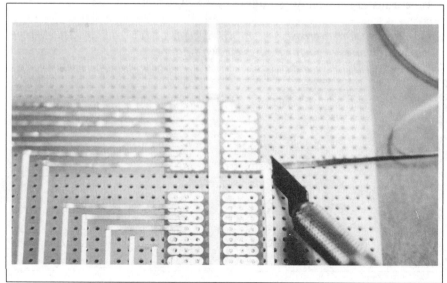

and refuse to flow together. This is the same action that's so much of an asset when soldering the closely spaced pads on the IC DIP pattern.

The second method requires less precision when cutting the tape. Here, the tapes are overlapped and burnished flat. Figure 2.10 illustrates good and bad examples for overlap joints. (With both methods of joining tapes and tapes to other patterns, it's essential that the ends be absolutely flat. There must be no curl where they meet or overlap. If any curl is overlooked, the joint, when soldered, might appear to be perfect but will usually be an open circuit.)

It is essential that every soldered junction be checked with a low-range ohmmeter *as soon as it is made!* If you wait until you've finished soldering all joints, you're likely to miss one or two, each of which is a potential problem.

Occasionally, a tape joint will lift when soldering heat is applied. If one does, it may be possible to save the joint by pressing down on the tape with the point of a darning needle while reapplying heat. Solder won't stick to the needle, which can be removed as the solder cools. Very narrow and short pieces of tape must be soldered with care or they may be picked up by the soldering iron. If this happens, the old solder must be heated and wiped off the surface with a cotton cloth. Before you make another try at it, this surface must be free of solder bumps and ridges.

When overlap joints are used, solder bridges the joint more readily if the lower tape is heated and solder is flowed onto it first. Solder can then be flowed over the edge and onto the upper tape to complete the joint. Tape runs that connect to DIP and other patterns should overlap about halfway across pad holes. If a hole is to accommodate a component lead as well as the tape, push a large darning needle through the

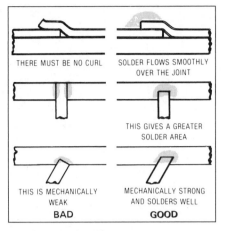

Fig. 2.10. Drawings illustrate good and bad tape terminations. Shaded areas show where solder is to be flowed.

hole from the conductor side. This forms the tape to the hole contour and permits the component lead to enter the hole without pushing the tape off the pad.

Where tapes are connected to DIP pads at the inner rows of holes, the tapes should overlap the hole completely and then be punctured with the needle. This ensures a good soldered joint between IC or socket pin and copper tape.

If you're soldering a component lead to one of the spare holes of a double- or triple-hole DIP pattern, make sure the joint between the IC pin and copper tape is also secure to the copper tape pattern. It's possible to have a good soldered connection between IC pin and tape while having an open circuit between them and the pattern pad. Solder must be flowed onto the pattern as well as the tape. However, reserve soldering of connections to DIP pin holes until *after* the socket or IC pin is in place. Otherwise, the solder may prevent entry of the pins.

With tapes and patterns all in place, carefully inspect the circuit to make certain that it agrees with both the conductor pattern drawing *and* the schematic diagram. If inspection discloses an error in the schematic or the pattern drawing,

it's much easier to correct before any soldering has been done. You can now solder all connection points, including the pins of ICs or their sockets. Then carefully inspect every solder point, preferably with a jeweler's loupe. Look particularly for poor soldering and possible solder bridges, the latter most likely around IC solder pads. Having done this and corrected any suspicious connection, you can proceed to install and solder into place the remaining components.

When you're done, once again carefully inspect your work. Look for bad solder joints, possible solder bridging between closely spaced conductors and pads, and particularly for *unsoldered* points.

You might be wondering if you can work up a double-sided circuit board using pressure-sensitive materials. The answer is yes—to a limited degree. The main difficulty isn't so much that you must perfectly register the patterns on both sides of the board (this isn't too difficult in any case, considering that you'll be working with perforated board and prepared patterns), but the fact that you can't make plated-through holes. If you're planning to build a project that contains ICs, you won't be able to use sockets, because the sockets will prevent you from gaining access to the patterns on the component side of the board. If you forego sockets and solder the ICs directly onto the board, you run the risk of damaging the ICs with excessive heat. The answer, of course, is to use Molex Soldercon pins, which substitute for sockets and obviate the possibility of causing heat damage.

Where tape runs in double-sided work require interconnection between traces on both sides of the board, you can puncture both and use pretinned hookup wire to form bridges. Insert the wire, solder it to the tapes on both sides of the board, and trim away excess length with flush cutters. Fig. 2.11 shows a completed Easy Circuit board after all connections have been soldered.

Conclusion

You'll find that you need very few and simple tools to produce printed-circuit boards using the system described. These consist of a fine-point tweezer, an X-ACTO® knife or Gillette ''Widget'' safety knife, a half-dozen or so bulletin-board push-pins, a couple of large darning needles, and a low-wattage soldering iron and appropriate accessories should do it.

Bear in mind, too, that E-Z Circuit material comes in many sizes and shapes for a variety of applications. For example, edge-connector boards are available for Apple II computer applications, complemented by insertion-type connector patterns. Other bus formats are available, too. Pressure-sensitive insulating tapes can be used to prevent short-circuits should you have any crossover points on your copper

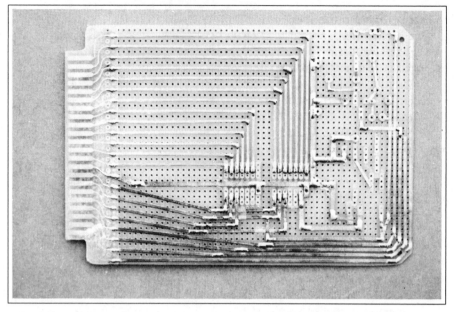

Fig. 2.11. This is what a completed Easy Circuit board looks like after all connections have been soldered. Notice how turns are made by angling the copper tapes. This photo shows examples of 90° and angled turns and an insulated crossover.

circuitry; copper power and ground distribution strips, which are nicely thick and wide, are among the many other adhesive strips and patterns one can use to simplify work.

The attributes provided by this method of making prototype experimental printed-circuit boards and single boards for construction projects should be appealing to many electronics experimenters and professionals who disdain the bother of photochemical work.

The simple photographic procedure described here will let you produce project front panels that are indistinguishable from those on commercial products

chapter **3**

Dress Up Your Projects

C. R. BALL, JR.

When was the last time you *really* finished a project, taking the time to give it a professional-looking front panel, with control legends and perhaps an eye-catching logo neatly and permanently rendered? If you're like many hobbyists, you just spray on a coat or two of enamel paint and label your panels with a dry-transfer lettering kit or a plastic tape labeler. Dry transfer lettering is okay at first, but it inevitably wears away and/or drops off, while tape labels give a project an unprofessional "klugy" look, no matter what other pains you might take to give it a classy appearance. Worse still, both types of labeling eventually wear away or drop off, leaving you with a project whose control functions are a complete mystery if you haven't used it for some time. This is obviously leading up to something.

That something is the fact that you *can* make very durable front panels that are indistinguishable in appearance from those you see on commercially made products. Using the procedure described here, you can make panels and decals that really dress up your projects, actually

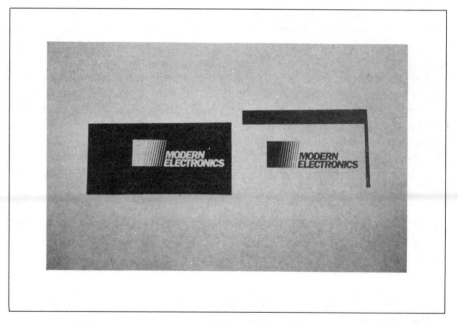

Fig. 3.1. Starting with positive art, first exposure and development produces the negative shown at the left. This negative is then used as original art to expose and develop the positive film shown at the right.

making you want to display them with pride. You can even use this procedure to make printed-circuit component identification overlays similar to the silk screening used on commercial pc boards. Best of all, you don't have to be specially trained to turn out professional-looking panels, and all materials

are readily available at reasonable cost.

Types of Nameplates

There are a number of processes for making professional-looking nameplates, all requiring easy-to-use light-

17

sensitive material. Some nameplate fabrication methods use the light-sensitive material for selectively coloring, etching or screening a panel. Another process uses the light-sensitive material as the finished nameplate image. These fabrication methods go by such names as anodizing, etching, silk-screening, and photo reproducing, respectively.

Anodized Nameplates are prepared by trapping various colored dyes into the "pores" of an aluminum nameplate panel. The pores are opened electrolytically by immersing the aluminum (as the anode) in a sulfuric-acid solution. Then the opened pores are selectively filled with colored dye through an exposed and developed light-sensitive material (photoresist mask). The pores are then closed by immersing the panel in a boiling-water solution, permanently trapping the dye pattern under the surface of the aluminum.

The anodizing process produces an extremely durable and attractive nameplate. Since you can use any thickness of aluminum, the nameplate can be self-supporting and, therefore, be used as part of the chassis or as a front panel.

Etched Nameplates, as the name implies, are formed by etching an image into an aluminum surface. The aluminum panel is first coated with a negative-acting photosensitive material (photoresist) that is not affected by the etchant. (Precoated panels are available from the sources listed in Table 3.1.) The panel is then exposed through negative or positive art and developed.

Following development, the aluminum is immersed in an etchant solution, usually caustic soda, that eats away the surface of the unprotected image areas. Then, after removing the photoresist, the etched areas can be ink filled. In the case of precoated panels, the coating is the image color and is selectively etched away.

Etched nameplates are extremely durable and can be self-supporting. Very colorful nameplates can be produced by flowing various colored inks into the etched image.

Silk-Screened Nameplates are produced by screening ink onto the surface of metal, plastic, or other material. The process begins by photographically transferring the artwork to a plastic film that, in turn, is secured to a silk screen. The screen is placed over the nameplate and ink is flowed through the open-mesh image areas of the screen. Aluminum must be anodized or treated with a chemical, such as Alodine 1000, to ensure that ink will adhere properly. Using epoxy inks, extremely durable nameplates can be made. Multicolor nameplates, of course, require a separate screen for each color.

Most nameplates on consumer electronic equipment are produced by the silk-screen process because they are easier and less expensive to manufacture in large quantities. However, because of the set-up time and equipment required, this process is not generally attractive to electronics hobbyists.

Photo Nameplates consist of a brushed-aluminum sheet between $7/100$ inch (1.78 mm) and $14/100$ inch (3.56 mm) thick or a $4/100$ inch (0.10 mm) thick transparent or colored polyester sheet. The aluminum or plastic sheet is coated on one side with a colored light sensitive material called an emulsion and an adhesive on the other side. (A removable backing protects the adhesive side until the prepared sheet is ready for placement.) The emulsion is exposed through negative or positive artwork, developed with a one-step rub-on chemical process, and finally coated with a clear protective spray or covered with a clear laminating film. The finished nameplate is easily cut to size with scissors and secured to a sub-panel, case, or chassis by its adhesive backing.

Many colors and color combinations are available on aluminum and plastic. Although the durability of photo nameplates is not as good as the other types, ease of

Table 3.1. Nameplate Materials and Manufacturers

Item	Manufacturer	Item	Manufacturer
Anodized nameplate supplies	Metal Photo Corp., 18531 South Miles Road, Cleveland, OH 44128	Silk-screen supplies	Various
Etched nameplate supplies	Kepro Circuit Systems, 630 Axminister, Fenton, OH 63026	Photo nameplate supplies	Kepro Circuit Systems, 630 Axminister, Fenton, OH 63026
	Fotofoil Division, Miller Dial Corp., 4400 North Temple City Boulevard, El Monte, CA 91734		3M Decorative Products, Bldg. 223-1S, 3M Center, St. Paul, MN 55144
		Drafting film, dry transfer lettering, templates, etc.	Bishop Graphics, 5388 Sterling Center Drive, Westlake Village, CA 91359

fabrication and low investment cost make photo nameplates the best choice for experimental and proto-type applications.

Because of its ready adaptability to home experimenting, the remainder of this article concentrates on the photo technique. We will discuss it in detail to provide you with all the information necessary to make professional nameplates for home and work projects.

Making a Photo Nameplate

The key to any attractive nameplate is good artwork. The finished product can be only as good as your original artwork. The kind of artwork you need depends on the type of final image you want.

Artwork ultimately takes one of two forms—positive or negative. Positive art is usually the original or an exact replica on transparent film. Negative art, on the other hand, is a photographic reversal of the original (positive) art. Figure 3.1 shows the difference between positive and negative art.

Nameplate material is negative-acting, with the final image being the reverse of the artwork used. For example, a piece of nameplate material exposed and developed using the positive artwork shown at the left in Fig. 3.1 will have a final image like that shown at the right for negative art.

You begin preparing your artwork by making an actual-size sketch of the nameplate. (If the nameplate is small or is to have fine detail, you may want to make a sketch twice actual size for ease of drafting.) After verifying the dimensions and placement of lettering, place a piece of clear or translucent drafting film, available from most art or office supply dealers, over your sketch.

Using your sketch as a guide, apply dry-transfer lettering as shown in Fig. 3.2. Alternatively, you can

use a drafting pen and a template. Pc drafting tape can be used to group or outline various areas of functions. Once you have completed transferring the details from your sketch to the film, the latter becomes your original artwork. If the original is other than actual size, you will have to take the artwork to a lithographer or print shop to have an actual-size positive or negative made. However, if the original art is actual-size and you want a negative of it, simply use the reversing film procedure discussed later in this article.

If you are planning to duplicate a nameplate for a project that appeared in a magazine article and want to avoid having to redo the art, again simply have a print shop make a positive or negative.

General Information

Although photo nameplates can be safely and easily made, certain precautions should be observed when handling the chemicals and the exposure light because both the developer and sealing spray are flammable, avoid using them near an open flame and do not smoke in their vicinity. If you have sensitive skin (or even if you do not, for that matter), wear rubber gloves when using the developer. Also, both chemicals are somewhat toxic and should be used in a well-ventilated area and should at all costs be kept out of the reach of children.

Care should also be taken to protect your eyes and skin from prolonged exposure to the ultraviolet light if you use a sun lamp. Wear sunglasses when the lamp is on, and minimize skin exposure to avoid sunburn. Keep in mind that as little as five minutes close to an UV source can result in sunburn.

Almost any ultraviolet light source can be used to expose the photo-nameplate material. You can, of

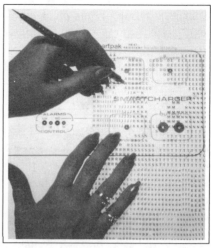

Fig. 3.2. After penciling your layout onto paper, cover with transparent film and use dry-transfer lettering and other drafting aids to transfer the drawn image. If the image is very small or contains lots of fine detail, work twice life size and then have the image photographically reduced.

course, make a sizable investment in either 3M's Model EU800 ($375) or Kepro's Model BTX-200 ($445) exposure box. Or you can use a blue-print machine to expose thin nameplate material. However, you can obtain effective exposure results with a common 375-watt sun lamp, as long as nameplate sizes are kept down to 8 inches (203 mm) by 10 inches (254 mm) or less. Sunlamps are available in most drug, hardware, and department stores for about $30.

When using a sunlamp, keep in mind that most use bulbs have an internal starting mechanism that prevents them from starting unless they are cool. If you turn off the bulb after use, you will have to leave it off for approximately 15 minutes before attempting to turn it on again.

Nameplate material does not require strict darkroom conditions, but fluorescent and other sources of ultraviolet light should be avoided when handling undeveloped material. Yellow "bug" lights make excellent safe lights for handling unexposed material.

Nameplate Material

Photo-nameplate material is manufactured by 3M and Kepro (see Table). The Dynamark™ brand manufactured by 3M offers the widest range of materials with 13 basic color combinations on polyester or aluminum and in sizes up to 24 by 48 inches (610 by 1219 mm). (The instructions given below are specifically for the 3M products, although most apply equally to the Kepro product.)

A starter kit from 3M contains all nine colors on 10 by 12 inch (254 by 305 mm) polyester film, four sheets of aluminum in various colors, overlay film, reversing film, grey scale, developer, developer pads and laminating sheets. The kit costs about $50. All you need to add is a light source, your artwork, and two pieces of glass. Individual colors and sizes are also available.

When using a sun lamp, two sheets of glass are needed: one to hold the artwork in close contact with the nameplate material during exposure, and the other to use as a developing surface. These glass sheets should be at least twice the size of the nameplate you are making. Various sizes are available at hardware stores. (When you purchase the glass, do not get the tinted type. The tint filters out the UV light you need for exposing the photosensitive material.) Paper towels will also be helpful for cleaning up left-over developer and drying developed nameplates.

Before exposing the actual nameplate (details for this are given in diagram form in Fig. 3.3), it is necessary to determine the proper exposure time for the material color and light source you are using. To do this, select the material you are going to use for your nameplate

under safe lighting conditions. Cut a piece slightly larger than the grey scale. (If you don't have the 3M kit, grey scales are available at most photography stores.) If you are using the yellow reversing film to make a negative, cut a similar piece. Place the nameplate material emulsion side up on a smooth, flat surface. Place the grey scale on top, and cover with a piece of glass. (*Caution:* Handle the nameplate material and reversing film *only* under safe light conditions until the image is developed.)

Fig. 3.3. To make a panel, label or overlay that is identical to (a positive of) your original art, perform all steps in both columns, starting at the upper left. For a negative image, simply start at the top of the right-hand column, using your original film as the "original art" called for.

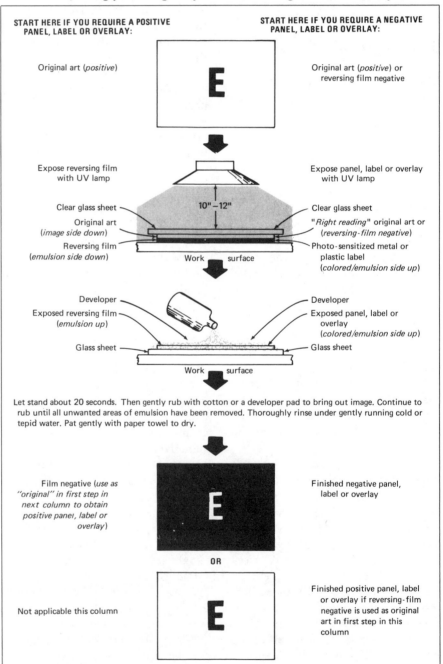

Using the following exposure times as a starting point, expose the grey scale for the selected amount of time:

Material color	Exposure time in minutes
red	2½ to 3
blue	1½ to 2
green	3 to 3½
black	15 to 20

These are approximate exposure times for a 375-watt sunlamp located 10 to 12 inches (254 to 305 mm) from the exposure surface. When using positive art, increase these times by 10%. Keep in mind that these times are guidelines only and are not intended to replace grey-scale tests and that actual exposure time will vary with the UV bulb used, its age and the distance to the exposure surface.

Position the sun lamp 10 to 12 inches (254 to 305 mm) from and parallel to the glass. After exposure, move the light source to a location away from your work area to prevent further exposure. Remove the glass and the grey scale. Place the exposed material, still emulsion side up, on another piece of glass and pour onto it enough developer to cover the surface (Fig. 3.4). Wait about 20 seconds and then gently rub the developer with a piece of cotton or a developer pad until the image appears (Fig. 3.5).

Compare the developed image to the original grey-scale exposure mask. If you are using plastic material, the image should be solid through step 2 on the mask. For metal material, the image should be solid through step 3, and for reversing film, it should be solid through step 4.

If you do not obtain the proper results, repeat the test and adjust exposure time accordingly. Longer exposures cause more steps to be solid and vice-versa.

Once you have established the proper exposure time for the material and light source being used, make

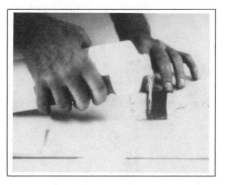

Fig. 3.4. Place exposed material, emulsion side up, on a sheet of glass and pour enough developer to soak it.

a note of the time, distance from light source and material color/type for present and future reference.

Making a Nameplate

Cut a piece of the nameplate material so that it is at least ¼ inch (6.35 mm) larger than the actual nameplate all around. Repeat the procedure for using the grey scale and expose the nameplate. If the name-

Fig. 3.6. The three stages in producing a finished nameplate. At top is pencil drawing; at center is original artwork; at bottom is finished panel.

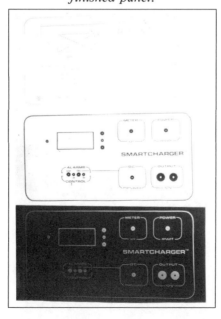

Fig. 3.5. Allow developer to stand for 20 seconds. Then gently rub with cotton or pad to bring out image.

plate is large, rotate the light during exposure to be sure all areas receive equal amounts of light. In such a case, it may be necessary to increase exposure time slightly. Develop the nameplate or reversing film as before. If areas that should not wash away do, indicating underexposure, during development, increase exposure time by 10% and try again. Be sure to make a note of the time that works best and save for future use. Figure 3.6 shows a nameplate sketch, artwork prepared from the sketch and the finished nameplate. Examples of a variety of nameplates that give you some idea of what you can do with these materials are shown in Fig. 3.7.

Fig. 3.7. Shown here are examples of finished labels to give you an idea of the kind of work that can be done with the photo-chemical materials. Note the grey scale at the lower left.

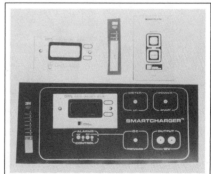

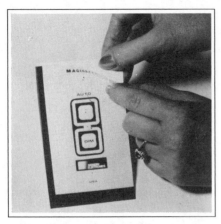

Fig. 3.8. Once you have trimmed two adjacent sides, remove protective backing, starting at finished corner.

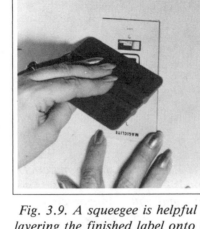

Fig. 3.9. A squeegee is helpful in layering the finished label onto the panel, working out air bubbles as you go.

Fig. 3.10. After burnishing down the finished label onto the actual panel, use a knife to trim away all unwanted material from holes and cutouts.

There are two ways of protecting the finished nameplate. One is to spray several light coats of a clear acrylic, such as Krylon, or the matte or glossy sprays from 3M over the entire surface of the nameplate. The other is to layer on adhesive-backed clear laminating film, such as that supplied in the 3M starter kit. Both are best applied in a dust-free environment and before the nameplates are trimmed to final size. Other ways to mount the laminating film are detailed in 3M Instruction Bulletin #4-4.

Mounting the Nameplate

Use scissors to trim two adjoining edges of the nameplate. Starting with the corner formed by the trimmed edges, peel the protective sheet from the adhesive backing (Fig. 3.8). Align the two trimmed edges with the proper edges of the panel. Finish removing the protective sheet and smooth the nameplate onto the panel. A squeegee is helpful in removing air bubbles (Fig. 3.9).

Once the nameplate is attached and smoothed, holes and other areas can be trimmed, using an X-ACTO® or similar knife (Fig. 3.10). The nameplate and panel can then be mounted to the equipment.

Pc component identification can also be made into a nameplate on clear plastic and attached to the component side of a pc board in the same manner as attaching a name-plate to a metal or plastic panel. Component leads will then punch through the plastic when they are mounted.

Summing Up

As you can see from the foregoing, making of professional appearing nameplates, decals and pc board overlays is really a simple, straightforward procedure. If you've already fabricated your own pc boards, using the photographic technique and materials, you'll be right at home with the procedure and materials employed in panel making. The results, of course, are well worth the effort and small additional cost.

Part **2**

Home Electronics

The Touchmaster

J. DANIEL GIFFORD

You've probably seen—and played with—one of those fascinating lamps that are controlled by the touch of a finger on their metal surfaces. They seem to be irresistible to everyone. As an electronic hobbyist, you've probably wondered how they work or, more likely, how you could build one. Here's how.

The "Touchmaster" discussed here is a small module that can be added to any lamp that has room to hide it in. It will control an ordinary 3-way bulb or, if you like, two separate bulbs, all with the barest touch of a finger.

The first touch will light the 3-way bulb's low-wattage filament or the first of two bulbs, depending on which type of lamp you use it in. The second touch will light the high-wattage filament or second bulb, and the third will light both filaments or bulbs. Either filament or bulb (or both, in the latter case) can be as much as 100 watts. (If you can contrive adequate heat sinking, much higher wattage bulbs can be used, but it's not recommended unless you're expert at this.)

This simple 3-way lamp is controlled by the touch of a finger on the brass band of the wooden base that contains the Touchmaster module.

The Touchmaster is also completely safe: the ac and dc halves of the circuit are completely isolated from each other via the power supply transformer and the output optocouplers. Just follow the construction precautions noted in this chapter.

Circuit Description

There are four parts to the Touchmaster circuit (Fig. 4.1). The first is the power supply for the control side. A 12-volt center tapped transformer supplies approximately 9 volts dc to the circuit through full-wave rectifier *D2* and *D3*. Capacitors *C2* and *C3* filter and smooth the dc; since the circuit is all CMOS, no regulator is needed.

The second part of the circuit is the touch switch, formed from the four gates of *IC1*, a CD4093B Quad CMOS Schmitt Trigger NAND gate. All four gates have their input tied together and thus act as Schmitt Trigger inverters. (If desired, a CD4584B or 74C14 Hex CMOS Schmitt Trigger Inverter IC

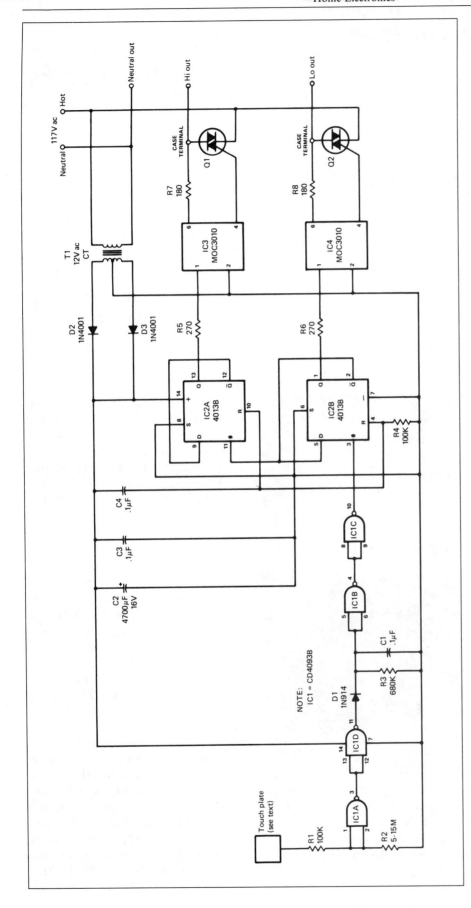

PARTS LIST
Semiconductors
D1—1N914 diode
D2, D3—1N4001 rectifier diode
IC1—CD4093B quad CMOS
Schmitt trigger NAND gate
IC2—CD4013B dual D-type
flip-flop
IC3, IC4—MOC3010 triac-
output optocoupler (Radio
Shack No. 276-134)
Q1, Q2—200-volt, 4-ampere
triac (Radio Shack No. 276-1001
or similar)
Capacitors
C1, C3, C4—0.1-μF
polypropylene/disc
C2—4000-μF, 16-volt
electrolytic
Resistors
R1, R4—100,000 ohms
R2—5M to 15M ohms (see text)
R3—680,000 ohms
R5, R6—220 ohms
R7, R8—180 ohms
Miscellaneous
T1—12-volt center-tapped, 120-
mA transformer (Radio Shack
No. 274-1360 or similar); case
(see text); perforated board; 14-
pin IC sockets (3); 5-point barri-
er strip; 2 pc-board pins; MOV
transient suppressor (Radio
Shack No. 276-570 or similar—
see text); machine hardware;
hookup wire; solder; etc.

may be used instead; be certain to
tie the two unused inputs to circuit
ground.)

The four inverters are used in
pairs to form two Schmitt Trigger
buffers. The input of the first buffer is tied to circuit ground via *R2*, a
5 to 15 megohm resistor, and to the

*Fig. 4.1. Touchmaster lamp
controller schematic. Note
polarization of the ac line input.
For safety, this must be
maintained by means of a
polarized or grounded plug.*

touch control surface via *R1,* a 100-kilohm resistor. *R1* limits the input current and prevents possible static damage to *IC1's* inputs, while *R2* determines the input impedance and, thus, the touch sensitivity of the circuit. *R2's* value must be found experimentally once the circuit has been built and installed: generally, the larger the area of the touch surface, the smaller the value of this resistor.

The output of the first buffer is normally low until the touch-control surface is touched. Then the body of the person touching it acts as an antenna and picks up the 60-Hz power line hum that radiates from the lamp itself and from the power lines of the building around it. This hum is rectified and amplified by the first buffer and emerges as a 60-Hz square wave. This waveform is rectified into dc by *D1* and charges *C1* until it reaches the input threshold (about 6 volts) of the second buffer. When this threshold is reached, the second buffer switches high and remains high until the finger is removed from the control surface. At this time, the 680 kilohm resistor, *R3,* rapidly discharges *C1* until the second buffer's low threshold (about 4 volts) is reached, whereby its output again drops low. The charging and discharging of *C1* takes about 0.05 second each way, so even three very fast taps on the touch surface will bring the lamp to full brightness.

The third part—and core of the Touchmaster—is a two-bit binary counter formed from the CD4013B CMOS Dual D-type flip-flop. The two flip-flops are connected to divide by two or toggle: the first clock impulse will drive the Q output high (and the $\overline{Q}$ output low); the second impulse will drive the Q output low. The touch switch is connected to the clock input of the first flip-flop (the low filament controller), and the $\overline{Q}$ output of the first flip-flop is connected to the clock input of the sec-

ond (the high filament controller). We now have a 4-state binary counter that is clocked by successive touches on the touch surface.

The counter starts at 00, or off, and the first touch will advance it to 01 (low filament on), the second to 10 (high filament on), the third to 11 (both on), and the fourth back to 00. The components *R4* and *C4* act as a power-on reset. Therefore, when the lamp is plugged in or after a power failure, the lamp will be in the 00 or off state. The time constant of the RC pair is such that a power-line flicker or momentary power loss will not cause the lamp to reset.

The fourth and final part of the Touchmaster circuit is the power output section. Outputs of the counter drive the input sides of the two triac optocouplers, *IC3* and *IC4.* Output sides of the optocouplers drive the two power triacs, *Q1* and *Q2,* that, in turn, control power to the lamp(s). Triacs are fairly efficient devices, so very small heat sinks can be used with output loads up to the recommended 100 watt limit. About 1 to 1½ square inches of dissipation area for each device is needed; if insulators are used, a common 2 to 3 square-inch heat sink may be used instead. A pinout of the triacs is shown in Fig. 4.2.

Fig. 4.2. Pinout of the triacs specified.

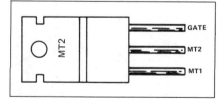

As mentioned earlier, there is no limit to the amount of power that the Touchmaster can control, as long as adequately rated triacs are used and adequate heat sinking is provided them. The devices specified in the parts list can handle up to 500 watts each with adequate heat sink-

ing. Most lamps, however, have limited space for heat sinks and even more limited ventilation to carry away the heat, so 100 watts per bulb or filament will be the practical limit for most applications.

Construction

Construction of the Touchmaster revolves around two points: space and safety. The space available to mount the module and the shape that the circuit board must be will be dictated by the lamp that the Touchmaster will be mounted in.

The shape of the perf board may need to be square, rectangular, long and narrow, or even circular in order to fit into the base or body of the chosen lamp. It's best to pick or design the lamp first and then build the Touchmaster to fit: don't make the (author's) mistake of building the module to fit a standard board or case and then try to fit it into a lamp. (Incidentally, the prototype in Figs. 4.3 and 4.4 was built about twice as large as necessary, both to allow possible reworking of the circuit and to more plainly show the layout.)

The second construction point, safety, is by far more important. What we have here is an ungrounded metal surface on one end and an ac power line at the other: a dangerous combination if strict precautions are not followed. The Touchmaster is inherently safe by virtue of its isolated design, but if it is improperly constructed, a chance accident could result in the touch surface and the ac power coming in contact.

The primary protection against this happening is clearly shown in Fig. 4.4. A gap is left on the circuit board between the ac and dc halves, bridged only by the transformer and optocouplers. No matter how the layout is modified, this "no man's land" must be maintained, and no wire may cross it or come near it. This wide and total separation of

Fig. 4.3. The Touchmaster module. Note how the two opto devices share a common 14-pin socket. The screw-terminal barrier strip could be replaced with solder pins instead. Note also the MOV spike-suppressor (black disc near transformer) used on this prototype to prevent false switching from line transients.

Fig. 4.4. Underside of the module shows the required "no man's land" between the ac and dc halves of the circuit. Eliminating this gap means risking a shock!

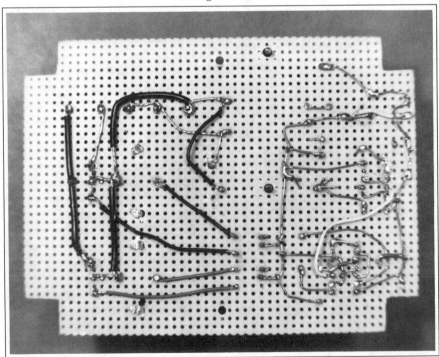

the circuit's halves ensures that no fluke of loose wire or faulty insulation can result in a mishap.

The second safety precaution is that the complete ac side of the module, if not the entire device, must be enclosed in a nonconducting environment. In some lamps, a separate case for the Touchmaster may be unnecessary if a hiding place enclosed in wood, plastic, or ceramic is available. If the lamp is metal or the space is tight, a separate plastic case should be used to shield the module against metal parts.

No matter how the ac circuitry is shielded, some provision for ventilation must be provided. The transformer and triacs do not produce much heat, even with a full 100-watt load on both outputs, but the heat they do produce must have an outlet. If a case is used, a number of small holes will preserve the safety of the enclosure, yet permit the heat to escape. Most lamps, even well-constructed ones, have enough gaps between their parts to dissipate the released heat without additional holes.

One addition may be needed on the Touchmaster module. If you have a noisy ac environment (lamps flicker, TVs and radios exhibit static, etc.) some protection against transients may need to be included to prevent such transients from causing the lamp to switch states by itself. If you have such a noisy environment, or if you want to guard against such occurrences, a metal-oxide varistor (MOV) such as Radio Shack's No. 276-570 or -571 should be installed across the incoming ac power conductors. Such a device will eliminate most, if not all such false switching.

Installation

Once a space has been found or made for the Touchmaster and the module has been built to fit, it should be firmly mounted in the space using screws and standoffs or a strong adhesive such as epoxy. Some provision should be left to remove the circuit board for repairs. Use of a barrier strip like that on the prototype is recommended for the ac and lamp connections.

The touch surface must be of metal, or course, but it must be isolated from any other metal parts of the lamp that are grounded or in contact with the lamp sockets. This isolation can be achieved a number of ways, the simplest of which would be a metal band, patch, or decorative piece on a wooden or ceramic surface. Something along this line can be added to or designed into almost any sort of lamp. A good second choice is to use an existing metal part of the lamp, such as a base, support, or separator and, if necessary, isolate it using fiber or plastic washers, sheet plastic, electrician's tape, or other means. If an all-metal lamp is used, the lamp socket and its support tube can be isolated from the rest of the lamp. Then, a touch on the lamp anywhere from its base to the shade finial will control it.

When the board is constructed, resistor R2 should not be soldered in. Instead, a pair of pins spaced about 0.6 inch apart should be installed in its place. When the module is installed and the touch surface is connected, temporarily install a 15-megohm resistor across the pins and check the touch response of the lamp. If it switches before the finger actually reaches the surface or jitters through several states on one touch, reduce the value of R2 and try again. When a value is found that lets the lamp switch cleanly without either jitter or hesitation, solder it in place and finish assembling the lamp.

Note that in the schematic, a distinction is made between the hot and neutral conductors of the ac cord. This polarization must be maintained; in keeping with standard wiring safety practice, the outgoing neutral connection must be made to the lamp socket shell, *not* the center contact. (A 3-way bulb will not work properly unless the neutral connection is made to the shell.) For 3-way lamps, the standard switched socket must be replaced with a switchless 3-wire socket. The center terminal is for the high filament, and the ring terminal is for the low.

A polarized plug must be used to keep the hot and neutral connections straight. Even better would be a grounded plug, with the ground lead connected to all the metal parts not used for touch control.

An Automatic LED Street Number Sign

HANK OLSON

During the daylight hours, anyone walking or driving past your house may not have trouble reading your street number. But it's a different story altogether after the sun goes down and darkness descends. If you don't have a lighted number, it may be impossible for a visitor to find your home in a developed community, especially if you live in a tract community where all homes are built on the same general design. If you have or anticipate having this problem, a solution is the automatic illuminated LED street number sign described here.

This project provides even illumination, unlike signs in which an incandescent lamp supplies backlighting. As a bonus, you don't ever have to remember to turn LEDs on and off. A built-in light detector automatically samples ambient lighting and does the switching for you according to light level. Furthermore, the LED sign consumes very little power, even when fully on, making it economical to operate.

About the Circuit

Shown in Fig. 5.1 is the complete schematic diagram of the automatic LED Street Number Sign. Power for the circuit is supplied by the full-wave bridge power supply shown at the upper left. Incoming 117 volts from the ac line is stepped down by transformer *T1*, rectified to pulsating dc by bridge assembly *RECT1*, and filtered to dc by capacitor *C1*.

The dc output at the junction of dropping resistor *R2* and filter capacitor *C1* supplies power to the LED numeral array shown in the dashed-line box at the upper right. Power for the control circuit is

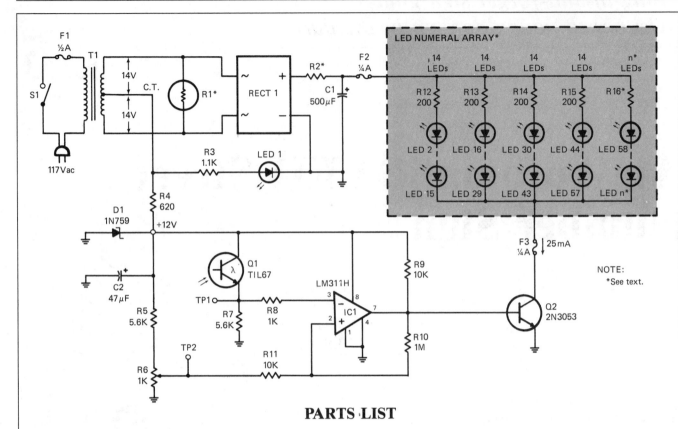

Fig. 5.1. Overall schematic diagram of the Automatic LED Street Number Sign. The boxed-off section at the upper right is an LED array that makes up the sign's LED numerals.

PARTS LIST

Semiconductors
D1—12-volt zener diode
IC1—LM311H comparator (N.S.C.)
LED1—Green light-emitting diode
LED2 thru LEDn—Red light-emitting diode (Hewlett-Packard No. 5082-4655 or similar)
Q1—TIL67 phototransistor (Texas Instr.)
Q2—2N3053 transistor
RECT1—50-PIV, 2-ampere bridge rectifier

Capacitors
C1—500-μF, 50-volt electrolytic
C2—47-μF, 25-volt electrolytic

Resistors (all 10% tolerance)
R1—RY57 thyrite varistor (Automatic Electric)
R2—½-watt (see text)
R3—1100 ohms, ¼-watt
R4—620 ohms, ¼-watt
R5, R7—5600 ohms, ¼-watt
R8—1000 ohms, ¼-watt
R9, R11—10,000 ohms, ¼-watt
R10—1 megohm, ¼-watt
R12 thru R15—200 ohms, ¼-watt
R16—See text
R6—1000-ohm, pc-mount trimmer potentiometer

Miscellaneous
F1—½-ampere fuse with pigtail leads

F2,F3—¼-ampere fuse with pigtail leads
S1—Spst power switch
T1—14 volt center-tapped transformer (Triad No. F90X or similar)

Perforated board and solder posts; 8-pin DIP socket for IC1; ac line cord and strain relief; solder-post pins for *TP1* and *TP2*; suitable plastic or metal enclosure; fast-set epoxy cement; silicone adhesive; machine hardware; hookup and bell wire; etc.

picked off the center tap of *T1*, current limited by *R4*, and regulated to +12 volts before delivery to phototransistor *Q1* and comparator *IC1*.

The supply potential delivered to the LED numeral array is intentionally limited to a nominal 30 volts dc, with current limiting, to conform to the National Electrical Code. This permits use of No. 18 bell wire between the control circuit and LED numeral array.

By using only high-efficiency gallium-arsenide-phosphide or gallium-phosphide LEDs, which need draw only about 5 mA to be visible, the design procedure can be simplified. With such LEDs, a drop of between 1.8 and 2.0 volts results when a given LED is forward biased by 5 mA. It is a simple matter, therefore, to determine the maximum number of LEDs that can be placed across the nominally 30-volt line.

Taking 1.9 volts as an average forward bias, the maximum number of LEDs that can be placed across the 30-volt line is 30/1.9, or 15. Since some series resistance must be included in any such calculation this number should be reduced to 14. Therefore, the maximum number of LEDs connected in series across the 30-volt line is 14.

Though you can't construct much of a street-number display from only 14 LEDs, additional series strings of LEDs can be connected in parallel with the first, as shown, until you have all the LEDs you need. The maximum number of series strings of LEDs connected in parallel should be limited to five, giving

you a total of 70 LEDs from which to compose your house number.

With 70 possible LEDs, you can figure a minimum of four LEDs per segment per numeral, arranging the numerals in the traditional seven-segment layout, even if your house number is 88888, which represents the most intensive use of LEDs. Figure 5.2A illustrates the LED count for each numeral. Note here that selected LEDs in certain segments of many of the numbers have been omitted to give the numerals a more rounded appearance, rather than the squared-off boxy look you'll find in traditional LED numeric displays for meters, frequency counters, and other such electronic devices. Coincidentally, this approach reduces the number of LEDs needed to construct numerals with rounded edges, like 2, 5, 6, 8, 9, and 0.

If you have fewer numerals in

your street number, or your street number consists of less-intensive segment use numerals (like 1, 4, and 7), you can use five and possibly even six LEDs per segment to increase legibility and/or character size, as shown in Figs. 2B and 2C, respectively. Bear in mind that the greater the number of LEDs used per segment, assuming no increase in character size, the greater the legibility of the numeral.

Resistors *R12* through *R16* in Fig. 5.1 serve as current limiters for the series strings of LEDs. Note that there are five such strings shown connected between the positive bus of the power supply and the collector of driver transistor *Q2*. Each string must contain 14 LEDs or their equivalent. Since not all street numbers will require 70 LEDs, it would be wasteful to include 70 LEDs in your numeral array. It may be possible to reduce the number of

Fig. 5.2. Drawings illustrate layouts for numerals composed of four (top), five (center), and six (bottom) LEDs per segment. Increase in LED count can increase numeral size, legibility, or both.

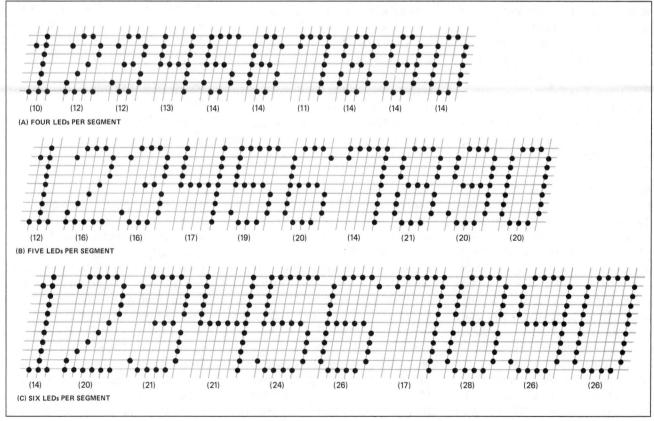

series strings required, depending on your LED needs. Also, it will be the rare case in which all series strings will require 14 LEDs, as indicated by *LEDn* in Fig. 5.1. In a case like this, where there are fewer than 14 LEDs in a series string, the value of the current limiting resistor (*R16* in Fig. 5.1), will have to be adjusted to make up for the loss of a LED or LEDs.

Before you can determine what value resistor to use in a string containing less than 14 LEDs, you must know that the potential on the nominally 30-volt positive bus from the power supply is actually 27.6 volts. This potential is fixed by the value of resistance used for *R2* and the current drawn by the series-parallel arrangement of the LED numeric array.

The voltage at the top end of the power supply bus must be adjusted by *R2* (more about this under "Construction") to yield the required 27.6 volts. This resistor dissipates only about 0.1 watt in normal service. However, if the 27.6-volt bus should short to ground, the ½-watt resistor would have to dissipate more than 5 watts and would quickly burn open like a fuse. There are ¼-ampere fuses (*F2* and *F3*) in both LED array lines, but these are to protect the electronics against any possible fault-to-ac-line problems, rather than to protect the circuit from overload damage.

Determining the value of resistance to use for *R2* is complicated somewhat by the rather unorthodox arrangement of the components at the output of the rectifier. Instead of having dropping resistor *R2* follow filter capacitor *C1* in the traditional manner, *R2* precedes *C1*. This arrangement makes determination of *R2*'s value more difficult, but it offers the benefit of reduced ripple current in *C1,* resulting in longer life for the capacitor.

In simple terms, the potential at the high end of *R2* will normally be somewhere between +30 and +40

volts. Knowing the number of series strings in the LED numeral array and the current drawn by each (5 mA), you can obtain the approximate value for *R2* and adjust it as needed until the potential at the low end of the resistor measures 27.6 volts.

The values of *R12* through *R15,* all the same in the 14-LED series strings in Fig. 5.1, have been determined for you and are indicated in both the schematic diagram and the Parts List. The value of *R16,* however, must be calculated separately, depending on the number of LEDs in its series string. Let's assume you need 13 LEDs in the final string. Multiply 13 by 1.9 volts (the average potential dropped across each LED) to obtain 24.7 volts. Subtract 24.7 volts from the actual 27.6 volts on the nominally 30-volt bus to obtain 2.9 volts. Since the current that is to flow through the string is to be 5 mA, use Ohm's Law for resistance to determine the value of the resistor as follows: $R = E/I = 2.9$ volts/5 mA = 580 ohms.

Similarly, you can calculate the value needed for *R16* for any number of LEDs fewer than 14 in the string. For example, if you need only 10 LEDs, the voltage dropped across them would be 19 volts. Subtracting this from 27.6 volts, you obtain 8.6 volts. Then, using the Ohm's Law formula, you obtain $R = E/I = 8.6$ volts/5 mA = 1720 ohms.

You can easily determine the number of LEDs needed to make up your street number by adding together the number required for each digit, depending on how many LEDs you want to use for each segment. If your street number is, say, 3456 and you've decided to use four LEDs per segment (Fig. 5.2A), you would add 12 + 13 + 14 + 14 to obtain 53 LEDs. This requires three series strings of 14 LEDs each plus a single string of 11 LEDs (with a 1340-ohm resistor in the last string). If you had a less LED-intensive

number like 1417 and decided to use six LEDs per segment, your LED count would be 66, requiring four strings of 14 and one string of 10 LEDs, with a 1720-ohm resistor in the last string (Fig. 5.2C).

The remainder of the electronics are for controlling the LED numeral array. Phototransistor *Q1* (Fig. 5.1) serves as an automatic switch that toggles on and off, depending on whether the sun is below or above the horizon. Whichever condition is detected is fed to the inverting (−) input of comparator operational amplifier *IC1*. In turn, *IC1* toggles on and off LED array driver transistor *Q2*.

With a darkness condition, *Q1* conducts very little current, bringing the input at pin 3 of *IC1* to near ground potential. This turns on *Q2,* allowing current to flow through the LED array and light the LED numerals. In daylight, *Q1* triggers into conduction. When the voltage on *TP1* becomes more positive than that on *TP2* (*TP1* and *TP2* are test points), *IC1's* output changes state and goes to near ground potential. This causes *Q2* to stop conducting and turn off the LED array. Resistor *R10* adds a small amount of hysteresis that prevents *IC1* from being indecisive at or near its on/off transition levels.

Construction

This is a relatively simple and straightforward project to build. Its circuitry, excluding the LED numeral array, can be assembled on a small piece of perforated board, using solder posts and an IC socket.

The best place to start construction is fabrication of the panel on which the LED numeral array is to be mounted. The panel can be made from ³⁄₁₆ inch (4.76 mm)-thick linen phenolic or other opaque insulating plastic sheet. Preliminary to machining the panel, lay out your numerals on a piece of paper, striving for eye appeal and legibility and sized appropriately for the distances from which your sign must be read. You can use the standard boxy seven-segment layout common to commercial displays, or you can make the numerals more rounded. In either case, give them a slight slant of between 7° and 10°. Mark off the locations where the LEDs are to be located, working actual-size. Try for equal spacing between LEDs as shown in the illustrations in Fig. 5.2. While you're at it, also indicate where in the layout the current limiting resistor for each LED series chain is to be.

Tape your template over the LED numeral array panel and use a sharp center punch to transfer the LED pattern to the panel. Tap lightly on the punch to avoid cracking or splitting the panel. (Do *not* at this time transfer the locations for the resistor leads to the panel.) Remove the template.

If you're using the commonest type of LED, the so-called T-1¾, use a ³/₁₆-inch (4.76 mm) bit to drill holes through the panel at each center-punched location. If you've decided to use a different type of LED, larger or smaller in diameter, you'll have to select a bit sized accordingly.

Once the holes are drilled, replace the template on the panel and transfer the locations for the current-limiting resistors to the panel with the center punch. Remove the template and use a ¹/₃₂- or ³/₆₄-inch (0.79 or 1.19 mm) bit to drill the holes.

Push the domed lens end of the LEDs into the holes from the rear of the panel. The lip around the base of the LEDs will prevent them from falling all the way through and will permit the domes to protrude about ³/₃₂ inch (2.38 mm) beyond the front surface of the panel. Orient the LEDs for easy interconnection and apply a spot of fast-setting clear epoxy cement on opposite sides to anchor the LEDs to the panel. When the cement sets, wire the series strings of LEDs as shown in Fig. 5.1, connecting the cathode of the first LED in the string to the anode of the next, and so on to make as many 14-LED strings as needed. Install and wire in the current-limiting resistors.

Now assemble the control-circuit/power-supply board. Keep in mind that phototransistor *Q1* must be located where it can sample ambient light. If you plan to mount this board behind the LED array panel, you'll have to drill two extra holes in the latter, in which to mount *Q1* and *LED1*. *LED1* is used here as a circuit-condition indicator. Run hookup wires from the leads of *Q1* and *LED1* to the appropriate points in the control circuit. If you're using a pc-mount transformer for *T1*, it can mount directly on the circuit board; otherwise, mount *T1* on one of the walls of the box that houses the project.

The only item you won't be able to mount on the circuit board just yet is *R2*, which will have to be selected after the project is powered up. In the meantime, wire into *R2*'s location on the board a 5000-ohm rheostat and set it for maximum resistance.

When you install polarized components, make certain that you orient them as detailed in Fig. 5.1. These components include electrolytic capacitors *C1* and *C2*, zener diode *D1*, integrated circuit *IC1*, light-emitting diode *LED1*, and transistors *Q1* and *Q2*. Use a low wattage soldering iron and only enough solder to assure good electrical and mechanical connections.

Before mounting the electronics in the box you've chosen for your project, wire together the entire circuit and plug it into a convenient ac outlet. Connect a dc voltmeter (or a multimeter set for dc volts) with its common lead going to circuit ground and its "hot" (+) lead going to the junctions between *R2* and *C1* and close *S1*. Slowly adjust the setting of the rheostat for a reading of 27.6 volts. Disconnect the meter and pull the project's plug from the ac outlet.

Now, without touching the setting of the rheostat, remove it from the circuit. Use an ohmmeter to measure the resistance at which the rheostat is set. The reading you obtain is the value of the resistor you must use for *R2*. Select a fixed ½-watt resistor with a value as close as possible to the reading and install it in the *R2* location in the circuit. This completes electronic assembly of the project.

Under normal operating conditions, the potential on the +27.6-volt line to the LED numeral array will go to a level greater than +30 volts when the display is off during daylight hours. It may even go as high as +40 volts above ground. However, it will still be within National Electrical Code limits because current in the circuit is much below the 3.2 ampere NEC specification.

The box you select for your project should easily accommodate the LED numeral array panel and control-circuit/power-supply (and the transformer if it's to be mounted off the board), plus a transparent sheet of red plastic about ¼ inch (6.35 mm) in front of the LED display. The plastic sheet serves two purposes: it protects the display from the elements, and it enhances the contrast of the display.

There's only one adjustment to be made to make the project fully operational. That is to set *R6* so that the LED display is off under full daylight conditions.

If you're planning to locate your street number sign outdoors, it's a good idea to completely weatherseal it. To do this, apply about a ⅛ inch (3.18 mm) bead of silicone adhesive along all seams of the box and around all hardware that goes through the box.

In Closing

The automatic LED street number sign described here is a maintenance-free project. It will give you many years of service without the need for attention. The LEDs are rated to deliver a million operating hours, and the circuit has been designed for minimum electrical wear and tear on components. So all you have to do is plug the line cord into an ac outlet and turn on the power.

Fuel Miser Reduces Heating Costs

ANTHONY J. CARISTI

If you're like most of us, you've seen your home heating bills go up and up year after year, apparently with no end in sight. But there is something you can do right now to reduce your heating costs dramatically, and that's to enhance the efficiency of your present heating system.

How? By adding to it an electronic cycling device that I call a fuel miser, a remarkable little gadget that will automatically regulate your furnace with ruthless, digital precision, yet keep you just as warm and cozy as you've always been. It's also easy to build, simple to install and suitable for use on either gas or oil heating systems.

Sound too good to be true? Not at all. Let me explain.

A typical furnace, you see, operates only in an "off" or "full speed ahead" state. So when the thermostat calls for heat, your furnace instantly, automatically cranks itself up to 100 percent of capacity. It responds as if the weather outside is as cold as it's ever going to be, a figure generally set at about −10 °F, for much of the country.

Some of this "full speed ahead" operation is tempered by a feature called heat anticipation, which is built into your thermostat and causes the furnace to shut off shortly before the thermostat registers your desired temperature. That helps some; the fuel miser helps more.

The real problem here, it turns out, is your furnace's heat exchanger. No matter how much heat your furnace generates, no matter how long it generates it, your heat exchanger can transfer just so many BTUs of heat energy into your hot water, steam or warm air system in a given amount of time. After the heat exchanger has reached a certain temperature level, any further burner operation simply results in more heat loss up the chimney.

The fuel miser enables you to select a "duty cycle" for your burner that can range from 10 percent to 100 percent of capacity, selectable in increments of 10 percent—nothing more. But once set, it will allow the thermostat circuit of your heating system to operate normally only for the duty cycle you have selected.

The rest of the time, your thermostat will be prevented from turning on your burner. However, residual heat from the heat exchanger will continue to flow into your heating system. The on-off cycle of the fuel miser is so fast, in fact, that the heat exchanger will always have sufficient heat, just as it would with a full-speed, lower-efficiency, noncontrolled furnace.

Gas-operated furnaces respond especially well to relatively short bursts of demand. The Fuel Miser has thus been designed so that each 10 percent increment of heating time here is 45 seconds, with a complete cycle taking 450 seconds, or 7½ minutes.

Oil furnaces are more restrictive in their cycling requirements; each system must be permitted a short cooling period each time the burner turns off. For oil systems then, the timing cycle of the fuel miser is set at 3 minutes for each 10 percent increment of duty cycle. The total time for one complete cycle for an oil burner system is therefore 30 minutes.

The selection of either of these timing cycles is accomplished merely by connecting one jumper wire in the fuel miser's circuit board.

How It Works

As you can see from the schematic diagram and the timing chart shown in Figs. 6.1 and 6.2, the fuel miser is

simply a clock dedicated to performing a specific task. IC1, a 555 timer chip, operates as an astable multivibrator at a frequency of about 22.7 hertz. This frequency is divided by *IC2*, a 12-stage binary divider, to provide a frequency of 0.022 hertz for gas systems or 0.006 hertz for oil systems. These frequencies represent periods of 45 seconds and 160 seconds (each period is the reciprocal of its frequency).

The selected output of *IC2* feeds a decade Johnson counter, *IC3*, which counts from zero to nine over and over again. *IC3* has 10 decoded outputs, one for each count, and a divided-by-10 output, pin 12, as illustrated in the timing diagram. One of the decoded outputs of *IC3* is selected by the duty cycle switch

Fig. 6.1. Schematic diagram shows that Fuel Miser is simply a clock performing a special task.

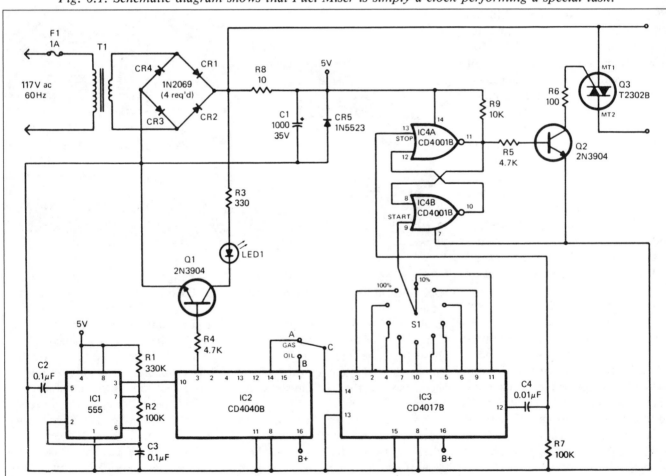

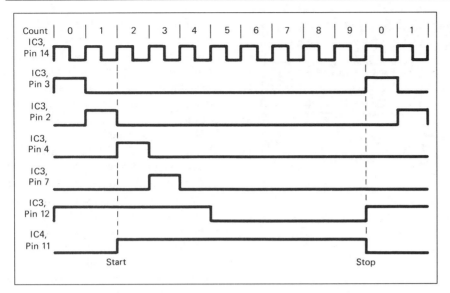

Fig. 6.2. Timing diagram for Fuel Miser.

and is used to trigger a latch circuit, *IC4A* and *IC4B*.

At this point the thermostat circuit of your furnace would be enabled. The divide-by-10 of IC3 is differentiated and used to reset the latch circuit. This disables the thermostat circuit.

If the output pulse of pin 4 of *IC3*, for example, is selected to start the sequence, the output pulse at pin 12 will stop the sequence eight decoded pulses later. Thus, the latch circuit output, pin 11 of *IC4*, will have a logic 1 level 80 percent of the time and a logic zero level 20 percent of the time.

This logic signal is fed to *Q2*, which acts as a switch to turn triac *Q3* on and off. *Q3* is the controlling switch that permits your thermostat to operate or not operate in accordance with the duty cycle selected by S1. *Q3* has a sufficient voltage rating and current-carrying capacity to handle both 24-volt and 117-volt thermostat circuits.

Construction

The fuel miser can be constructed on a printed or wiring circuit board measuring about 3½ by 5 inches (89 by 127 mm). A printed circuit layout is illustrated full size in Fig. 6.3, as viewed from the copper side of the board. The parts layout, as seen from the component side of the board, is shown in Fig. 6.4.

The layout of this circuit is not at all critical. It would be good practice, though, to use sockets for the integrated circuits and triac instead of soldering these components directly into the circuit, especially if the PC pattern is used. Such practice makes servicing the Fuel Miser easy, if it's ever necessary.

It's also important to pay strict attention to the orientation of the integrated circuit chips. Pin 1 of these components is usually indicated on the top of the plastic package by a small dot or numeral 1. In Figs. 3 and 4, pin 1 of each chip is identified by a small dot.

When you have finished constructing the circuit, examine it very carefully to be sure that there are no solder splashes that might short out one copper path to another, or two adjacent IC pins. Check also the position of each diode to make sure it's placed in the circuit as shown in Fig. 6.4.

There is one jumper wire that must be placed in the circuit for the appropriate type of heating system that the Fuel Miser will control. For gas systems, connect the jumper wire between points A and C as

---

PARTS LIST

Semiconductors
CR1 thru CR4 silicon diode, 1N2069 or similar
CR5—5.1-V zener diode, 1N4733 or similar
IC1-555 timer
IC2—CD4040B 12-stage binary counter
IC3—CD4017B Johnson counter
IC4—CD4001B Quad 2-input, NOR gate
LED1—Light-emitting diode
Q1, Q2—2N3904 transistor or similar
Q3—T2302B triac (RCA or similar)

Capacitors
C1—1000-µF 35-V electrolytic capacitor
C2, C3—0.1-µF ceramic capacitor

C4—0.01µF ceramic capacitor
Resistors ¼-W, 10%
R1—330 ohms
R2, R7—100k
R3—330 ohms
R4, R5—4.7k
R6—100 ohms
R8—10 ohms
R9—10k
Miscellaneous
F1—1-A fuse
S1—Rotary switch, 10-position 1 pole
T1—6-V transformer

Note: The following parts are available from A. Caristi, 69 White Pond Rd., Waldwick, NJ 07463: pc board, $7.75; triac T2302B, $3.75; CD 4040B, $3.75. Please include $1.00 for postage. NJ residents add tax.

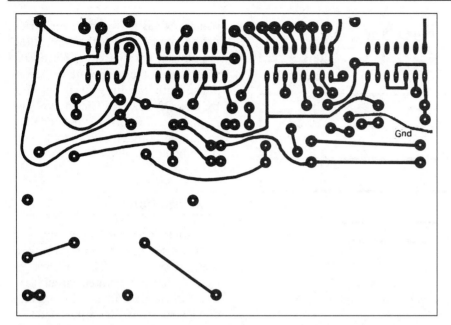

Fig. 6.3. Actual-size etching-and-drilling guide for Fuel Miser pc board.

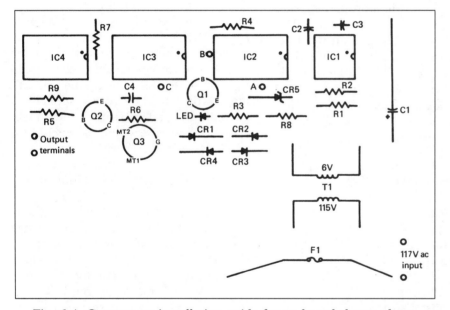

Fig. 6.4. Component installation guide for pc board shown above.

Before you connect the Fuel Miser into your furnace circuit, turn it on by applying 117 volts of ac power to the transformer primary. The LED should flash about once a second. If it does, your Fuel Miser is probably wired correctly.

If you do not get the flashing signal from the LED, disconnect the electrical power and examine the circuit for bad solder connections or short circuits between adjacent pins on the IC chips. Also check the diodes, transistors and ICs to be sure that they are not placed backwards in the circuit. You will have to substitute new IC chips for those already in the circuit if one or more of these chips is defective.

Installation

Once completed, the Fuel Miser can be installed anywhere near your furnace or your thermostat. Turn off all electrical power to the furnace and the Fuel Miser before making the installation. For all heating systems that operate with a two-wire thermostat, all you need do to connect the Fuel Miser is to open one of the thermostat connections and connect the output terminals of the Fuel Miser in series with the thermostat. This is illustrated in Fig. 6.5.

In some oil burner systems, three-wire thermostats are used. These thermostats have two sets of contacts that close at slightly different temperatures and are designed so that the burner starts only when both contacts are closed.

In these systems, the thermostat is usually wired to a relay whose contacts operate the oil burner motor. This means that the Fuel Miser's output terminals must be connected in series with the relay coil. This is shown in Fig. 6.6, which illustrates a typical three-wire oil burner. A photo of the author's assembled board is shown in Fig. 6.7.

shown in Fig. 6.4. For oil burner systems, connect the jumper between points B and C. Be sure to use only one jumper wire in your circuit.

For ease of assembly into a cabinet, you may mount the duty cycle selector switch directly on the circuit board and wire it into the circuit. This will enable you to mount the board to the front of the cabinet with the switch shaft protruding

through a hole drilled for that purpose. Use spacers to mount the circuit board.

Note that you may want to mount the LED on the panel of the cabinet so you can view it during operation to make sure it's working properly. After your assembly is complete, you will then want to label the switch positions, from 10 percent to 100 percent in increments of 10 percent each.

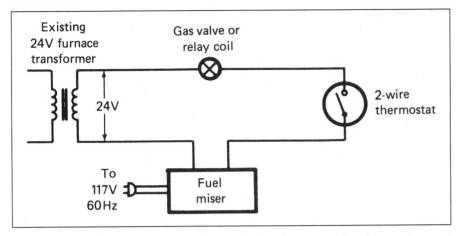

Fig. 6.5. Installation details for two-wire thermostat heating system.

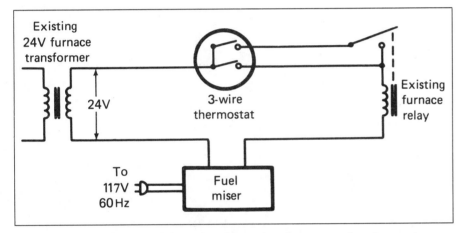

Fig. 6.6. Installation details for three-wire thermostat heating system.

After you have made the necessary connections, whatever your system, apply power to both the Fuel Miser and your furnace. Set the Fuel Miser's switch to the 100 percent position, and check your furnace for normal operation when heat is called.

Next, set the Fuel Miser's switch to the 10 percent position. Now set your thermostat to its highest setting and time the cycle of burner operation. For gas systems, the burner should operate about 45 seconds and be off for about 7 minutes. For oil systems, the burner should operate about 3 and be off for about 27 minutes.

When you've checked out your Fuel Miser, it's time, of course, to set it into operation. It is suggested that you start with a setting of 70 percent for a day or two. With some experimenting, you will quickly settle on a duty cycle that provides you with sufficient comfort while substantially reducing your heating bill.

You will probably find that during severe winter weather, your preferred setting will normally approach the higher end of your new heating scale. During milder weather, though, you'll probably find you can take full advantage of the lower settings—and lower costs.

Fig. 6.7. Photo of author's prototype shows project assembled on perforated board. Note the use of sockets for all ICs and transistors. All wiring is performed on under side of board. A homemade pc board can also be used.

chapter **7**

Experimenter's Radio-Control System

ROBERT C. FROSTHOLM

Most radio-control (R/C) system plans published in books and magazines are fixed in design, usually to control model airplanes, cars, boats, etc. There are no such limitations imposed on the Experimenter's Radio-Control System presented here. This is a basic transmitter/receiver system with "open end" outputs that *you* adapt to suit your particular needs. In addition to allowing you to control the usual hobby models, the system can be made to control heating/cooling systems and automatic sprinklers, implement sophisticated robotics, and even set up a digital local-area network. In fact, the uses to which the system can be put are limited only by your inventiveness and knowledge of electronics.

Unlike other R/C systems you may have seen in the past, the Experimenter's Radio-Control System has very few components, the credit for which goes to a pair of matched encoder/transmitter and receiver/decoder integrated circuits from National Semiconductor. With these two ICs and a few extra components, you can build the full system in just a few hours.

Our basic system provides four output channels. Its two digital channels provide simple on/off switching, while its two analog channels provide proportional control.

Encoder/Transmitter

A complete six-channel digital-proportional encoder and r-f transmitter on a single DIP chip makes up the heart of the transmitter. This National Semiconductor LM1871 chip (*IC1* in Fig. 7.1) is intended for use

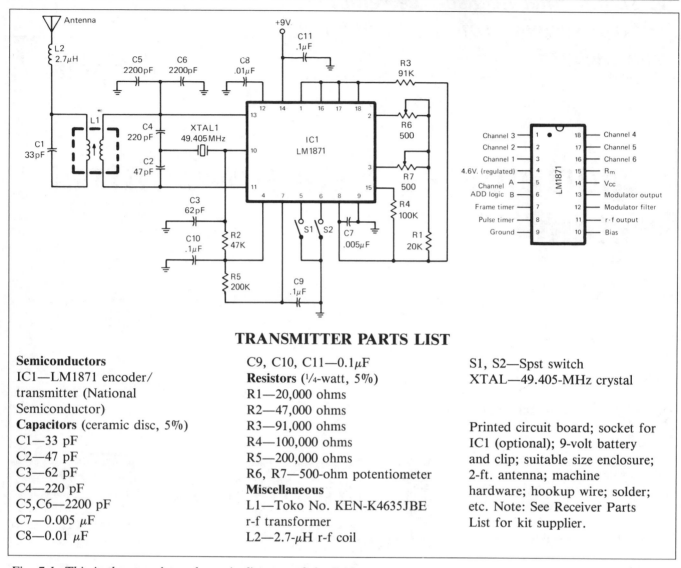

TRANSMITTER PARTS LIST

Semiconductors
IC1—LM1871 encoder/
transmitter (National
Semiconductor)
Capacitors (ceramic disc, 5%)
C1—33 pF
C2—47 pF
C3—62 pF
C4—220 pF
C5,C6—2200 pF
C7—0.005 µF
C8—0.01 µF

C9, C10, C11—0.1µF
Resistors (¼-watt, 5%)
R1—20,000 ohms
R2—47,000 ohms
R3—91,000 ohms
R4—100,000 ohms
R5—200,000 ohms
R6, R7—500-ohm potentiometer
Miscellaneous
L1—Toko No. KEN-K4635JBE
r-f transformer
L2—2.7-µH r-f coil

S1, S2—Spst switch
XTAL—49.405-MHz crystal

Printed circuit board; socket for
IC1 (optional); 9-volt battery
and clip; suitable size enclosure;
2-ft. antenna; machine
hardware; hookup wire; solder;
etc. Note: See Receiver Parts
List for kit supplier.

Fig. 7.1. This is the complete schematic diagram of the R/C transmitter. Pulse widths are set by potentiometers R6 and R7 for the two analog channel and by switches S1 and S2 for the two digital channel outputs.

as a low-power, license-free, non-voice communications device for use on 27 or 49 MHz. In addition to the radio-control hobby, toy and industrial applications, the encoder can provide a serial input of six words for hard-wire, infrared, and fiber-optic communications links.

Potentiometers *R6* and *R7* in Fig. 7.1 are used to set the pulse widths of the two analog channels, while switches *S1* and *S2* allow you to set the binary-coded pulse position modulation for the digital channels (see Fig. 7.2). Thus, the two digital channel outputs (in the receiver) are determined by the number of pulses

Fig. 7.2. Shown here are details of digital channel encoding and decoding via pulse count modulation. Transmitter conditions in first two columns generate the receiver responses indicated by entries in the last two columns.

LM1871 (TRANSMITTER)			LM1872 (RECEIVER)		
PIN CONDITIONS		TRANSMITTED WAVEFORM	BINARY PULSE COUNT	DIGITAL OUTPUTS	
PIN 5 (CH A)	PIN 6 (CH B)	← T_F →		CH A	CH B
Open	Open		100	Off.	Off
Ground	Open		101	On	Off
Open	Ground		110	Off	On
Ground	Ground		111	On	On

transmitted, rather than by the width of the channel.

Two timing circuits make up the transmitter's encoder. The waveforms for these are shown in Fig. 7.3. Frame time is determined by the values of R5 and C9 at pin 7 of *IC1*; pulse time at pin 8 is determined by the values of *C7* and *R4*. The relationships are as follows:

Frame time $T_F = R5C9 + 0.63R4C7$
Modulation time $T_M = 0.63R4C7$
Channel Time $T_{CH} = 0.63R3C7$

Frame, modulation, and channel times should typically be set for 9.5, 0.5 and 0.5 milliseconds, respectively.

Class C was chosen as the operating mode for the crystal controlled oscillator/transmitter. Resistor *R2* provides base bias current from V (regulated) pin 4 of *IC1*. R-f feedback in the oscillator is via series-mode third-overtone crystal *XTAL1*, which controls the frequency of oscillation. With this arrangement, the best alignment method would be to tune *L1* for minimum supply current while observing the carrier envelope.

Receiver/Decoder

The receiver is based on National Semiconductor's companion LM1872 radio-control receiver/decoder chip, a crystal-controlled superheterodyne design that offers good sensitivity and selectivity (see Fig. 7.4). In concert with the LM1871 transmitter, the LM1872 provides four independent information channels. The two analog channels are pulse-width modulated (PWM), while the two digital channels offer simple on/off control (see ''Modulation Methods'' for more details.)

Each digital channel provides sufficient power to directly drive a 100-mA load. Instead of providing direct control, each of the LM1872's analog outputs goes to its own separate SN76604 pulse-width demodulator/servo amplifier. The SN76604 has on-chip transistors that are capable of driving a 400-mA load. This servo amplifier is unique in that it provides bidirectional output capability from a single-ended power supply.

In the Fig. 7.4 circuit, the r-f signal from the transmitter is demodulated and decoded by negative-edge triggering of a cascade of three binary dividers. The dividers count the number of pulses to determine the number of information channels being transmitted.

Single conversion, with agc, generates a 455-kHz i-f and provides 58 dB of gain. The *L5/C13* input circuit prevents strong out-of-band TV and FM signals from cross-modulating the desired signal. The decoder portion extracts the time information from the carrier for the analog channels and the pulse-count information for the digital channels.

At the core of the decoder is a three-stage flip-flop binary counter chain identified by the letters A, B, and C. Referring to Fig. 7.5, when the r-f carrier drops out for the first T_M modulation pulse, the falling edge advances the counter. During the period T_M, sync timing capacitor *C20* is held low by a transistor inside *IC2* (Fig. 7.4). When the carrier comes up for the first variable analog pulse (T_{CH}), *C20* begins to charge toward the V + /2 threshold but does not reach this point before T_{CH} ends. When T_{CH} does end (carrier dropout), the counter advances for the second analog channel and repeats the sequence. Thus, the width of each analog pulse output equals the sum of a fixed T_M pulse and a variable T_{CH} pulse width.

Following transmission of the second analog channel, a variable quantity of from one to four fixed 500-microsecond width pulses that contain the digital channel information are transmitted. At the conclusion of the frame, a sync pulse is sent. This pulse is much longer in duration than the sync pulse timer's period and ultimately resets the counter to ready it for the next frame. The transmitter will continue to send successive frames of information as long as power is applied.

Construction

Though neither the transmitter nor the receiver is very complicated, in terms of numbers of components, printed-circuit board construction is highly recommended. There are two reasons for this. One is to keep the assembled circuits as compact and lightweight as possible. The other is to keep down r-f interactions. You can fabricate your own pc boards, using the actual-size etching-and-drilling guides given in Fig. 7.6, or purchase an entire kit, which includes ready-to-use pc boards, from

Fig. 7.3. These are the transmitter encoder's timing circuit waveforms.

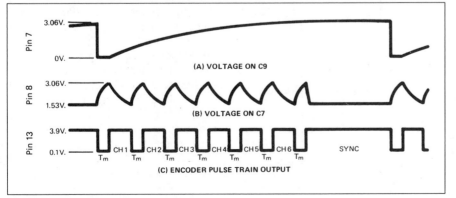

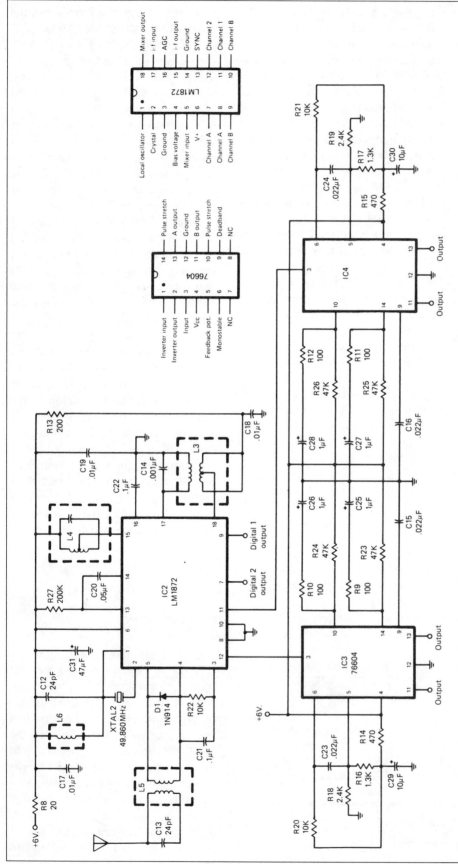

RECEIVER PARTS LIST

Semiconductors

D1—IN914 diode

IC2—LM1872 receiver/diode (National Semiconductor)

IC3, IC4—76604 demodulator/ servo amp (Texas Instruments)

Capacitors

C12, C13—24-pF ceramic disc

C14—0.0001-μF ceramic disc

C15, C16—0.022-μF Mylar

C17, C18, C19—0.01-μF ceramic disc

C20—0.05-μF ceramic disc

C21, C22—0.1-μF ceramic disc

C23, C24—0.33-μF Mylar

C25 thru C28—1-μF, 6-volt electrolytic

C29, C30—10-μF, 6-volt electrolytic

C31—47-μF, 6-volt electrolytic

Resistors (¼-watt, 5%)

R8—20 ohms

R9 thru R12—100 ohms

R13—200 ohms

R14, R15—470 ohms

R16, R17—1300 ohms

R18, R19—2400 ohms

R20, R21, R22—10,000 ohms

R23 thru R26—47,000 ohms

R27—200,000 ohms

Miscellaneous

L3—Toko No. RMC202313NO center-tapped r-f transformer

L4—Toko No. RMC402503NO r-f coil

L5, L6—Toko No. KEN4028 DZ r-f transformer

XTAL2—49.860-MHz crystal

Printed-circuit board; suitable enclosure; four C- or D-cell batteries (see text) and holder; antenna; machine hardware; hookup wire; solder; etc.

Note: The following items are available from Advanced Analog Systems, Inc., 790 Lucerne Dr., Sunnyvale, CA 94086: No. AAS-2712 complete kit of parts, including circuit boards but not batteries and enclosures, for $75.00; No. PCB1871 etched and drilled pc boards for transmitter and receiver for $15.00; No. C1781 Toro coils (L1 and L3 thru L6) for $25.00 California residents, please add 7% tax.

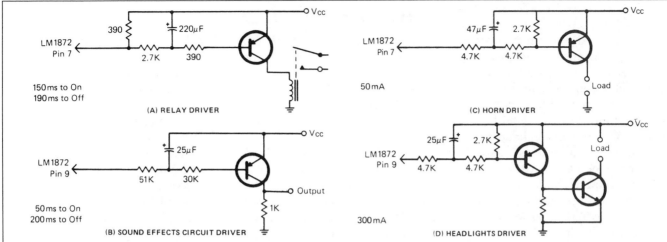

(A) RELAY DRIVER

LM1872 Pin 7

390   220µF

2.7K   390

Vcc

150ms to On
190ms to Off

(B) SOUND EFFECTS CIRCUIT DRIVER

LM1872 Pin 9

25µF

51K   30K

Vcc

Output

1K

50ms to On
200ms to Off

(C) HORN DRIVER

LM1872 Pin 7

47µF   2.7K

4.7K   4.7K

Vcc

Load

50mA

(D) HEADLIGHTS DRIVER

LM1872 Pin 9

25µF   2.7K

4.7K   4.7K

Vcc

Load

300mA

Interfacing to the Real World

For the Experimenter's Radio-Control System receiver's digital outputs to do anything useful, they must be interfaced with the so-called "real world." Shown here are four typical examples of simple interfaces for the digital outputs of the LM1872 (*IC1* in Fig. 7.4) at pins 7 and 9. These simple circuits—and others you might think of—can be assembled on small pieces of perforated board and housed within the receiver's enclosure or external to it.

Circuit (A) is an example of an interface that can provide on/off control for high-power loads. Power for the load, independent of the receiver's battery supply, is routed through the relay's contacts. Circuit (B) provides a direct on/off *signal*, rather than the mechanical make/break action of circuit (A). Circuits (C) and (D) source current for medium- and relatively high-power loads, respectively. Other interfaces will suggest themselves.

the source given in the Receiver Parts List.

Circuit assembly on the pc boards is a simple straightforward procedure (see Fig. 7.7 for details). You simply plug each component into the indicated holes on the board, making sure to properly orient it, and solder its leads or pins to the foil pads on the underside of the board. You can use the DIP sockets for the ICs if you wish, but this is not essential.

You can house the transmitter and receiver in any size boxes, preferably metal, that will comfortably accommodate them, their battery supplies, antennas and any controls

Fig. 7.4. This is the complete schematic diagram of the receiver/ decoder. Digital channel outputs are taken from pins 7 and 9 of IC2. Analog channel outputs first go through demodulator/servo amplifiers IC3 and IC4.

Fig. 7.5. Timing waveforms available at various points within the receiver.

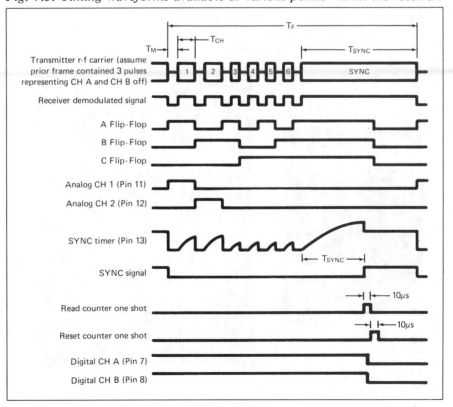

Modulation Methods

As explained in the main text, the Experimenter's Radio-Control System employs both digital and analog control elements.

There are many different ways to communicate in a digital format. Computers and microprocessors, for example, use pulse position modulation (PPM) in which at a specific point in time a pulse is either present (logic 1) or absent (logic 0). If a pulse arrives too soon or too late, it often goes undetected. Hence, the pulse's *position* in time is of critical importance.

The digital channels in this project use a form of pulse position modulation known as *pulse-count modulation* (PCM). At the transmitter, switches *S1* and *S2* (see Fig. 7.1) are closed for a logic 1 or open for a logic 0. The LM1871 detects the status of the switches in *S1/S2* sequence and internally converts this to a pulse train as follows: one pulse for open/open; two pulses for closed/open; three pulses for open/closed; and four pulses for closed/closed. The pulse train is then used to turn on the r-f carrier for transmission in bursts.

At the receiver, the transmitted carrier bursts are detected and converted back into pulses. The receiver then counts the pulses and decodes the count to latch the digital outputs as follows: one pulse for off/off; two pulses for on/off; three pulses for off/on; and four pulses for on/on.

The analog section employs pulse-width modulation (PWM). Pulse-width modulation is simply a means of changing the width (time duration) of a pulse to convey the desired information. Perhaps the most common form of PWM is Morse code, in which an ideal dash is three times longer than a dot. With Morse code, only two pulse widths are employed. In our R/C system, pulse widths can vary over a 1-to-2-millisecond range (mandated by FCC regulations to limit side-band interference). This is sufficient for the typical hobby servo, which centers with a 15-millisecond pulse and requires a 1.0-millisecond pulse for full left and a 2.0-millisecond pulse for full right positioning.

In the Experimenter's Radio-Control System, analog information is provided by potentiometers *R6* and *R7* in Fig. 7.1, which apply voltages to the two analog channel inputs. Unique applications could replace the pots with thermostat controls, humidity sensors, pressure transducers, or any other analog voltage source. The width of the generated pulse is directly proportional to the magnitude of the analog voltage developed at the source.

Fig. 7.6. Actual-size etching-and drilling guides for transmitter (left) and receiver (right) to use when making your own printed-circuit boards.

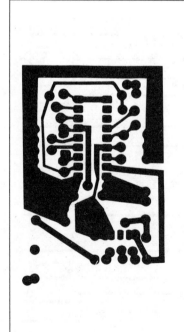 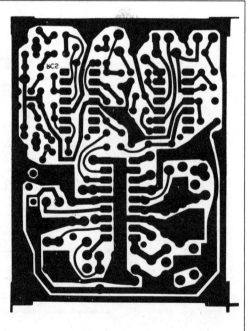

and interfacing that may be required for your application.

Using the System

A 2-foot antenna is recommended for most applications. This will give roughly a 200-foot communicating range. If you wish to increase the range of the system, you can increase the length of the receiving antenna. Additional range can also be obtained by increasing receiver sensitivity. Decreasing input transformer *L5*'s turns ratio, for example, will couple more signal into the mixer, but at the expense of a lower tuned-circuit Q, due to mixer loading. Moving the primary tap on mixer transformer *L3* farther from the supply side and/or decreasing the primary-to-secondary turns ratio will also increase gain. Changing

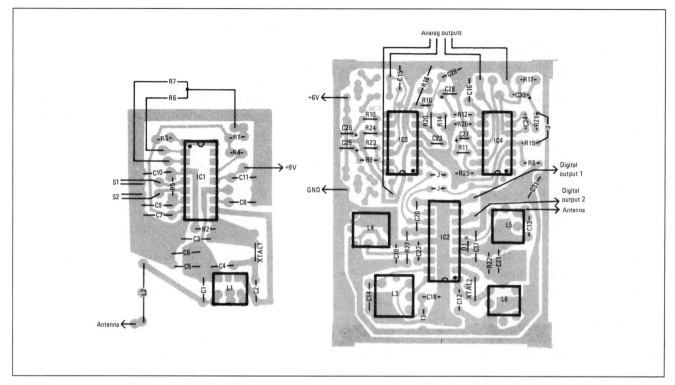

Fig. 7.7. These are the component installation and orientation guides for the encoder/transmitter (left) and receiver/decoder (right).

L3 to a 5:1 ratio coil (the specified coil gives a 32:1 ratio) will double 49-MHz sensitivity from 6 to 12 microvolts.

The receiver's digital outputs have significant drive capability. They are capable of sinking 100 mA with a saturation resistance of 7 ohms. Alternatively, they can source 100 mA at up to 1 volt above ground for driving grounded npn transistors and silicon controlled rectifiers (SCRs). For higher currents, the digital outputs can be summed by connecting together pins 7 and 9 of *IC2*.

The 455-kHz intermediate frequency was chosen for convenience. Actually, system i-f can be as low as 50 kHz or as high as 1 MHz, obtainable by changing the values of the appropriate components.

Receiver alignment is quite simple, requiring just a voltmeter capable of tracking down to about 25 millivolts and a general-purpose oscilloscope with a minimum bandwidth of 1 MHz.

The alignment procedure is as follows. Adjust the slug in *L6* while using an oscilloscope to monitor the local oscillator signal at pin 2 of *IC2*. As you adjust *L6*, you will note that signal amplitude increases, reaches a peak and then abruptly falls off. For proper alignment, adjust the coil's slug in the opposite direction from the drop-off point, just below peak.

To adjust *L3, L4,* and *L5,* use the r-f signal from the transmitter. Before proceeding to adjust these coils, however, it is necessary to defeat the agc by temporarily grounding pin 16 of *IC2*. Use the amplitude of the i-f signal at pin 15 to guide in alignment. It is sometimes advantageous to monitor this signal on the unused output of *L4* to prevent the i-f from shifting as you touch pin 15.

Place the transmitter at a sufficient distance from the receiver so that the measured voltage on pin 15 of *IC2* is less than 400 millivolts (less than 50 millivolts if you are monitoring *L4*'s secondary). Adjust *L5, L3,* and *L4* for maximum signal strength. Repeat adjusting these coils until you observe no further increase in amplitude.

Applications Suggestions

The Experimenter's Radio-Control System described here consists of a basic encoder/transmitter and receiver/decoder without interfacing to the outside world. Since this is conceptually an *experimenter's* R/C system, we have left applications implementation to your ingenuity.

The system described is excellent for remote radio control of the usual model airplanes, boats, cars, etc. By adding some very minor interface circuitry at the decoder outputs of *IC3* and *IC4,* it is possible to remotely control lights, appliances, heating systems, automatic sprinkler systems, and much more. For such applications, no modification of the transmitter is necessary.

For more ambitious—and

knowledgeable—experimenters, other applications might include simple robot control; complex robot control (tie the transmitter into a personal computer and program the floor plan of your home, for example); conversion of video games to eliminate the cable attached to the joysticks; a carrier-current digital local-area network (FSK or on/off carrier modulation) communications link using local house ac wiring; remote temperature monitoring with associated heater/air conditioning control; etc.

Some simple interfaces to help you get started are given in circuits A through D in "Interfacing to the Outside World." If your primary interest is to adapt the system for motor drive (as needed for model airplanes, boats, and cars), important information is given in the "Motor Drive Notes" box.

Whichever way you decide to use the Experimenter's Radio-Control System, you will find it both highly flexible and eminently adaptable.

Motor Drive Notes

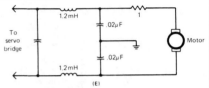

For applications in which motors are used, the receiver and drive motors are powered by the same battery. Because of high current drain, alkaline cells are preferred. An alkaline C cell can deliver 400 mA, a D cell 700 mA, for 10 continuous hours. Comparable carbon-zinc cells will last only one or two hours.

Since dc motors generate wide-spectrum noise, this can have an adverse effect on the receiver's r-f and i-f sections. Also, high peak-current demands by a motor under heavy load can affect battery terminal voltage. This can be critical as cell voltage drops toward its end-of-life 0.9-volt level. Fortunately, sensitive circuit elements in the receiver are referenced to the supply line, and the LM1872 has good common-mode rejection characteristics.

Most notable problems will occur with very inexpensive motors in which a metal stamping is used for commutator brushes. The brushes have very-light, single-point contacts that cause a great deal of arcing and, hence, electrical noise. If a motor is located several inches from the receiver, you may have to use a noise-suppression network like that shown here. In projects where space considerations force close proximity between motor and receiver, use low-noise motors with wire or carbon brushes. Various types of small dc servo motors are available from local hobby dealers and mail-order houses.

A standard TV/video-game r-f
modulator plus a home-brew dual-
IC receiver lets you use cable to
transmit analog or digital signals
over long distances

chapter **8**

A Simple Cable Communications System

DUANE M. PERKINS

Transmission of high-frequency signals over a coaxial cable is easily achieved using a vhf carrier. The "transmitter" for such a system is a readily available Aztec Model UM1285-8 (or similar) r-f modular commonly used to transmit pictures from a home computer or video game to a TV receiver. The modulator is a relatively inexpensive item that doesn't require any "construction" on your part. It's designed so that you can simply use the signal you want to transmit to modulate the video carrier. Then all you need to complete the system is a receiver at the other end of the cable. We'll tell you how to build this receiver inexpensively from components you can obtain from local electronics parts stores and mail-order houses.

Although the r-f modulator is designed to serve as a transmitting device for pictures from a video signal source to a TV receiver, it isn't restricted to just this use. It can also be modulated with any analog and/or digital signal that falls within the 4-MHz bandwidth of the commer-

cial broadcast TV video (picture) signal. Since the modulator can accommodate high frequency dc pulses, the system is a natural for digital transmission. An obvious application here would be high-speed transmission of data from a home computer over a substantial distance. Time- or frequency-division multiplexing would allow for simultaneous transmission of multiple signals.

About the Receiver

A suitable receiver for your cable communication system can easily be built with the aid of two ICs that greatly simplify assembly, since they contain all of the circuitry required for their separate functions. These ICs are the MC1350 i-f amplifier and the MC1330 video detector. Just add a few capacitors, resistors, and coils, plus a suitable

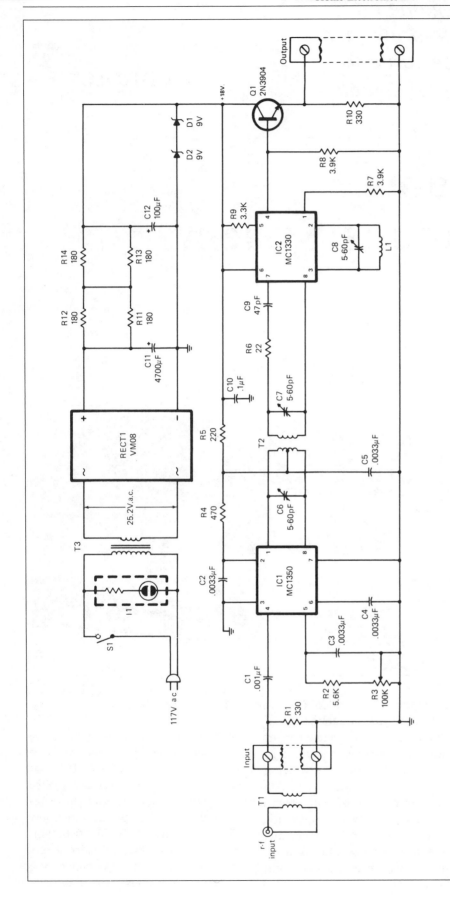

PARTS LIST

Semiconductors
D1, D2—9-volt, 1-watt zener diode
IC1—MC1350 i-f amplifier
IC2—MC1330 video amplifier
Q1—2N3904 or similar npn silicon transistor
RECT1—VM08 or similar bridge rectifier

Capacitors
C1—0.001-μF disc
C2 thru C5—0.0033-μF disc
C6, C7, C8—5 to 60-pF trimmer
C9—47-pF disc
C10—0.1-μF disc
C11—4700-μF, 35-volt electrolytic
C12—100-μF, 35-volt electrolytic

Resistors
(¼-watt, 10%)
R1, R10—3300 ohms
R2—5600 ohms
R4—470 ohms
R5—220 ohms
R6—22 ohms
R7, R8—3900 ohms
R9—3300 ohms
R11 thru R14—180 ohms
R3—100,000-ohm linear-taper potentiometer

Miscellaneous
I1—Panel-mount neon-lamp assembly
L1—R-f coil (see text)
S1—Spst slide or toggle switch
T1—75-to-300-ohm TV matching transformer
T2—R-f transformer
T3—25.2-volt, 300-mA transformer
Suitable size aluminum case (Radio Shack No. 270-238 or similar); printed-circuit board; 4-contact barrier block; ac line cord with plug; control knob for R2; 22-gauge magnet wire; ½" (12.7 mm) spacers (4); rubber grommets; rubber feet (4); machine hardware; hookup wire; solder; etc.

power supply, and you have a complete receiver (see Fig. 8.1). The coils are all hand wound, using magnet wire, and are easy to make. A 75-to-300-ohm TV matching transformer provides the means for coupling the input from the 75-ohm cable to the receiver.

To match the capability of the transmitter, the receiver must be capable of demodulating a carrier on the 61.25-MHz channel-3 or 67.25-MHz channel-4 frequency to deliver a dc output signal with frequency components that do not exceed the 4-MHz bandwidth.

Considering what it does, the receiver circuit shown in Fig. 8.1, along with its ac-line-operated power supply, is really quite simple. Though the MC1350 specified for IC1 is described by the manufacturer as an i-f amplifier, in our receiver we use it as an r-f amplifier.

Transformer T1 isolates the cable from the receiver's ground (this may not be necessary) and doubles the input voltage. If you wish, you can connect the cable directly to the input, though there will be a loss of half the gain. If you make a direct connection to the input, change the value of R1 to about 75 ohms.

R-f transformer T2 couples the amplified r-f signal from the output of IC1 and delivers it to the input of detector IC2, which further amplifies the signal prior to demodulation. Detector output at pin 4 of IC2 has a peak to-peak amplitude of about 6.5 volts, which is fed to Q1. The purpose of emitter-follow-

Fig. 8.1. In this overall schematic diagram of the receiver, circuit design is greatly simplified by the use of specialized i-f amplifier (MC1350) and video amplifier (MC1330) integrated circuits. Coils L1 and the primary and secondary of T2 are hand wound.

er stage Q1 is to lower output impedance to about 300 ohms.

High-frequency ac signals can be matched to a 75-ohm coaxial cable with another matching transformer connected to the output of the receiver at the emitter of Q1 through a suitable coupling capacitor. Subcarriers can be pulled off in this manner and sent to a suitable receiver/demodulator.

Potentiometer R3 controls the r-f amplifier's gain as needed to compensate for cable attenuation in long runs. Lowest gain is ample for a short cable run. However, cable losses of 18 dB or more, which occurs at about 900 feet with RG-59/U, can be compensated for by adjusting R3 to increase gain.

Power for the circuit is derived from the 117-volt ac line through a power supply, shown at the top in Fig. 8.1. This is a simple, straightforward supply in which a pair of zener diodes (D1 and D2), each rated at 9 volts, regulate the 18 volts dc required by the circuit. Power-on indicator I1 is optional.

Construction

Careful consideration must be given to the high frequencies and high gain involved in the circuit when building the receiver. This is particularly important with regard to L1 and T2. Any coupling between these two components is almost certain to result in undesired oscillations. Therefore, it's necessary to arrange your layout so that L1 and T2 are physically separated from each other and that their axes are in 90° opposition. Construction is best done on a printed circuit board, an actual-size etching-and-drilling guide for which is given in Fig. 8.2. Also shown in Fig. 8.2 is the components placement/orientation diagram.

Before you begin construction, prepare the coils that make up L1 and T2 by closely winding 22-gauge

magnet wire on a ¼ inch (6.35 mm) form, such as the shaft of a potentiometer. Wind five turns for each half of the primary and 10 turns for the secondary of T2 and 10 turns for L1. Then carefully scrape away the enamel coating from each end of each coil and the center tap of T1's primary and tin with solder. Note that these coils all have an air core.

Referring to the components placement/orientation diagram in Fig. 8.2, install the components exactly as shown. Make sure all are properly oriented and indexed before soldering them into place. Note that the primary and secondary coils that make up T2 mount in-line, rather than parallel to each other as is usually the case with transformers.

Remove ¼ inch (6.35 mm) of insulation from each end of three 4 inch (102 mm) lengths of red insulated and four 4 inch (102 mm) lengths of black insulated hookup wires. Loosely twist together three red/black wire pairs. Remove an additional ¼ inch (6.35 mm) of insulation from only one end of the black wire in one pair and install and solder the *opposite* ends of these wires in the holes labeled To R3 on the components placement diagram. Plug one end of each of the remaining wire pairs into the holes labeled From T1 and OUTPUT and solder into place. (Note: Use the red wire for signal "hot" and the black wire for signal ground in all three cases). The fourth black wire goes to the hole external S1.

Temporarily set the pc board assembly on the floor of the aluminum enclosure in which the project is to be housed and mark the locations in which its mounting holes are to be drilled. Remove and set aside the board and drill the holes. Machine the front panel (the side of the box nearest the trimmer capacitors) to accommodate I1, R3, and S1. Make sure you locate these holes where the components that mount in them won't interfere with or touch the

Fig. 8.2. Shown at the left is the actual-size etching-and-drilling guide to use when home fabricating the receiver printed-circuit board. The illustration at the right gives details for installing and orienting components.

components on the circuit board. If you wish to avoid having to cut a rectangular hole for a slide switch, use a toggle switch for *S1* so that only a single round hole need be drilled. Then drill the five holes through the rear wall, sized according to the needs of the hardware for the barrier block and the rubber grommets for the input and output wire pairs and the line cord.

Mount the barrier block on the outside real wall of the box (Fig. 8.3). Strip ¼ inch (6.35 mm) of insulation from each lead of *I1*. Tightly twist together the fine wires in each lead and sparingly tin with solder. Remove the retaining nut from *I1* and mount the lamp assembly in its holes on the front panel. Repeat this procedure for the two conductors at the unfinished end of

the ac line cord and then separate the conductors for a distance of about 3 inches (76.2 mm).

Pass the free end of the ac line cord through its rubber grommet, feeding it from the outside into the box. Tie a knot about 4 inches (102 mm) from the prepared end to serve as a strain relief. Connect and solder either lead of the line cord to either *T3* primary lead. Crimp and solder the other ac line cord lead to one lug of *S1*. Mount *S1* on the front panel. Then locate the single fourth black wire and one lead of *I1* and crimp both to the other lug of *S1*. The other *I1* lead goes to the *T3* primary lead not connected to *S1*.

Mount *R3* on the front panel, pointing its lugs upward and in line with the top lip of the box. Viewing the project with the front panel fac-

ing you, the lugs on *R3* are now 1, 2 and 3 from left to right. Locate the red/black twisted-pair wires for *R3* (the one with the extra ¼ inch (6.35 mm) of insulation removed from the black wire). Pass the bare conductor of the black wire through lug 2 and crimp it around lug 3 and solder both connections. Crimp and solder the red wire to lug 1.

Feed the remaining two pairs of red/black twisted-pair wires through the two small rubber grommets in the rear wall of the box and solder to the ends of each wire a spade lug. Slip the spade lugs under the screw heads of the barrier block and tighten.

Carefully measure the locations of the trimmer capacitor (*C6, C7,* and *C8*) adjustment slots. Transfer these locations to the top of the box and drill a ⅛ inch (3.18 mm) hole at

Fig. 8.3. Interior view of project. Note that 4-contact barrier block mounts on rear panel. Position pc board with large filter capacitor along rear panel.

each point. These holes provide access for a tuning wand to the capacitors for easy tuning of the receiver.

Aligning the Receiver

Before attempting to align the receiver, check for proper operation by measuring the voltages at certain key points. Plug the line cord into a convenient ac receptacle and set $S1$ to on. The approximate voltages you should obtain are as follows:

Voltage	Measurement Point
18	IC2 pin 6, Q1 collector
15	IC1 pins 6 & 8
13	IC2 pin 5
11	IC1 pin 2
8	IC2 pin 1
6.7	IC2 pin 4, Q1 base
6.2	Q1 emitter
4.3-5.3	IC1 pin 5 over full range of R3

Once you've verified that the voltages are approximately correct, connect 75-to-300-ohm transformer $T1$ to the receiver's INPUT terminals. Then connect the r-f modulator (transmitter), set to channel 3 or 4, depending on channel activity in your viewing area, to the input of $T1$. Connect a suitable power supply to the transmitter and turn it on.

Begin alignment by using the full output of the transmitter. To do this, ground the video modulation input to the transmitter's case. Set the receiver for minimum gain and use a voltmeter to monitor the receiver's output. Tune each coil circuit inside the receiver for minimum output voltage, adjusting $C8$, $C7$ and $C6$ in that order. Repeat the tuning procedures as often as necessary until you obtain no further reduction in output voltage. However, it isn't necessary to try for the last few millivolts, since oscillation

may occur if tuning is peaked too precisely. Just tune for less than 1 volt of receiver output.

After completing rough alignment, unground the transmitter's video modulation input and feed in positive-pulse modulation while observing receiver output on an oscilloscope. Refine alignment to obtain best output, which should be about 6.5 volts peak-to-peak with 100% modulation. It may be necessary to stagger-tune slightly to obtain good waveform reproduction and avoid oscillation. Try changing the spacing between the turns of the hand-wound coils and/or between the primary and secondary of $T2$ if necessary.

When properly aligned, the receiver should produce an output signal that is very clean and has fast rise and fall times and sharp corners. Use the highest-frequency pulses your scope will reproduce without significant high-frequency attenuation. In the final analysis, however, all you need tune for is best alignment for your application, which may not even require maximum gain.

Parting Comment

In addition to the video carrier, the r-f modulator can also put a 4.5-MHz audio carrier on the cable. With a suitable FM receiver, such as TV audio, the sound carrier can also be used simultaneously with the video carrier for voice, FSK or tone transmission. The sound carrier, however, is 22 dB below the level of the video carrier and can be used only for transmission of an ac signal in the audio spectrum. As such, it is of only secondary interest.

Part **3**

Audio/Video Electronics

Adding this accessory to your hi-fi system recovers ambience information from recordings and adds delay to provide realistic sound

chapter **9**

"Surround-Sound" Enhancer

JOHN H. ROBERTS

Ambience—so-called "room sound"—is the missing ingredient that makes even the best stereo system sound flat and lifeless when compared to live-performance sounds. Over the years, various techniques have been devised and employed in consumer products to simulate or recreate the ambience of the live performance. To some degree, all have been successful. Until now, however, few have offered the advantages of the Delay Enhanced L-R Decoder described here.

What makes this Decoder project a superior performer is that it uses two of the time-honored techniques that have met with relatively large success. It offers both time delay and L-R matrix (ambience-recovery) capabilities in the same accessory. Combining the two techniques results in a system that works better than either alone.

Performing L-R matrix recovery before adding time delay cuts the expense of using two complete channels, with no deterioration of the ambience information. Adding delay to the L-R matrix corrects that system's localization problems.

Some Background

Artificial reverberation, generated by either mechanical or electronic delays, offers some improvement over the unprocessed sound signals normally delivered to the speakers of a hi-fi system. However, even the most elaborate delay system requires adjustments to make the simulated reverberation match different recordings, the result often sounding unnatural. Discrete and matrixed four-channel recording had the capability of reproducing ambience but was not properly utilized and, hence, fell out of favor.

Fig. 9.1. The Dynaquad™ L-R ambience-recovery scheme places the rear speakers in parallel with the speakers used in the front.

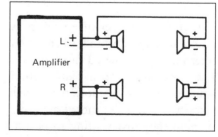

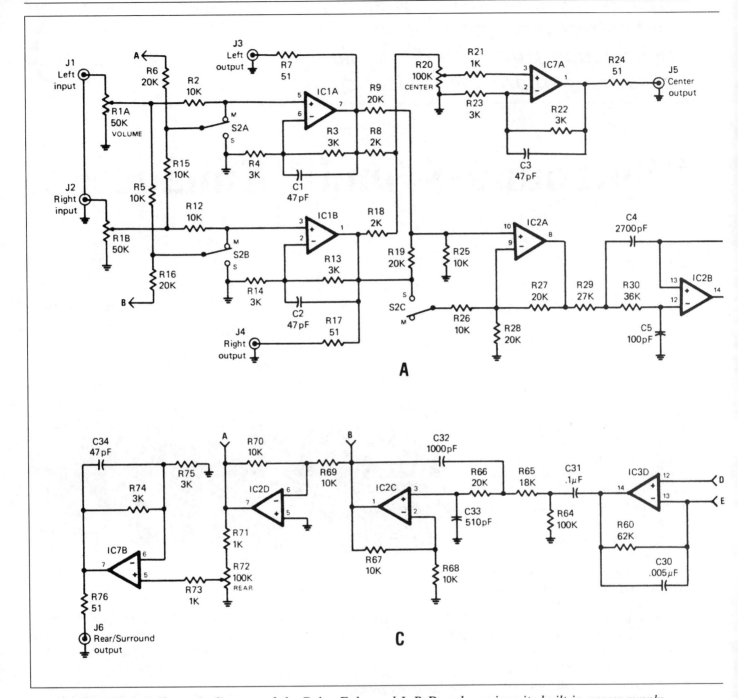

Fig. 9.2. Entire schematic diagram of the Delay Enhanced L-R Decoder, minus its built-in power supply. Arrowed letters in each part match up with the same arrowed letters in other parts (A goes to A, B to B, etc.). Numbers shown in small boxes are voltages that can be measured with a good circuit, provided here in case you have to troubleshoot.

A certain amount of ambience is automatically captured whenever a microphone is located more than a few feet away from any sound source. Therefore, most recordings already contain significant amounts of ambience just waiting to be un-

locked. To unlock it, you need a special signal processor.

Two popular techniques to extract this ambience information from conventional recordings are *time delay* and *L-R matrix*. Pure time delay, not to be confused with delay gener-

ated artificial reverberation, was discovered by E. Roerbaek Madsen, who was searching for a way to dramatically improve audibility in conventional recordings.

Some consumer hi-fi delay devices of the late 1970s were based on the

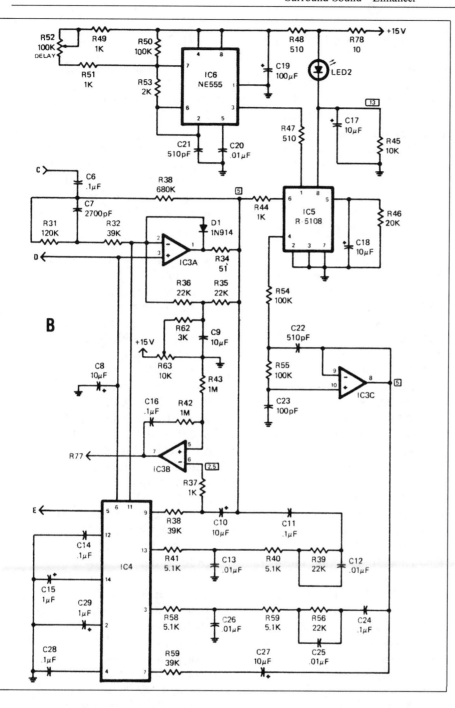

By subtracting the output of one microphone from the other, the almost identical sounds would cancel out, leaving predominantly ambience. This system improved the ambience situation quite a bit, but it suffered from poor front imaging and localization. That is, sounds occasionally appeared in the back that were not supposed to be there.

A note of caution: If you wish to experiment with the passive L-R matrix, keep in mind that the rear speakers will be in parallel with those in front and may present an unacceptably low impedance to your power amplifier. Additionally, peaks occurring in only one channel may upset the protection circuitry of the other, which must then sink the full current being sourced, even if it is sitting at 0 volt.

The Haas Effect

Haas, an early researcher into psychoacoustics, characterized how we perceive and localize sounds. He determined that, to avoid being confused by the echoes caused by reflections when trying to localize the direction from which a sound is coming, the brain ignores all but the first sound it "hears" for a small fraction of a second. All reflections arriving during this time period, called the Haas Fusion Region, are fused into the first sound, thus increasing its apparent loudness.

As a result of this "fusion," you perceive one louder sound coming from the direction of its first arrival. Reflections and echoes arriving after fusion, delayed by 20 to 30 milliseconds, are once again perceived as separate sounds. Their density and rate of decay contain information that your brain uses to gauge the nature of the acoustic space you are occupying.

Madsen principle. This approach reproduced a delayed version of the front signal through additional speakers located off to the sides or rear of the main front speakers in the listening room. It is interesting to note that this technique also works with mono recordings.

L-R matrix, perhaps better known as Dynaquad™, was a passive system that simply connected a pair of rear speakers differentially across the "hot" or + terminals of the left and right output channels of an amplifier (see Fig. 9.1). This system operated under the principle that sounds coming directly from an orchestra arrive at both microphones almost simultaneously, while room-reflected sounds arrive from various odd angles with relatively large time differences between the two microphones.

PARTS LIST

Semiconductors
D3 thru D6—IN4002 rectifier diode
D7—1N914 signal diode
IC1, IC7—NE5532 or TL072 dual op amp
IC2, IC3—TL074CN quad op amp
IC4—NE572N dual compander
IC5—R-5108 2048-stage ASR (Reticon)
IC6—NE555 timer
IC8—78M15 +15-volt regulator
IC9—79M15 −15-volt regulator
LED1,LED2—Light-emitting diode

Capacitors
C1, C2, C3, C34—47-pF, 10%, disc
C4, C7—2700-pF, 5%, polystyrene
C5, C23—100-pF, 5%, polystyrene
C6, C11, C14, C16, C24, C28, C31—0.1-μF, 5% polystyrene
C8, C9, C10, C17, C18, C27, C38, C39—10-μF, 35-volt electrolytic
C12, C13, C25, C26—0.01-μF, 5%, polyester
C15, C29—1-μF, 25-volt electrolytic
C19—100-μF, 16-volt electrolytic
C20—0.01-μF disc
C21, C22, C33—510-pF, 5%, polyester
C30—0.005-μF, 5%, polyester
C32—1000-pF, 5%, polystyrene
C35, C36—1000-μF, 35-volt electrolytic
C37, C40 thru C49—0.1-μF disc

C50—0.022-μF, 600-volt disc
Resistors (all ¼-watt, 5%):
R2, R5, R12, R15, R25, R26, R45, R67 thru R70—10,000 ohms, carbon film
R3, R4, R13, R14, R22, R23, R62, R74, R75, R77—3000 ohms
R6, R9, R16, R19, R27, R28, R46, R66—20,000 ohms
R7, R17, R24, R34, R76—51 ohms
R8, R18, R53—2000 ohms
R10, R11, R78—10 ohms
R21, R37, R44, R49, R51, R71, R73—1000 ohms
R29—27,000 ohms
R30—36,000 ohms
R31—120,000 ohms
R32, R35, R36, R39, R56—22,000 ohms
R33-680,000 ohms
R38, R59—39,000 ohms
R40, R41, R57, R58—5100 ohms
R42, R43—1 megohm
R46—20,000 ohms
R47, R48—510 ohms
R50—180,000 ohms
R54, R55, R64—100,000 ohms
R60—62,000 ohms
R65—18,000 ohms
R1—Dual 50,000-ohm, linear-taper potentiometer
R20, R52, R72—100,000-ohm linear-taper potentiometer
R63—10,000-ohm trimmer potentiometer
Miscellaneous
F1—¼-ampere pigtail fuse
J1 thru J6—Phono jack
S1—Dpdt push-push pc-mount switch

S2—4pdt push-push pc-mount switch
T1—28-volt, center-tapped transformer

Printed circuit board; sockets for ICs; suitable enclosure; line cord; strain relief; control knobs; panel lens for LED1; machine hardware; hookup wire; etc.

Note: The following items are available from Rhoades National Corp., P. O. Box 1316, Columbia, TN 38402 (tel. 615-381 9001): Assembled model, $249.: No. P-250-DL complete kit of parts for $179.00; No. P-250-B etched and drilled pc board for $19.00; No. P-250-T 28-volt, c.t. pc-mount transformer for $7.00; No. R-5108 Reticon 2048-stage ASR IC for $30.00; NE5532N dual op amp for $2.25; TL074CN quad bi-FET op amp for $2.50; NE572N dual compander for $3.25; 78M15 regulator for $1.50; 79M15 regulator for $2.50; No. P-2X50KB dual 50,000-ohm, linear taper potentiometer for $2.50; No. P-100KB 100,000-ohm linear taper potentiometer for $1.00; No. S-1 dpdt pc-mount switch for $1.00; No. S-2 4pdt pc-mount switch for $1.50 Add $1.00 S&H for orders of less than $10.00, $2.00 on COD orders. Tennessee residents, please ad 7.5% sales tax.

In the Delay Enhanced L-R Decoder presented here, the mechanism that allows the time delay to cure the passive L-R matrix's front localization problem is the same mechanism that caused it in the first place, namely the Haas effect (see "Haas Effect").

In the passive L-R system, sounds from the rear speaker will reach you before the sounds from the front speakers because they are closer. Because of the Haas effect, your brain will attempt to lock onto these rear sounds, causing you to hear false localization.

Delaying the sounds being fed to the rear speakers by 20 to 30 milliseconds will ensure that the sounds from the front speakers will always arrive at the listener's position before the sounds from the rear do. In fact, when properly adjusted, this project should make it so that you never actually hear the rear speakers as discrete sound sources. What you will get, then, is ambience that simply "surrounds" you as you listen.

The L-R matrix plus delay works equally well with a wide range of program sources, including many that were not originally recorded using stereo microphones.

About the Circuit

The schematic diagram for the ambience-recovery system is shown in three parts, in Fig. 9.2A, B, and C. The system is designed to work with a wide range of both mono and stereo program sources. The output of the ambience/surround channel, available at J6 in Fig. 9.1C, offers a full 12-kHz bandwidth. (Listening tests have revealed that the 6-kHz bandwidth used in past designs was inadequate for best ambience extraction from CD and other high-quality recordings.)

In addition to the normal L-R + delay, or surround, mode, a stereo synthesizer is built in to enhance playback of monophonic program sources. Jacks J3 and J4 in Fig. 9.2A provide the outputs for both normal stereo and synthesized stereo, the latter when a mono source is connected to input jacks J1 and J2 and switch S2 is set to MONO. Also, an L + R, front-center fill, output is provided at J5 in Fig. 9.2A, for use in small movie screen applications and in hi-fi setups as a mono feed to a subwoofer.

For convenience of setup and use, the circuit includes a master volume control (R1 in Fig. 9.2A) and separate level controls for the front-center (R20 in Fig. 9.2A) and surround (R72 in Fig. 9.2C) outputs. Both outputs are capable of boost and cut relative to the master volume control. Hence, it is a simple matter to correct for differences in sensitivity between the front and rear speaker systems. Once relative gains are set, the level controls track the master volume control for routine system level changes.

This circuit uses the newest ASR integrated circuit, the R-5108 from Reticon, to extract ambience signals from stereo sources. This device, shown as IC5 in Fig. 9.2B, has 2048 stages of delay, which is twice as long as the popular SAD-1024 and half as long as the SAD-4096. This new chip has the biphase clock drivers and output sample-and-hold circuit built into a smaller chip that is housed inside a compact 8-pin DIP package.

Input and output filters, tuned for −3 dB at 12 kHz, condition the audio in the surround channel to avoid sampling rate aliasing and to smooth out the output waveform. An NE572N, IC4 in Fig. 9.2B, companding noise-reduction chip is used around the delay chip for noise-free performance with even the most dynamic sources available. The NE572N is an improved version of the popular NE570.

NE555 timer IC6 in Fig. 9.2B generates the time base for the system. The frequency of this time base controls how long an audio sample takes to work its way through the ASR. Potentiometer R52 provides the means for adjusting the clock frequency to vary the system delay time. High-slew-rate op amps are used throughout the system to deliver maximum audio fidelity.

The power supply for the system is shown in Fig. 9.3. Note that this

Fig. 9.3. This is the power supply, showing full regulation of the +15- and −15-volt lines. The lower portion of the diagram shows power connections to ICs.

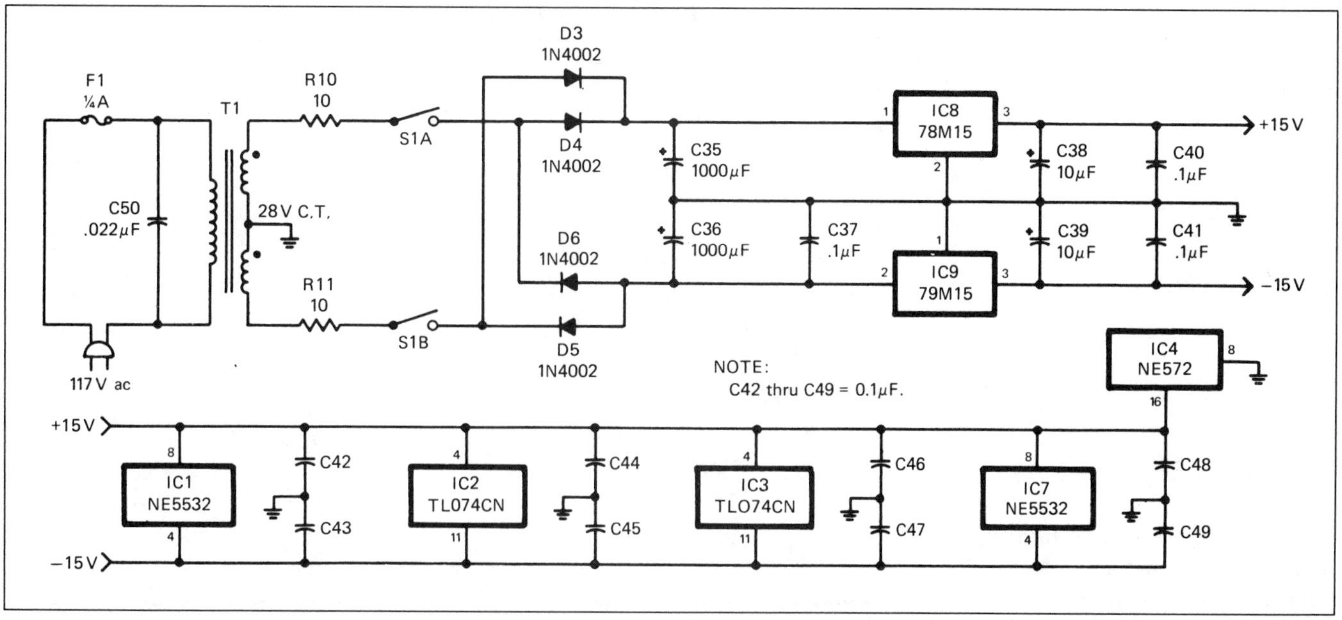

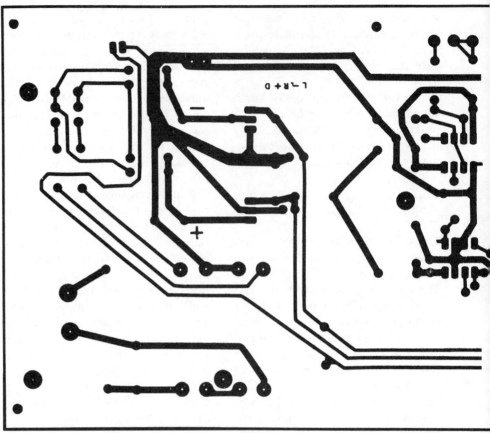

Fig. 9.4. This is the actual-size
etching-and-drilling guide for the
pc board.

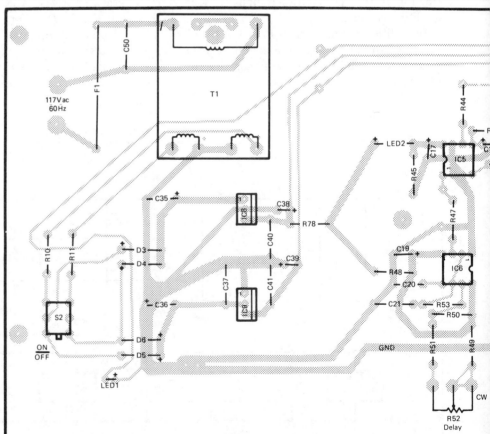

Fig. 9.5. When installing
components on the pc board, be
certain to orient them as shown.

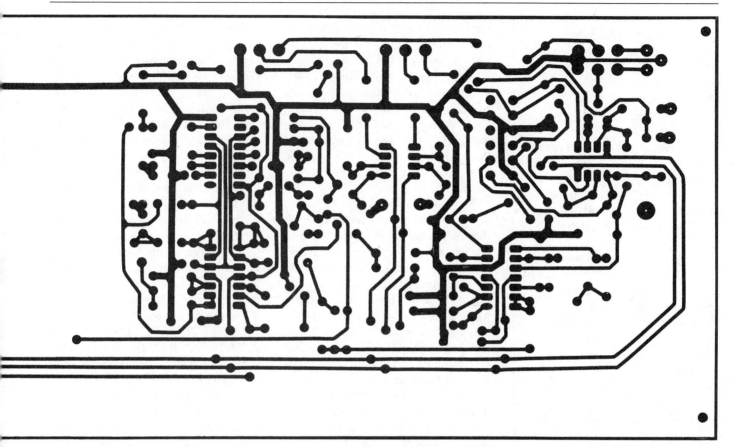

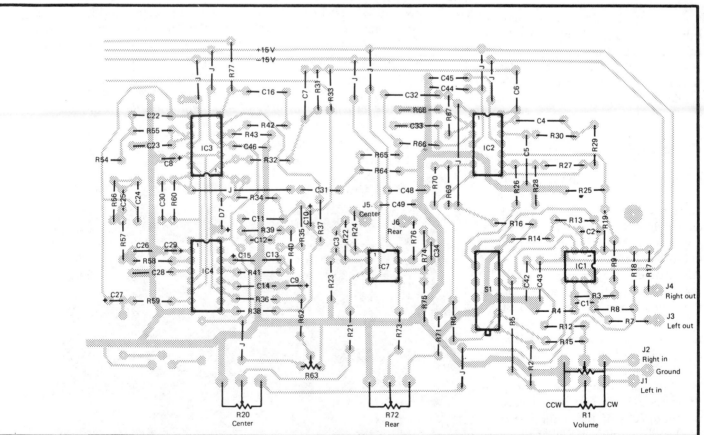

Specifications

Input impedance	10k ohms or greate
Output impedance	50 ohms
Maximum output into hi-fi load	8 volts
into 600 ohms	7.5 volts
Gain (each output)	+6 dB to full off
Delay time	5 to 30 ms, adjustable
THD + direct	<0.01%, 20 Hz to 20 kHz
delay	0.5% nominal, 100 Hz to 10 kHz
Noise (IHF A)	
direct	<−100 dBV
delay	−91 dBV
Frequency response	
direct	dc to 20 kHz +0/−0.25 dB
delay	20 Hz to 12 kHz ± 3 dB

full-wave bridge circuit provides full regulation of both the +15- and −15-volt buses. The schematic also shows the pins to which the buses connect on the ICs.

Construction

Owing to its complexity, it is highly recommended that you assemble the delay system's circuit on a printed-circuit board. You can fabricate your own board, using the etching-and-drilling guide given in Fig. 9.4. Alternatively, you can purchase a ready-or-installation board from the source given in the Parts List. Whichever way you go, you will note from the components-placement guide in Fig. 9.5 and the photo of the interior of the project in Fig. 9.6 that all components except the various input and output jacks mount directly on the circuit board.

There is nothing critical about as-

sembly, except that you must carefully observe the polarities and orientations of the integrated circuits, diodes, light-emitting diodes, and electrolytic capacitors before soldering them into place. Sockets are recommended for all ICs, though you can, if you wish, install these devices directly on the pc board and solder their pins to the copper pads.

Approach assembly logically. Start component installation with the lowest-profile devices first and work your way up to power transformer *T1*. That is, install first the jumper wires (indicated by the *J*s in Fig. 9.5) using bare solid hookup wire, except between pin 1 of *IC2* and the junction between *R16* and *R69* and between pin 14 of *IC3* and *C31*, both of which must be *insulated* solid hookup wire. Next, install the resistors and diodes, followed by the IC sockets (if you have decided to use them) or the ICs themselves, trimmer potentiometer *R63*, and the low-profile capacitors.

Before installing *LED1*, trim its lead to 1½ inches (38 mm) long, taking care to remember which lead is

which (it is best to somehow mark the cathode lead for easy identification). After installing and soldering the lead to the copper pads on the board, bend the leads first back away from the lip of the board and then forward, about half way along their lengths. When you are finished, the LED should be about ³⁄₈ inch (9.5 mm) above and its body parallel with the board's surface. Be careful not to flex the LED's leads too much or they will break away from the device's body or the board.

The largest components should be mounted last on the board. These include electrolytic capacitors *C35* and *C36* and transformer *T1* in the power-supply section and controls *R1* (VOLUME), *R20* (CENTER), *R52* (DELAY), and *R72* (REAR). Temporarily set aside the pc board assembly.

As with the pc board, you can fabricate your own low-profile enclosure or purchase it ready-to-use, including all machining and labeling, with the complete kit of parts from the source given in the Parts List. If you decide to make your own enclosure, make sure you drill

Fig. 9.6. All input and output jacks mount on the rear wall of the enclosure. The switches, controls and LED mount on the front panel. All other components mount on the pc board.

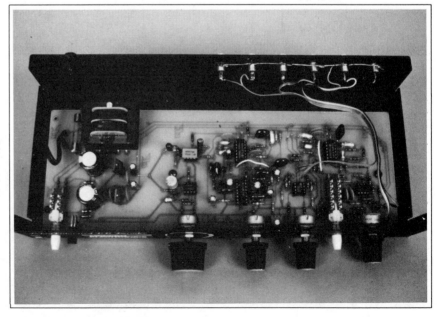

the holes for the controls, switches, *LED1*, input and output jacks, and the line cord in the proper locations. Use the circuit-board assembly to take all measurements for this operation.

Once machined, the enclosure should be spray painted and, when the paint completely dries, labeled. If you use a dry transfer lettering kit, apply two or three *light* coats of clear spray lacquer to the front and rear panels to protect the lettering. Be careful not to make the lacquer too thick or runny or the lettering will lift off and dissolve.

When the enclosure is ready, install the input and output jacks on the rear panel and wire together all ground lugs with bare solid hookup wire. Then pass the free end of the line cord through its hole and secure it in place with a plastic strain relief. (If you prefer, you can line the hole with a rubber grommet, pass the free end of the line cord through, and knot it about 7 inches (178 mm) from the free end.) In any event, leave 6 inches (152 mm) to 7 inches (178 mm) of loose wire with which to work.

Retrieve the pc-board assembly and install and solder into place seven separate lengths of hookup wire, or use a seven conductor, preferably color-coded, ribbon cable to the appropriate points on the circuit board. Make the wires long enough to reach their respective jacks, plus some slack, when the board is in its mounting location inside the enclosure. Twist together the fine wires in first one and then the other free end of the line cord. Make sure that all fine wires are twisted into the bundles. Then lightly tin each bundle with solder. Slip these wires into the holes provided for them in the pc board, solder them to the copper pads, and trim away any excess.

Carefully align the shafts of the controls and the buttons on the switches with their respective holes

Dolby Sound Movies

Movie sound tracks are usually recorded in discrete left, right, center (front), and surround (rear) channels. Special effects, like earthquake sounds, can bring the count up to six discrete channels. When these movies are mixed down to the ordinary two-channel stereo track format, the center channel is matrixed onto the left and right channels in-phase, while the surround channel is matrixed onto the left and right channels out-of-phase.

When this stereo mix-down is played back through a stereo system, the mostly dialog center channel is projected from the left and right speakers at equal volume and appears localized between the two. The surround signals also come out of the left and right speakers. But because they are out-of-phase, they appear to take on a diffuse quality with wider apparent separation. If this stereo mix-down is played back through a monophonic system, the surround signal cancels out.

Theater installations use reduced bandwidth (−3 dB at 6 kHz), Dolby B noise reduction, and logic separation enhancement on the surround channel. This is done to accommodate the significant number of movie-goers who must sit directly beneath one of the surround speakers and would not otherwise receive an acceptable balance of front to surround signals.

in the front panel and slide the board into place. Start hex nuts onto the control shafts but leave them quite loose. Tilt the board upward from the rear. Using ¼ inch (6.35 mm) spacers and No. 4 machine hardware, mount the board to the floor of the enclosure. Before tightening any hardware, make certain that the buttons on *S1* and *S2*

work without binding. This done, tighten the board mounting screws and the hex nuts on the controls. Then press a red panel lens into the remaining hole in the front panel and carefully push *LED1* into the lens. Install knobs on the front-panel control shafts.

Using Figs. 9.2 and 9.5 to guide you, connect the free ends of the wires coming from the printed-circuit board to the appropriate jacks on the rear panel (Fig. 9.6).

Hookup and Use

The delay system is best connected between the outputs of a preamplifier and the inputs of a power amplifier. However, it can also be used effectively in a tape-monitor loop.

The rear speaker system and its driving amplifier need not be as powerful and wide ranging as the front speaker systems and amplifier. Typically, an amplifier for the rear source need not have more than 25 percent to 50 percent of the power of that used up front. The rear speaker need not be critical in performance, nor need it be matched to the speaker systems you use for the front, since the surround channel rolls off above 12 kHz and very low frequencies tend to be recorded in-phase and, thus, are suppressed in the surround channel.

To set delay time, begin with the DELAY control set to its midpoint position (straight up). This will be about the 30 millisecond position. You can optimize the delay time for your room by listening to a recording with impulse-type sounds, like record scratches (they are good for something, after all). When the delay time is set for too long a duration, you will hear discrete repeats or echoes. If it is set for too short a time, the image will shift to the rear speaker. When the setting is correct, the rear speaker will aurally disappear as an actual sound source.

In Closing

The project described previously will extract ambience from any stereo program source and deliver spectacular "surround sound" effects from stereo-encoded movies. At least one of the new stereo TV programs, NBC's *Miami Vice*, uses surround sound; others are expected to follow. In the meantime, you can switch in the stereo synthesizer for the old-fashioned monophonic TV programs and still enjoy enhanced sound reproduction.

Practical installation methods to obtain better sound reproduction and additional listening areas with extra speaker systems.

chapter 10

Adding Extension Speakers to a Stereo System

NORMAN EISENBERG

Everyone knows that the normal complement of speaker systems for stereo reproduction is a pair—one for each channel. Furthermore, many stereo system owners have discovered that using additional ("extension") speakers can prove to be both useful and enjoyable. There are, of course, two basic reasons for adding extra speaker systems to a stereo setup. One is to enhance the sound in the same room in which the main speakers are located. The other is to supply stereo sound to another room. The two aims aren't mutually exclusive; you can do both—*if* you go about it properly.

Most of today's stereo receivers and integrated amplifiers have provisions for connecting extra speaker systems and then selecting them or the main pair or both pairs with a front-panel switch. Owners' manuals usually refer to this feature, but just as often provide little or no information on some important conditions involved when extra pairs of speaker systems are added. These considerations include speaker impedances, available power from the amplifier, relative volume, and the gauge and length of the cables used to interconnect speaker systems and amplifier or receiver with which they are used.

The Parameters

For most consumer-grade audio equipment, the standard amplifier output load is 8 ohms. This is the impedance for which the amplifier's output power is stated in the list of technical specifications. It also happens to be the nominal impedance of the vast majority of speaker systems.

Because they're constant-voltage devices, most receivers and amplifiers can supply more than their rated power into loads whose impedances are less than 8 ohms. How much power they can deliver, however, and with how much distortion and into how low impedance the load before the danger point is reached varies considerably from one amplifier to another. Unfortunately, even though this information is frequently of critical importance, rarely do manufacturers include it along with the other technical specifications.

With some professional-grade, heavy-duty amplifiers, you'll see a specification for 4-ohm loads. You might also see a statement to the effect it's safe for the impedance to go as low as 2 ohms. Supplementary information might even give you legitimate power data at these low-impedance speaker loads.

Most user's manuals for typical home stereo amplifiers and receivers are rather vague on this subject. The best I have come across in recent years promises 62.5 watts per channel into 8 ohms and 90 watts per channel into 4 ohms. This manual also cautions the user to connect only 8-ohm or greater speaker systems to the amplifier when using remote speakers. The cautionary note

takes pains to specify that both remote *and* main speaker systems must have a minimum of 8-ohms impedance.

More typical, unfortunately, is the manual for many recent receivers and amplifiers that simply states remote speaker systems can be hooked up and selected with a front-panel switch. This is a very idealistic (and unrealistic) view. Things just aren't that simple. If you were to take a statement like this on face value, you could blithely blow your amplifier or speakers or both!

In the real world, very few—if any—things are perfect in design. Speaker systems, particularly, aren't. When a manufacturer specifies his speaker system to have an 8-ohm impedance, this is a *nominal* figure. The speaker system may, indeed, have an 8-ohm impedance—but only at selected frequencies. In fact, the impedance may quite readily drop to 7 or 6 ohms at certain frequencies. This would present no problems for the driving amplifier if only one pair (stereo) were connected to it, since even the most skimpily designed receiver can usually cope with a 4-ohm load. When you connect *two* such pairs of speaker systems in parallel to each of the receiver's outputs, the amplifier section could be in very real trouble. As for using three pairs of speaker systems, forget it!

Estimating Impedances

To estimate the total impedance presented to an amplifier (including the amplifier section of a receiver), note the equations in Fig. 10.1. Bear in mind that these equations represent "best-case" approximations when it comes to speaker systems, since actual impedance when a speaker reproduces music will vary across the audio range, often

Estimating Total Impedance

The following equations can be used to determine *nominal* total impedances (Z_t), but don't assume you can blithely combine any number of speaker systems in series-parallel arrangements and hit the mark. In these equations, Z_1, Z_2, . . . Z_n represent the nominal impedances of the individual speaker systems.

For any number of speaker systems:

$$Z_t = \cfrac{1}{\cfrac{1}{Z_1} + \cfrac{1}{Z_2} + \cfrac{1}{Z_3} + \cdots \cfrac{1}{Z_n}}$$

For two speaker systems in parallel:

$$Z_t = \frac{Z_1 \times Z_2}{Z_1 + Z_2}$$

For speaker systems in series:

$$Z_t = Z_1 + Z_2 + Z_3 + \cdots Z_n$$

Fig. 10.1. Equations for estimating the total speaker impedance presented to the outputs of an amplifier.

dipping below the rated nominal value.

If your owner's manual isn't explicit on the safe lower limit of impedance you can apply to the outputs of your amplifier or receiver, try to get the information from the manufacturer. Failing this, play it safe and assume that no impedance of less than 4 ohms total should be used with the amplifier as-is.

Similarly, consider the power available to drive the combination of main and extension speaker systems. You can't assume, for example, that a receiver rated for, say, 80 watts per channel when driving one pair of speaker systems (one per channel) will obligingly pump out double that power so that each of two speaker systems on each channel will be getting 80 watts of power. Things just don't work that way. Except for the most rigorously designed, heavy-duty professional-grade amplifiers, chances are that there will be a drop of at least 3 dB for each added speaker system per channel. Hence, the 80 watts per channel delivered by the amplifier becomes more like 40 watts per channel with respect to each of two speaker systems connected to a given channel.

Keep in mind that the more speaker systems you try to run off the same output channel, the closer you come—in terms of reduced load impedance and increased demand on available power reserves—to the safe operating limit of a given amplifier or receiver. When that limit is reached or exceeded, the amplifier will shut itself down, if you're lucky, or self-destruct, perhaps taking the speaker system with it if no safeguards are built in.

While it's generally safe to make use of the extra speaker outputs on today's receivers and amplifiers, the watchword (unless you can get specific advice to the contrary from the manufacturer) is to use no more than one extra pair of speaker systems. Like the main pair, the added pair should have an impedance of 8 ohms.

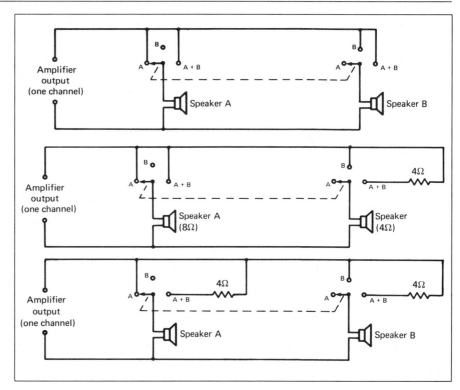

Fig. 10.2. You can build your own switching arrangement for selecting either or both speakers connected to the output of an amplifier—for 8-ohm-only systems (top), for mixed 8/4-ohm systems (center), and for 4-ohm-only systems (bottom).

Going Beyond Two Pair

If you wish to use more than one extra pair of speaker systems, or if your equipment doesn't have a built-in speaker-pair selector, you'll need a separate switching setup. You can make your own speaker switch (see Fig. 10.2) or buy one already made up from most hi-fi equipment dealers.

Typical of the ready-made speaker-switching accessories on the market today are the Model 30-5006 that handles up to three pairs of stereo speaker systems and Model 30-5002 that handles up to five pairs, both from Audiotex. If you have a separate power amplifier, you can use Adcom's Model GFS-1

switcher (Fig. 10.3), which handles up to three speaker systems.

Beyond Switching

Using a speaker switching device will effectively handle impedance relationships, but it can't solve the power-drain problem. With regard to power, you must exercise some common sense. For instance, assume you're running three speaker systems from one side of an amplifier and the amplifier itself is rated to deliver 60 watts of power per

Fig. 10.3. If you prefer a ready-to-install speaker switching box, you can use the Adcom Model GFS-1 shown here or a similar product from another manufacturer.

channel. When all three speaker systems are being used simultaneously, each can get no more than 20 watts. This may be enough to drive the speaker systems adequately for your purposes, but don't expect to hear consistently loud and clear crescendos from all three, or even just one of the three.

With any switching arrangements in which several speaker systems are driven from the same amplifier, you have the additional problem of having to adjust the relative volumes from each speaker. For example, suppose you have set up the added speaker systems to provide a wider stereo spread in the same room in which your main speakers are located. Depending on program material, room acoustics, and the positions of all four speaker systems, it may be necessary to play one or even a pair of speaker systems louder than the others. The volume control on your receiver or amplifier may be able to serve as a master level control, but it can't be used to adjust the volume of sound emanating from any *one* of the speaker systems.

The solution, of course, is to use an "L pad" (Fig. 10.4). This is a

ers. When you buy one, get the best you can afford, and make sure its impedance is the same as that of the speaker system whose volume it will control. Wiring an L pad into your hi-fi setup is a simple enough procedure. Logically, it should be located fairly close to the speaker system it's to control.

An L pad, of course, can't increase the volume beyond the level set by the master volume control in the amplifier. So it may take some juggling between the settings of the two controls before you can get the balance you want. Remember, too, that when you turn down the L pad to silence an extension speaker system, the control will still be taking power from the line. Hence, even though the one speaker system is muted, the other speakers in the system won't be getting full power.

Another Approach

The whole switching setup can be avoided if you're willing to use a fancier and costlier type of setup—an additional power amplifier for each pair of added speaker systems.

The easiest, though most complex and costly, way to go is with a separate preamplifier and separate power amplifier for the main speaker systems. You can then use the preamp to drive whatever other individual power amp(s) you add to the setup.

If the added power amps have their own input level controls, so much the better. If they don't, you can still use L pads in the lines that go to the speaker systems connected to them.

Instead of using power amps for the extra speaker systems, you can use integrated amplifiers that *do* have volume controls. This choice offers redundancy that can prove to be a boon in terms of flexibility for elaborate extra speaker system arrangements.

Added amplifiers can be run from a receiver as well as from an integrated amplifier (see Fig. 10.5). An unused tape monitor jack, or the circuit-interrupt option, can be adapted for feeding signals from the main system into an added amplifier that's driving the extension speakers. The disadvantages of going this route include added equip-

Fig. 10.4. To control the volume from extension speakers, you will need an L pad for each speaker you add.

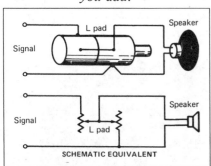

dual-sectioned volume control that maintains correct impedance match while adjusting the volume of an individual speaker system. L pads are sold by many hi-fi equipment deal-

Fig. 10.5. The safest, most flexible way to add speakers to an existing system is through a separate amplifier.

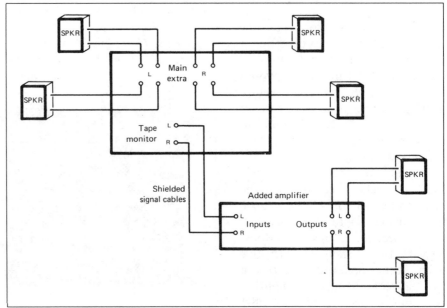

ment complexity and installation space, as well as cost. On the plus side is the fact that this type of setup gives you full control over each speaker system, independently of the others and with optimum relationships of impedance, power, and damping for *all* the speaker systems.

Where They're Used

One of the most popular uses for extension speaker systems is in supplying stereo sound to one or more rooms other than the main listening room. If only one such "remote" setup is planned, the simple use of the existing speakers B outputs on your receiver or amplifier will suffice. Of course, the cautions regarding speaker impedances explained previously still apply, and you'll have to insert L pads in the lines feeding the remote speaker systems to be able to control the volume without having to use the control on the amplifier.

If your hi-fi equipment doesn't have provisions for connecting an extra pair of speaker systems to it, you'll have to use one of the switching arrangements described previously.

When more than one remote setup is planned, a more elaborate switching arrangement is needed. Probably your best bet would be to buy a multiple-speaker switch after discussing your needs with your local audio equipment dealer. It would be better but more costly to introduce an additional amplifier into the system. Under no circumstances should you try to add several remote speaker systems directly to the outputs of a power amplifier by coming up with a series-parallel arrangement that *seems* to present the correct impedance on the basis of arithmetic computation. Many a well-intentioned hi-fi buff has done just this only to have caused very

expensive damage to his hi-fi system.

Without the main listening room itself, there are two good reasons for using additional speaker systems. One is to enhance the stereo effect by using extension speaker systems as "flankers." Positioned along the side walls and flanking the two main speaker systems, the extension speakers can lend a dramatic highlight to large-scale musical works. They create a "big stage" effect that adds a rich ambience to the sound while washing out a lot of system response problems resulting from deficiencies in room acoustics.

Should center filling be the only application you plan for your extension speaker systems, you can probably achieve your goal by using the extra speaker outputs on your present equipment. You'll need L pads to obtain the kind of balance you want, of course. If you want flanking in your main listening room *and* remote listening in another room, you'll have to plan on using an accessory speaker switcher or get an additional driving amplifier.

A need for speaker flankers is indicated, in most instances, for installations in which the main speaker systems are relatively close together or are fairly directional in their dispersion patterns. At the opposite extreme is the situation where the main speaker systems are too far apart and don't provide a consistently solid center image or aural focus. What results from a situation like this is a "hole" in the middle of the stereo spread.

The hole-in-the-middle problem can be effectively dealt with by using a center-fill speaker system that provides A-plus-B (left-plus-right) channel signal. Center filling makes the stereo presentation more substantial or solid by providing a "wall of sound" effect. Again, musical perception is improved, and

many problems of otherwise poor room acoustics are solved.

The concept of a center-fill speaker that handles an A-plus-B (monophonic) signal suggests the use of just one speaker system to do the job. Don't become a victim of this logic! Hanging a single speaker system onto the outputs of a solid-state amplifier can be tricky at best and downright dangerous at worst. Because a common ground may be involved in the two channels in solid-state amplifiers, manufacturers do not recommend bridging the channels with a speaker system.

Ruling out a single speaker system, you can obtain a perfectly workable A-plus-B fill by using two speaker systems. Simply stack one atop the other and plant the pair in the same location in which you'd put a single speaker system (see Fig. 10.6). Each speaker system in the

Fig. 10.6. To obtain center-channel fill, stack speaker systems as shown here.

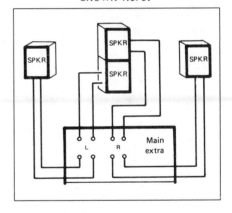

stacked pair gets its own left or right channel signal from the left and right outputs of the amplifier or receiver. But since the two signals are so closely coupled physically, they form an acoustic mix that is perceived as a monophonic source containing the signal in channel A plus that in channel B.

As with all the other varieties of added speaker system hookups, the center-fill arrangement can be driven directly from the extra speaker outputs on your present stereo equipment. Alternatively, the speaker systems can be driven by their own separate amplifier driven from the tape-monitor or preamp output on the main amplifier. Again, use L pads for controlling the volume of the added speaker systems.

Table 10.1. *The Cable Run Range in Feet Is Shown Between the Two Lines*

Speaker Impedance in ohms	Cable Gauge for cable run in feet			
	0–30	31–40	41–70	71–100
4	18	16	14	12
8	18	16	14	14
16	20	18	16	14

A Final Consideration

When adding extension speaker systems, you must consider the thickness (gauge) of the cables delivering power to them from your amplifier. This is particularly important for installations where the add-on systems are far removed from the driving amplifier. Cables that aren't thick enough can reduce total power delivered to the speaker systems, resulting in a loss in listening volume.

In figuring the gauge to use for your cables, it's important that you take into account the *actual* cable lengths you'll be using. This is the actual length in feet, measured from the amplifier's output, routed along baseboards and doorways, and dressed around cabinets, etc., to the speaker systems. As a general rule of thumb, the longer the cable runs, the larger the thickness of cable needed.

Specific lengths of cable runs vary somewhat from one speaker manufacturer to another. The best advice is to follow the recommendations supplied with the speaker systems you purchase. If none are given, and you can't obtain them from the manufacturer, use Table 10.1 to determine what you should use. This table errs slightly on the side of caution, but you won't go wrong by using a thicker (lower gauge number) cable than might nominally be required.

chapter **11**

VCR Remote Controller Is a TV Turn-On

CHARLES NICOL II

I recently purchased a videocassette recorder that has a full-feature wireless remote-control system. However, this great convenience was somewhat diminished by the TV receiver with which I planned to use the VCR. It does not have a remote control capability, requiring me to still get up from my viewing chair to turn off my TV set when I was finished viewing. To circumvent this problem, I devised a modification of my VCR that would let me control ac power to my TV receiver.

My solution entails modifying some of the basic electronics inside most modern VCRs. If you are faint of heart or if your VCR is still within its warranty period, I do not suggest that you make the modification to be described. Otherwise, this may be a practical solution to a problem similar to mine. To perform this modification, your VCR must have on its rear panel a convenience ac receptacle that is powered at all times, regardless if your VCR is turned on or off. In addition, you need only three commonly available electronic components.

The Circuit

Shown in Fig. 11.1 is the circuitry needed to accomplish the modifica-

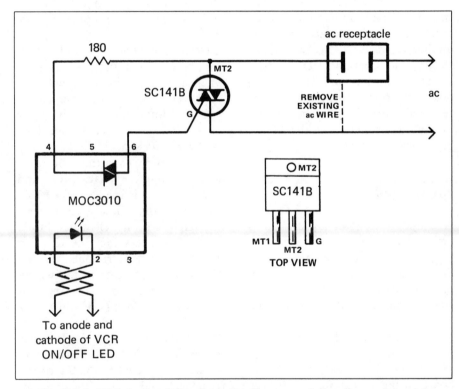

Fig. 11.1. This is the full schematic diagram of circuitry required to perform the VCR modification described in the text. Note that only three components are required, all inexpensive and readily available.

tion, along with instructions on where to install it. The main element in this circuit is the Motorola SC141B triac (Radio Shack No. 276-1001), which is triggered by the MOC3010 optical triac trigger (Radio Shack No. 276-134). The 180-ohm resistor simply reduces the 117-

volt ac line power to a safe level for the triggering device.

The triac operates as a bidirectional thyristor that can be gate triggered to be fully on or fully off (in this application). The SC141B in this circuit is rated at 200 volts, 6 amperes with proper heat sinking. It is ideal for switching ac voltages. In the Fig. 11.1 circuit, it is used to switch on and off the ac voltage to the receptacle on the rear panel of your VCR.

As shown in the diagram in Fig. 11.1, inside the MOC3010 optical triac trigger are a gallium-arsenide infrared emitting diode that is light coupled to a silicon bilateral switch. It takes a forward current of between 5 and 15 mA for the internal IR diode to trigger the bilateral switch. (For a slight increase in cost, the MOC3012, which triggers at 5 mA, can be substituted for the MOC3010.)

Triggering of the MOC3010 is accomplished by passing a current from the VCR's POWER LED through its internal IR diode. When the LED is on (indicating power is applied to the VCR), current flows through the internal LED and triggers the built-in triac. This in turn applies a voltage to the triac's gate terminal, triggering it on and applying full 117 volts ac to the VCR's accessory receptacle.

Installation

A 2 by 1 inch (50.8 by 25.4 mm) perforated board is of sufficient size to accommodate the triac, triac driver and resistor. A socket is recommended for the triac driver. Install a pair of solder pins on the board near the triac's MT1 and MT2 (main terminals 1 and 2) terminals. Wire the components together on the underside of the board, using solid hookup wire for all interconnections except those from the triac's MT1 and MT2 ter-

minals. Use heavy-duty stranded wire for these interconnections. Then connect and solder appropriate lengths of the same stranded wires to the solder pins on the top side of the board. Solid 22-gauge hookup wire is sufficient for interconnections between the triac driver and VCR's POWER LED. Clip a Radio Shack No. 276-1367 heat sink onto the triac.

Installation of the circuit requires that you open your VCR's cabinet to gain access to the connection points. Before you proceed, however, make sure that the VCR's power cord is unplugged from the ac line. Once the cabinet is opened, determine the best procedure for accessing the ac receptacle's wiring and the connection points to the POWER LED.

Determine where you will mount the board, selecting a location where it will not interfere with the VCR's electronics or mechanical elements. Mount the board with the aid of one or two sets of machine hardware and spacers.

Next, loosely twist the solid wires coming from the triac driver and route them to the power LED. Make sure that these wires do not interfere with the elements inside the VCR. Tack-solder the wires to the appropriate terminals on the LED. Then cut through the wiring to one of the lugs of the ac receptacle and strip ¼ inch (6.35 mm) to ⅜ inch (9.5 mm) of insulation from the cut ends. Tightly twist together the wires from MT2 of the triac and the wire connected to the lug of the receptacle and secure the connection with a wire nut. Do the same with the MTI wire and the wire for-

merly connected to the ac receptacle's lug.

Checking It Out

Plug your TV receiver's power cord into the VCR's accessory receptacle and the VCR's power cord into an ac wall outlet. Turn on your TV set and then your VCR. The latter's POWER LED should light and then, after a short interval, a picture should appear on your set's screen (you should hear sound immediately) if everything is okay. Then step across the room and turn off and then on and off again the VCR with its remote controller. The VCR and TV receiver should both turn off, on and then off, signalling that everything is operating as it should.

Once you are satisfied with the modification's operation, disconnect power to the VCR and reassemble its cabinet. Then make all cable connections between VCR and TV receiver and antenna. Plug the VCR's power cord into the ac line, and your system is ready for use.

In Conclusion

It should be noted that various makes and models of VCRs are different and that you may have to do some improvising to take advantage of the modification described here. For example, your VCR may not even have an accessory ac receptacle on its rear panel. In this case, you would have to install one.

Security Electronics

*An "engine-stall" anti-theft device
that you can install and forget with
confidence that it will work*

chapter **12**

How to Short-Circuit Auto Thieves

ANTHONY J. CARISTI

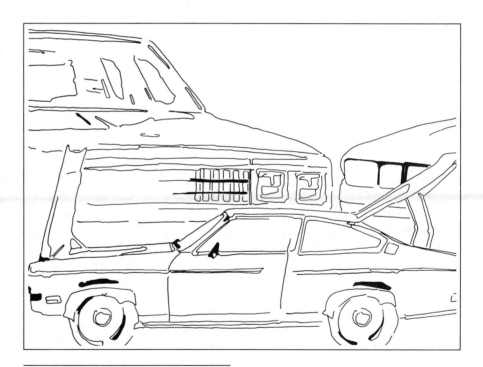

Installing an anti-theft device on your car or other vehicle makes good sense these days. But the best anti-theft device in the world is useless if you forget to turn it on.

The car anti-theft device presented here overcomes this problem. It sets itself automatically whenever the ignition is turned off! Also, it is inexpensive, reliable, and easy to build. And it works on all gasoline-operated vehicles with commonplace negative-ground electrical systems.

The heart of this theft-deterrent device is an Amperite thermal time-delay relay whose contacts are connected to a vehicle's ignition circuit. These contacts are normally open. However, they automatically close after a delay of about five seconds when the car is started unless a hidden reset button is pressed. Without the latter action, the car will simulate engine trouble, stall in a few seconds, and not be able to be started again with the ignition key. You can be sure that a would-be automobile thief won't bother staying around in order to fix it.

How It Works

The schematic diagram in Fig. 12.1 illustrates the logic portion of the circuit. Two NAND gates, IC1A and IC1B, are connected in a configuration called a bistable or latch circuit. This circuit has two stable states. In one, the logic level of the output terminal, pin 11 of the *IC1A,* is at zero-or 12-volt potential, depending upon the "set." When the circuit is in a reset mode, the logic level at pin 11 of *IC1A* is zero. $Q1$ and $Q2$, connected in a Darlington configuration, are thus cut off since there is no base current in $Q1$. Thus, no current can flow through the heater coil of the thermal relay, and the contacts stay open.

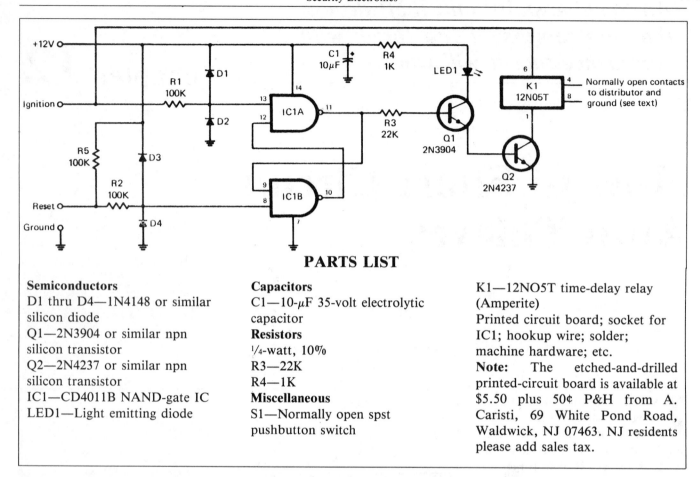

PARTS LIST

Semiconductors
D1 thru D4—1N4148 or similar silicon diode
Q1—2N3904 or similar npn silicon transistor
Q2—2N4237 or similar npn silicon transistor
IC1—CD4011B NAND-gate IC
LED1—Light emitting diode

Capacitors
C1—10-µF 35-volt electrolytic capacitor
Resistors
¼-watt, 10%
R3—22K
R4—1K
Miscellaneous
S1—Normally open spst pushbutton switch

K1—12NO5T time-delay relay (Amperite)
Printed circuit board; socket for IC1; hookup wire; solder; machine hardware; etc.
Note: The etched-and-drilled printed-circuit board is available at $5.50 plus 50¢ P&H from A. Caristi, 69 White Pond Road, Waldwick, NJ 07463. NJ residents please add sales tax.

Fig. 12.1. The install-and-forget vehicle anti-theft module is very simple in design, as illustrated in this schematic.

When the vehicle is stopped and the ignition turned off, the logic level to the ignition terminal of the circuit is set to zero, since this terminal is connected to the ignition-key circuit. This causes the output of *IC1A* pin 11 to go to +12 volts and drives *Q1* with a base current of about 0.5 mA. The LED then lights, indicating that the circuit is now armed. Hence, you can leave your vehicle without ever having to worry whether you set your anti-theft protection.

If a would-be thief decides to steal your car before you return, he (or she) will in some way energize your ignition system—either by hot wiring it or forcing your ignition key switch. Your car starts, but five seconds later stalls out since the heater of the time delay relay has been energized through the ignition circuit and *Q2*.

Of course, each time you return to your car, you must deactivate the circuit or you will face the same stall-out as a car thief would. This is accomplished by causing a momentary zero logic condition at the reset terminal of the circuit. The reset pulse forces the output of *IC1A* to go to zero volt, thus cutting off *Q1* and *Q2* and preventing the relay from operating.

Diodes *D1* through *D4* have been included in the circuit to protect *IC1* from possible voltage spikes that might come from the vehicle's electrical system.

Construction

The entire circuit can be placed on a small printed-circuit board measuring about 2 by 3½ inch (50.8 by 89 mm). Figure 12.2 is a full-size illus-

tration of the foil layout as seen from the copper side of the board. Figure 12.3 illustrates the component layouts as viewed from the component side of the board.

It is recommended that an IC socket be used for *IC1* rather than soldering the chip directly into the board. In the event that service is ever required, it would be extremely difficult to remove the chip if it were soldered in place. Be sure to follow the component layout exactly as shown for the IC, transistors, diodes, and electrolytic capacitor. These components are polarized and the circuit will not work if any of these parts are placed in the circuit in the wrong direction. Pin 1 of *IC1* is identified by a small dot.

The time-delay relay may be mounted directly to the top of the board (Fig. 12.4) using a small

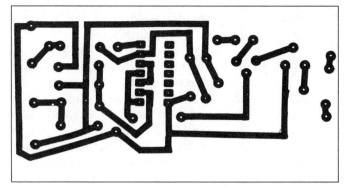

Fig. 12.2. This is the actual-size etching-and-drilling guide for homebrewing the pc board.

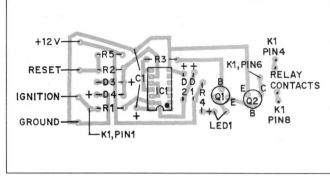

Fig. 12.3. After fabricating your pc board, use this drawing as a guide to component placement.

amount of silicone glue or some other similar adhesive. This type of mounting is an excellent method for this component, which has a glass envelope. To make connections to the relay, you can solder wires directly to the pins if you clean them thoroughly before you start. It's best to use an acid flux here (though *never* for any other electronic components, where rosin-core must be used). It is suggested that you solder the wires to the relay before you mount it to the board, thoroughly washing off solder connections with alcohol to remove any excessive flux.

You have the option of mounting the LED on the board or at a remote location. The best installation for the module would be in the engine compartment, hidden from view. In that case you might want to run a pair of wires to the passenger compartment so that you can view the LED, which provides a visual indication of the set or reset status of the circuit.

Initial Checkout

It would be a good idea, of course, to check out your module before you install it in your vehicle. To do so you will need a 12-volt dc power source and a pair of jumper test leads. Connect the dc power source to the +12 volt and ground terminals of the module. Observe proper polarity! Connect a jumper lead between the ignition terminal and +12 volts. Momentarily jump the reset terminal to ground with the second jumper lead. The LED should now be off.

Now remove the jumper lead between the ignition terminal and +12 volts and connect it between the ignition terminal and ground. The LED should light. Reconnect the jumper lead between ignition and +12 volts. The LED should remain lit. Now take the second jumper lead and momentarily connect the reset terminal to ground. The LED should be extinguished. This completes checkout of your module.

If your module does not work properly, disconnect the power source and recheck all the solder connections. Be sure there are no solder bridges that might short one copper path to another. Check all components for location and proper orientation. You might want to substitute another chip for *IC1*, in case the chip you used is defective.

Installation

The theft-deterrent module is connected into your existing ignition system as illustrated in Fig. 12.5. Since different manufacturers have

Fig. 12.4. Author's prototype was assembled on a piece of perforated board. You can do the same, or you can make your own printed-circuit board, using the etching-and-drilling guide that appears elsewhere in this chapter.

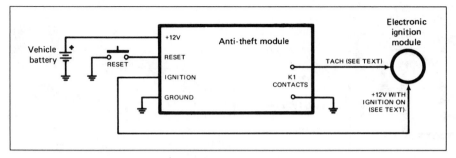

Fig. 12.5. How to install the anti-theft module in a vehicle.

slightly different ignition systems, follow only those instructions that apply to your vehicle.

The four connections located on one side of the module are the same for all vehicles, and should be made as follows:

The +12 volt terminal of the module should be connected to any hot lead of the vehicle that has +12 volts on it at all times, engine running or not. The ground connection of the module can be made to any exposed metal part of the car body or chassis. The ignition terminal of the module is connected to the power lead that feeds the ignition system when you turn the ignition key to its ON position. This point is easily accessible at the electronic module or coil of your ignition system or at the key switch behind the dashboard. The connection point should have voltage only when the ignition key is turned on, and should be zero when the engine is turned off. If in doubt, use a voltmeter to be sure.

To install a reset switch, the reset terminal of the module can be wired to a hidden pushbutton switch in the passenger compartment. It's much easier, though, simply to use your horn relay instead (see Fig. 12.6). The only disadvantage to this is that you must briefly sound your horn each time you start your car.

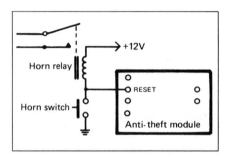

Fig. 12.6. The horn switch line is the simplest point in your vehicle to use for connecting the reset line.

On all cars, connect one side of the relay contact to ground. On General Motors vehicles with electronic ignition, connect the remaining relay contact to the terminal of the distributor marked TACH. This is the left-hand terminal of the dis-

tributor, looking at the terminal side of the distributor.

On Chrysler vehicles, you must determine which wire of two is the correct one to use. You can find out by briefly shorting one of the wires to ground while the engine is running. If the engine stops, you've just found the correct relay contact. If not that wire, it's the other.

On Ford Motor vehicles, the correct connection for the relay contact is the wire that runs between the coil and the distributor. This is also the contact for cars with ignition points.

If you drive an import, though, your best bet is to consult your dealer to determine how to connect the relay to its electrical system.

Final Checkout

When your installation is complete, check out the operation of the anti-theft module as follows: Start your car, then turn it off. The LED should be lit. Now start your car while the LED is still on. After a few seconds the engine should stall out. Press the reset button. The LED should be extinguished. Start your car. The engine should run normally.

Now that your vehicle is protected against theft and your forgetfullness, check with the insurance agent who handles your coverage. You may qualify for a reduced rate!

Portable Gas Detector . . . It Can Save Your Life!

LARRY D. GRAY

Have you ever thought you smelled gas and wished you had a way to check out your suspicion? Do you need to efficiently check the carburetor air-to-fuel mixture in your car but cannot justify spending the big bucks for a professional analyzer? Well, with the Portable Gas Detector described here, you can do both—and the project will cost you only about $35 to build. To top it all off, you can use the Detector as an alcohol breath analyzer.

About the Circuit

At the heart of the gas detector's circuit is a Figaro 812 solid state gas-sensor device (*GS1* in Fig. 13.1). The sensor uses n-type SnO_2, the resistance of which decreases with an increase in concentration of gas. The 812 has a high sensitivity to

Fig. 13.1. Circuitry for Gas Detector is very simple. Most of the work is done by gas sensor GS1; IC1 and LED2 through LED11 form the display.

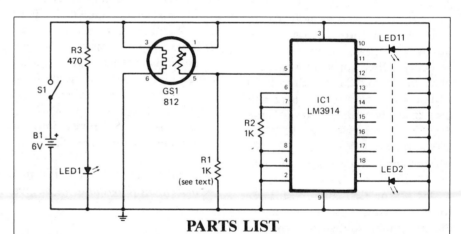

PARTS LIST

Semiconductors
IC1—LM3914 dot/bargraph display driver
LED1—Green 3-mm light emitting diode
LED2 thru LED11—Red 3-mm light-emitting diode
Resistors
¼-watt, 10%
R1, R2—1000-ohm
R3—470-ohm
Miscellaneous
B1—Four 1.5-volt AA cells in series (see text)
GS1—Figaro 812 gas sensor
S1—Spst toggle or slide switch
4³/₈″ × 2½″ × 1¼″(111 × 63.5 × 38 mm) plastic box; pc

board or perforated board and solder posts; four cell AA battery holder; chassis mount seven pin miniature tube socket; machine hardware; hookup wire; solder; etc.

Note: The following are available from QDI Inc., P.O. Box 205, West Union, OH 45693: Figaro 812 gas sensor for $14.95; etched and drilled pc board for $6.95; complete kit of all board mounted parts, including GS1, tube socket and pc board but not plastic case, for $29.95. Please include $2.00 for postage and handling.

toxic gases and organic solvents. Hence, *GS1* can sense very small concentrations of carbon monoxide and alcohol. Although it is not as sensitive to hydrocarbon products, like natural gas, it still gives good results.

Since *GS1* does all the work in this circuit, the only other items needed are the components that make up the eye-catching bargraph light-emitting diode display. Consequently, the circuit is quite simple. The LM3914 voltage comparator used for *IC1* is all that is needed to sequentially drive the display consisting of *LED2* through *LED11*.

Contained inside the LM3914 are 10 comparators. The first comparator is referenced 0.12 volt above ground. Each successive comparator is then referenced another 0.12 volt above the previous one. With this arrangement, an input of 1.2 volts is required for a full-scale display indication in which all 10 LEDs that make up the bargraph display are lit. Current through the display is controlled by *R2*. The 1000-ohm value specified for this resistor limits the current through the 10 LEDs to 10 mA.

Gas sensor *GS1* and resistor *R1* form a voltage divider that limits the maximum voltage delivered to *IC1* to 1.2 volts. When the sensor is exposed to air, its resistance is relatively high (about 50,000 ohms), and very little voltage (0.08 volt) is applied to the LM3914. As a combustible or toxic gas passes over the sensitive surface of *GS1*, sensor resistance drops, increasing the voltage dropped across *R1*. In turn, this causes *IC1* to light one or more display LEDs, the number being lit increasing as the voltage increases. The more combustible or toxic the gas, the lower the resistance of *GS1* and the greater the number of LEDs that light.

To avoid confusion, a green LED is used for *LED1* to indicate when

power is on. Resistor *R3* serves as a current limiter for this LED.

Power for the circuit is supplied by *B1,* which consists of four AA cells in series. While any type of AA cell can be used to power the project, alkaline cells are recommended if you expect to obtain reasonably long operating life, since *GS1*'s heater draws considerable current, though the rest of the circuit draws very little.

Construction

Owing to the simplicity of the circuit, you can use either a printed-circuit board or a perforated board and solder posts for assembly. If you decide to fabricate your own pc board, use the actual-size etching-and-drilling guide shown in Fig. 13.2. Whether you choose pc or perforated board construction, the components-placement guide, also in Fig. 13.2, should be used. It is not necessary (or advisable) to install *IC1* in a socket.

Gas sensor *GS1* plugs into a seven-pin miniature tube socket and,

therefore, presents no problems with regard to indexing during installation. Wiring details for this socket are shown in Fig. 13.3.

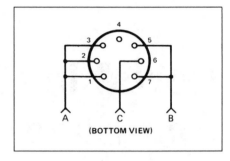

Fig. 13.3. Wire the gas sensor's socket as shown here; match the lettered points to the same points in Fig. 13.2.

Once the circuit has been assembled, it can be temporarily connected to the battery supply and tested before final assembly. Before proceeding to testing, however, machine the plastic box in which the project is to be housed to accommodate the battery holder on the floor of the box, the gas sensor (in its socket) to the top end, and the circuit board and power switch to the

Fig. 13.2. Actual-size etching-and-drilling guide is at left; components-placement diagram at right gives complete board assembly details.

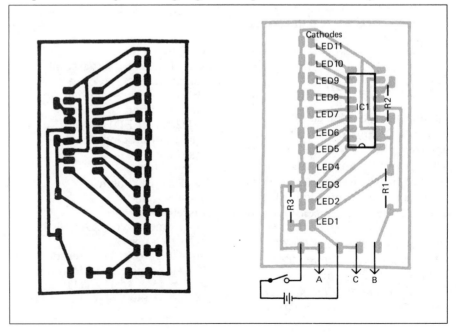

cover. Note that the circuit board mounts to the lid with no hardware. Instead, a single column of 11 holes into which the domes of the LEDs plug is sufficient to hold the assembly in place. Of course, the holes should be just large enough to provide a snug—not forced—fit. If you wish, however, you can apply a small drop of clear plastic cement to *LED2* and *LED11* to hold the assembly in place.

Testing and Use

When power is first applied to the circuit by closing *S1, GS1*'s heater element begins to warm up the sensitive surface. This display will initially light, sometimes to full scale, and then fall back to zero as the sensor stabilizes. This indicates that the sensor is ready to use. If during warm-up *LED2* or *LED3* remain on, this is an indication that the battery is getting weak and should be replaced.

Testing can be accomplished with a gas-type cigarette lighter. Simply press the gas-release button (do *not* rotate the spark wheel) and allow the escaping gas to come into contact with the gas sensor. If the battery is fresh and you have properly wired the circuit, the LEDs should give a full scale reading.

Having satisfied yourself that the Gas Detector is operating as it should, turn off the power and proceed to final assembly. Mount the battery holder on the floor of the plastic box with machine hardware. Do the same for the gas sensor's socket on the top of the box. Then carefully align the 11 LEDs with the holes in the box's lid and gently press home. Place a 1 inch (25.4 mm) length of plastic electrical tape over the exposed lugs of the gas sensor's socket to insulate it from the rest of the circuitry. Fit the lid onto the box and secure it in place with the supplied screws. Finally, plug *GS1* into its socket. If you wish, you can label the LEDs and put the legend "Gas Detector" onto the lid with a dry-transfer lettering kit and follow up with two or three light coats of clear lacquer to protect the lettering from scratches.

There are a couple of improvements you might want to incorporate into your Gas Detector. An obvious one is to replace the standard AA cells with rechargeable nickel-cadmium cells. If you do this, it is a good idea to also install an appropriate accessory jack to obviate the need to remove the cells for recharging.

Detector sensitivity can be increased by substituting a larger value resistor for that specified for *R1* in the Parts List. This will cause the voltage dropped across *R1* to be greater for a given concentration of gas. If you wish to have both the standard and the increased sensitivities, you can install a switch that will allow you to choose between the 1000 ohm and larger-value resistors as circumstances dictate.

chapter **14**

Microwave Leak Detector

RALPH NEAL

Microwave ovens have been around now for some years. There's always been some lingering concern about leakage due to seals on oven doors losing their effectiveness for one reason or another.

Simple detectors are available to check for possible leaks. They're usually in the form of a plastic wand with a go-no-go LED that lights when near a dangerously high level of microwave leakage. One can be made in only a few minutes time at a cost of less than one-fifth that of a commercial unit. The circuit uses only a microwave diode (D1), which is a 5082-2835 Schottky diode or similar one, and an LED (D2), which is a 1N82 or similar light-emitting diode.

The circuit is basically a microwave receiver tuned to the microwave oven's operating frequency. Tuning is accomplished by taking advantage of the natural resonance of the dipole antenna, in this case the very leads of the microwave diode itself. In the presence of microwave leakage, a voltage is generated across the diode, which acts as a de-

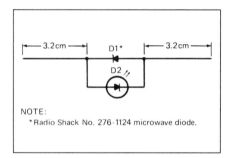

NOTE:
* Radio Shack No. 276-1124 microwave diode.

The circuit is very simple, consisting of a microwave diode and an LED.

tector. If this voltage is significant, it lights the LED.

The leak detector can be built on a small piece of perforated board or even a small piece of cardboard in only a few minutes time. As you can see from the diagram, each leg of the dipole must be close to 3.2 cm. in length for it to be tuned to the operating frequency of the oven (2400 MHz). To my surprise the lead lengths of the microwave diode were almost exactly that. Thus, all I needed to have a working leak detector was simply to solder the LED across the microwave diode.

When making this connection be careful to observe the polarity of

both diodes. Be sure that they are connected anode to cathode or the circuit will not function! When making the solder connection be sure to solder the LED leads as close to the body of the microwave diode as possible. Place a strip of tape over the legs that form the dipole antenna to protect it from possible damage.

Once the detector is built, you will, of course, want to check your own microwave oven for possible leaks. To perform this check, first place a small cup of water in the microwave oven. Then hold the detector in such a way that the dipole antenna is horizontal to the microwave oven. Turning on the microwave oven and taking care not to tilt the detector out of the horizontal plane, move the leak detector up and down in front of the oven door, keeping a close eye on the LED. If the LED lights up, you have found an area where the oven is leaking excessive microwaves. From the few ovens I have tested, most seem to leak at the door handle, with enough microwave radiation to set off the detector. Note that this lead detector does not measure the *amount* of microwave leakage, but only that significant leakage exists. When tested side by side with a commercial detector, the LED of the detector would light only when dangerous levels of leakage were indicated on the commercial detector.

Part **5**

Telephone Electronics

Phone accessory automatically calls a preprogrammed telephone number when your burglar/fire alarm or other sensor is tripped

chapter **15**

The Teleguard

ANTHONY J. CARISTI

The easy-to-build, low-cost project described here will guard you against a host of emergency situations while you are away—fire, theft, flood, power loss, etc. Upon its activation, it will automatically call a preprogrammed telephone number selected by you and alert the party being called to an emergency with a unique audio tone. The device, called "Teleguard," goes into action whenever a switch is closed. This might be a pushbutton that an invalid presses or the automatic operation of a sensor or thermostat.

Several important features are built into Teleguard to give you peace of mind. For example, the device will repeatedly call the number stored in its memory until it gets an answer, upon which it will transmit its unique "alert" signal. In addition, Teleguard has a power-failure indicator that monitors the ac power line. Should this LED extinguish, you know that power has been interrupted and that you have to reprogram the telephone number into memory to ensure continued protection. (A battery backup supply

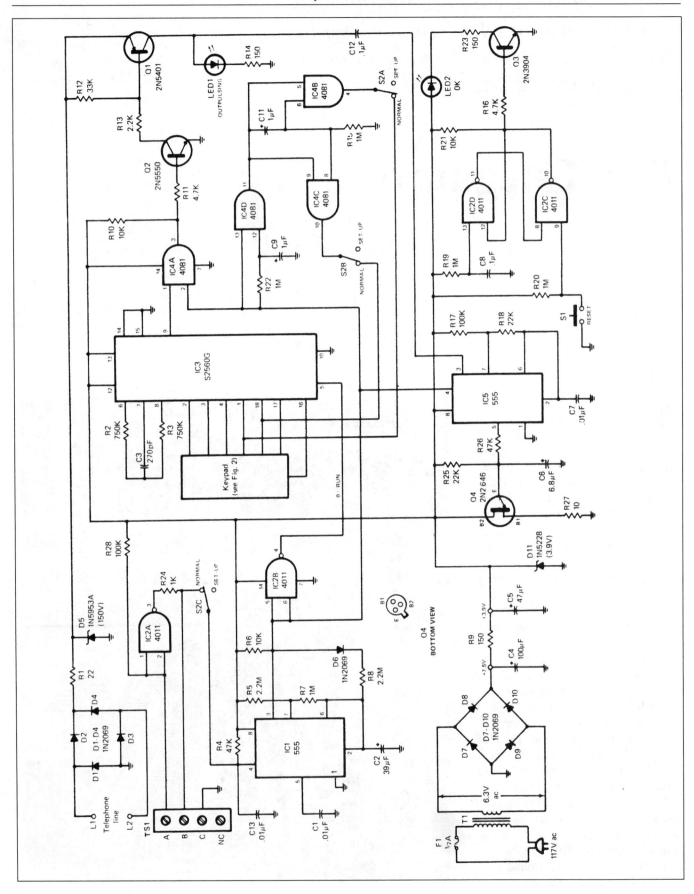

PARTS LIST

Semiconductors
D1 thru D4, D6 thru D10—IN2069 or similar silicon diode
D5—1N5953A or similar 150-volt zener diode
D11—1N5228 or similar 3.9-volt zener diode
IC1, IC5—555 timer
IC2—CD4011B quad NAND gate
IC3—S2560G telephone dialer IC (AMI)
IC4—CD4081 quad AND gate
LED1—Red light-emitting diode
LED2—Green light-emitting diode
Q1—2N5401 or similar pnp silicon transistor
Q2—2N5550 or similar npn silicon transistor
Q3—2N3904 or similar npn silicon transistor
Q4—2N2646 or similar unijunction transistor

Capacitors
C1, C7, C10—0.01-μF disc
C2, C5—47-μF, 10-volt electrolytic
C3—270-pF disc
C4—100-μF, 10-volt electrolytic
C6—6.8-μF, 10-volt electrolytic
C8, C12—0.1-μF disc
C9, C11—1-μF, 10-volt electrolytic

Resistors (all ¼-watt, 10%)
R1—22 ohms
R2, R3—750,000 ohms (5% tolerance)
R4, R26—47,000 ohms
R5, R8—2.2 megohms
R6, R10, R21—10,000 ohms
R7, R15, R19, R20, R22—1 megohm

R9, R14, R23—150 ohms
R11, R16—4700 ohms
R12—33,000 ohms
R13—2200 ohms
R17, R28—100,000 ohms
R18, R25—22,000 ohms
R24—1000 ohms
R27—10 ohms

Miscellaneous
F1—½-ampere slow-blow fuse
S1—Spst normally open, momentary-action pushbutton switch
S2—3pst toggle switch
T1—6.3-volt, 100-mA transformer
TS1—4-lug screw-type terminal strip
Keypad—3 by 4 matrix (Industrial Electronic Engineers Inc. No. KS 2585 or similar; see text)
Suitable-size plastic utility box; 6′ or longer telephone cord with modular plug at one end; printed-circuit or perforated board and solder posts; sockets for ICs; holder for F1; ac line cord with plug; ½″ (12.7 mm) plastic spacers (5); insulating plastic tubing; labeling kit; machine hardware; stranded hookup wire; plastic cable ties; solder; etc.

Note: The following are available from A. Caristi, 69 White Pond Rd., Waldwick, NJ 07463; pc board for $7.75; S2560G for $7.50; 2N5401 for $3.00; 2N5550 for $2.75; 2N2646 for $2.95. Add $1.00 to cover shipping and handling. NJ residents add sales tax.

can be integrated, of course, to

Fig. 15.1. The heart of Teleguard's circuit is IC3, a specialized digital IC that replaces rotary telephone dial.

maintain operation in case an ac power outage does occur.)

Teleguard can be left connected to your telephone line at all times with the assurance that it won't affect normal telephone service. It can also be reprogrammed at any time to dial the number of the location where you or the person you want alerted will be.

About the Circuit

At the heart of Teleguard's circuit (Fig. 15.1) is *IC3*, a specialized digital integrated circuit that has been designed to replace the standard rotary dial in a telephone. This chip transmits a series of pulses in accordance with a telephone number entered into its on-chip memory bank from a keypad similar to that found on the familiar pushbutton telephone. Any number, including area code, can be entered.

Once a number is stored in memory, it remains there for as long as power to the circuit is uninterrupted. However, you can deliberately change it simply by "dialing" in a new telephone number. Doing this replaces any previously entered number. When the circuit is tripped, the number stored in memory is automatically dialed out repeatedly (about every 90 seconds) until it is stopped at the receiving end.

The timing cycle that controls repeated dialing of the number in memory is provided by *IC1*, an ordinary 555 timer chip operated in its astable mode. When the number is dialed out, the *on* time of the circuit is approximately 60 seconds, while the *off* time is about 30 seconds.

A logic low fed to pin 4 holds *IC1* in the standby (not tripped) mode as long as the protective circuit connected to screw-type terminals, A, B, and C of terminal Strip *TS1* on Teleguard is intact. (Hookups from the external protective circuits are made from the screw-type terminals selectively, according to whether the circuits are normally open or normally closed arrangements. (More about the hookups later.) When the external circuit is secure, *IC2* is prevented from oscillating. When the circuit is triggered, by tripping the external protective circuit, *IC1* begins its timing cycle and continues to time out as long as the external circuits tells it an emergency exists.

Taken from pin 3, the output of *IC1* is an inverted pulse that is fed to on/off-hook pin 5 of *IC3* via *IC2B*. This pulse tells *IC3* when to begin dialing out its stored number. A logic fed to pin 5 causes *Q1* and *Q2* to switch on and connect *R14* and *LED1* to the telephone lines. The LED lights, indicating that a dial tone is available and outpulsing can begin.

A logic 1 fed simultaneously to pins 1 and 18 of *IC3* starts the outpulsing operation. This logic signal is provided by *IC4B, IC4C,* and *IC4D.* Delay network *R22/C9* delays the outpulsing signal by 1 second to allow the telephone line to activate the dial tone when *Q1* switches on. When the 1-second delay time has elapsed, pins 1 and 18 of *IC3* are fed a logic-1 pulse that causes the number in memory to be dialed out. Timer *IC1* holds *IC3* in the operate mode for a total of 60 seconds to permit the dialed number

time to ring and the party being called to answer.

When the *on* time of *IC1* ends, *IC3* is returned to the on-hook condition by a logic 1 fed to pin 5. This disconnects the called party. About 30 seconds later, *IC1* returns to the *on* state and the cycle repeats.

Oscillator *IC5* generates the audio signal tone that alerts the called party to an emergency situation at Teleguard's end of the line. With *IC5* enabled only during the *on* time of *IC1*, no tone is generated, so there is no interference with normal telephone operation.

An additional memory circuit is built into Teleguard to provide indication that the telephone number stored in memory is not lost due to a temporary power failure. This is provided by *IC2C* and *IC2D,* which are connected as a bistable or latch

circuit. When line power is first applied to Teleguard, pin 10 of *IC2* is held low by means of the delay voltage applied to pin 12, the result of the finite charge time of *C8*. Thus, *Q3* and power-line monitor *LED2* will be off. After programming the desired telephone number into Teleguard's memory bank, you can turn on *LED2* by pressing and releasing RESET switch *S1*. This causes *LED2* to light and indicate an OK condition, meaning that the number is now stored in memory. Should there be an interruption of power to Teleguard at any time thereafter, *LED2* will extinguish and remain off, even if power is restored to the circuit. If you note that *LED2* is off at any time, this tells you that the number held in memory has been lost and must be reprogrammed into *IC3* from the keypad.

Fig. 15.2. Calculator-type keypad with 3 by 4 switch matrix connects to IC3 as shown to permit the desired telephone number to be entered into memory.

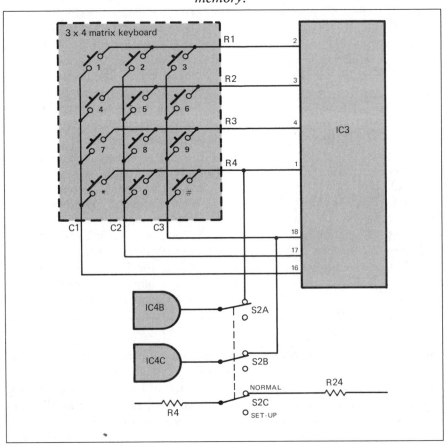

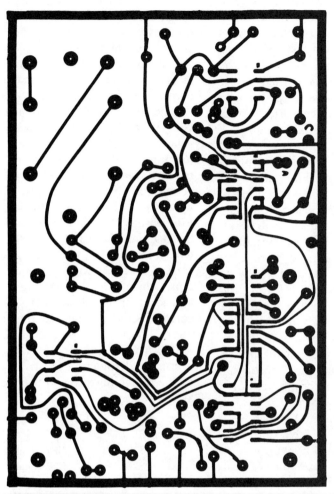 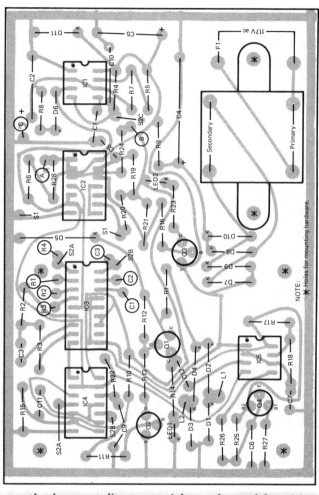

Fig. 3. Shown above is the full-size etching-and-drilling guide for Teleguard's printed-circuit board. The compo- *nent's placement diagram at right can be used for wiring the pc board or an alternative perforated board.*

board and push home. Drop a lockwasher onto each screw end and start a 6-32 nut on each. Gently tighten the hardware.

Checkout

Before you attempt to put Teleguard into service, you should perform some preliminary voltage checks with a dc voltmeter. Plug the line cord into an ac receptacle. Then, being careful to avoid touching any part of *T1*'s primary circuit, measure the voltage across *C4* and *C5*. You should obtain readings of about 7.5 and 3.9 volts, respectively. Clip the meter's common lead to the negative (ground) side of *C2* and measure the

voltages at pin 8 of *IC1* and *IC5,* pin 14 of *IC2* and *IC4*, and pins 12 and 13 of *IC3*. In all cases, the readings should be 3.9 volts. If you obtain the proper results, disconnect the meter from the circuit and unplug Teleguard from the ac line.

Allow *C4* and *C5* to fully discharge. Then install the ICs in their respective sockets, referring to Fig. 1 for identifications and the component-placement diagram in Fig. 3 for locations and orientations. Practice the usual safety procedures when handling the ICs, since some of them are CMOS devices that are easily damaged by static electricity discharges. Place the lid assembly on the

box and secure it in place with the supplied hardware. Finish assembly by labeling *S1* with the legend RESET, *S2* with the legends NORMAL and SET-UP, *LED1* with the legend OUTPULS-ING, and *LED2* with the legend OK. Use a dry-transfer lettering kit or a plastic tape labeler for this operation. If you use the dry-transfer method, spray two or three *light* coats of clear lacquer over it to protect the legends from scratching and peeling. Be sure to wait until each coat of lacquer is dry before spraying the next.

case, it is a good idea to use sockets for all ICs, both to protect them against heat and static damage during assembly and to permit easy troubleshooting in case of circuit failure. Also, if you decide to use perforated board, component layout and orientation should be basically the same as for the pc board (see Fig. 15.3).

Select a plastic box large enough to comfortably accommodate the project's circuitry. Before wiring the board, set it in the bottom of the box, orient and position it as it will be when assembly is complete, and mark the five locations where the mounting holes (indicated by asterisks in the component-layout diagram in Fig. 15.3) are to be drilled. Remove the circuit board and set it aside. Then drill the holes in the marked locations.

Decide which will be the top and bottom walls of the box. In the bottom wall, drill three holes—one for ac line cord entry, a second for telephone line entry, and a final one for mounting the fuse holder. Size these holes as needed. On the top wall of the box will be mounted screw-type terminal strip *TS1*. You will have to use a drill, coping saw, and file to cut a slot long and wide enough to provide clearance for the solder lugs and screws on the terminal strip and drill a separate pair of holes to permit the terminal strip to be anchored in place with machine hardware. Route the free ends of the ac and telephone line cords from the outside into the box and tie a knot in each to serve as strain reliefs. Then mount the fuse holder and terminal strip in their respective locations.

The keypad, switches and LEDs mount on the lid of the box. Trace the outline of the keypad's *inner* lip on the lid of the box. Then drill a ¼ inch (6.35 mm) hole in each corner of the traced cutout area, using a coping saw to cut away all unwanted material within the outline, and smooth the edges with a file. Avoid

removing too much material; you want the keypad to fit snug in the cutout. Drill the holes for the switches and LEDs, sizing the latter to accommodate panel-mount eyelet clips. Then apply a spot of fast-set epoxy cement at all four corners and midway between the corners of the keypad and press the keypad into its cutout. Allow the cement to fully set before handling the lid assembly.

Meanwhile, wire the circuit board according to the component-placement diagram in Fig. 15.3. Pay strict attention to the orientation of all polarized components (ICs, transistors, diodes, and electrolytic capacitors). Also, do *not* install or handle the ICs until all wiring has been completed. Start wiring by installing the resistors on the circuit board, followed by the diodes, IC sockets, capacitors and transistors, in that order. Then loosely mount *T1* in place with machine hardware, plug its primary and secondary leads into the appropriate holes, and solder.

Prepare nineteen 12 inch (305 mm) and three 8 inch (203 mm) lengths of stranded hookup wire by stripping ¼ inch (6.35 mm) of insulation from each end. Tightly twist together the fine wires at each end and lightly tin with solder. Install and solder one end of each of the 12 inch (305 mm) wires in all holes except those labeled A, B, C, L1, L2, and the unmarked hole between *R17* and *T1* in the Fig. 15.3 component placement diagram. Install one end of each of the 8 inch (203 mm) wires in holes A, B, and C.

Place the circuit board, component side up, to the left of the plastic box. Tightly twist together the fine wires in each conductor of the free end of the ac line cord and lightly tin with solder. Plug one of these wires into the *T1* primary hole and solder into place. Form a hook in the other wire, slip it into the side lug of the fuse holder, crimp shut and solder. Prepare a 3 inch (76.2

mm) length of heavy-duty stranded wire as you did for the 8 inch (203 mm) and 12 inch (305 mm) wires. Form a hook at one end, slip it into the rear lug of the fuse holder, crimp shut, and solder.

Trim away enough insulating outer jacket from the telephone line cord's free end to expose 3 inches (76.2 mm) of insulated conductors. Clip off and discard the black and yellow wires. Strip away ¼ inch (6.35 mm) of insulation from the red and green wires, tightly twist together the fine conductors in each wire, and lightly tin with solder. Plug either wire into the hole labeled *L1* and solder. Plug the other wire into hole *L2* and solder. (The coding of these wires is unimportant, since the *D1* through *D4* bridge in Fig. 15.1 will deliver the correct polarity signal to the telephone line.)

Finish wiring the project by connecting and soldering the free ends of the remaining wires to the board as follows:

From Board Pad	To
S2A	S2a toggle
S2B	S2B toggle
LED1, K	LED1 cathode
LED1, unmarked	LED1 anode
C1	C1 on keypad
C2	C2 on keypad
C3	C3 on keypad
R3	R3 on keypad
R2	R2 on keypad
R1	R1 on keypad
R4	R4 on keypad
S1	S1, either lug
S1	S1, other lug
LED2, K	LED2 cathode
LED2, unmarked	LED2 anode
A	lug A on TS1
B	lug B on TS1
C	lug C on TS1

Before connecting and soldering any of the wires to the leads of *LED1* and *LED2*, slip a 2 inch (50.8

mm) length of insulating sleeving over the wires. Tack-solder the wires to the leads of the LEDs, and push the sleeving up over the connections and bare wire leads to protect against short circuits. Gently press the LEDs into their eyelet clips.

Plug the free end of the stranded wire attached to the rear lug of the fuse connector into the free *T1* primary hole and solder.

Remove the hardware loosely securing the transformer to the circuit board. Feed five 6-32 by 1 inch (25.4 mm) machine screws through the mounting holes in the bottom of the box from the outside. (Be sure to keep *T1* from swinging free as you do this; otherwise, its lead may tear loose from the board.) Slide a ³/₈ inch (9.5 mm) or ½ inch (12.7 mm) plastic spacer over each screw end. Now align the screw ends with the holes in the circuit board and push through. Drop a lock washer onto each screw end and start a 6-32 nut on each. Gently tighten the hardware.

Checkout

Before you attempt to put Teleguard into service, you should perform some preliminary voltage checks with a dc voltmeter. Plug the line cord into an ac receptacle. Then, being careful to avoid touching any part of *T1*'s primary circuit, measure the voltage across *C4* and *C5*. You should obtain readings of about 7.5 and 3.9 volts, respectively. Clip the meter's common lead to the negative (ground) side of *C2* and measure voltages at pin 8 of *IC1* and *IC5*, pin 14 of *IC2* and *IC4*, and pins 12 and 13 of *IC3*. In all cases, the readings should be 3.9 volts. If you obtain the proper results, disconnect the meter from the circuit and unplug Teleguard from the ac line.

Allow *C4* and *C5* to fully discharge. Then install the ICs in their respective sockets, referring to Fig. 15.1 for identifications and the component-placement diagram in Fig. 15.3 for locations and orientations. Practice the usual safety procedures when handling the ICs, since some of them are CMOS devices that are easily damaged by static electricity discharges. Place the lid assembly on the box and secure it in place with the supplied hardware. Finish assembly by labeling *S1* with the legend RESET, *S2* with the legends NORMAL and SET-UP, *LED1* with the legend OUTPULSING, and *LED2* with the legend OK. Use a dry-transfer lettering kit or a plastic tape labeler for this operation. If you use the dry transfer method, spray two or three *light* coats of clear lacquer over it to protect the legends from scratching and peeling. Be sure to wait until each coat of lacquer is dry before spraying the next.

Setup and Use

Plug Teleguard's line cord into an ac receptacle and its other cord into the telephone line from the phone company, and switch *S2* to SET-UP. OUTPULSING *LED1* should now light, indicating that Teleguard has established connection to the telephone system. Dial the emergency number you have selected, using Teleguard's keypad. As you do this, *LED1* will flash in accordance with the digits being dialed. When *LED1* stops flashing, switch *S2* to NORMAL to put the system into its "guard" mode.

System operation can be checked by simulating an emergency condition. You do this by activating the external protective circuit (Fig. 15.4). Before you wire the premises to be monitored with switches and/or sensors, you can simulate the emergency condition simply by using a length of hookup wire to short terminal A to terminal C on *TS1*.

This simulates the closing of a normally open protective circuit (Fig. 15.4). If everything is okay, OUTPULSING *LED1* should pulse on and off in accordance with the telephone number. When outpulsing ceases, you can lift the receiver of the telephone that is on the same line as Teleguard and hear the special tone that denotes existence of an emergency condition. (Be sure to alert the party being called, should he or she answer the telephone, that this is only a test.)

Having verified that the system works with normally open protective devices, it is a good idea to also verify operation with normally closed devices. Again, you can do this locally simply by connecting a jumper wire from terminal A to terminal C of *TS1* with one wire and from terminal A to terminal B with a second wire. (This arrangement is

Fig. 15.4. Teleguard can accommodate both normally open and normally closed sensors, depending on how protective circuit is connected.

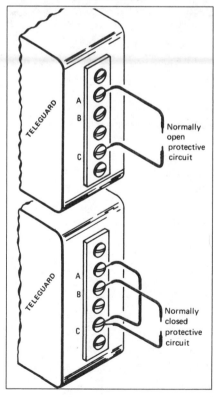

detailed in the normally closed diagram in Fig. 15.4.) To trip the circuit, simply disconnect wire from terminal B.

Once you know Teleguard is operating as it should, you can proceed to wire the premises to be protected with appropriate sensors and run conductors from the sensors to the project. An interior view

of the assembled Teleguard project is shown in Fig. 15.5.

Should you wish to change the telephone number stored in Teleguard's memory at any time, simply do the following: (1) set *S1* to SET-UP; (2) dial in the new number with the project's keypad *after LED1* extinguishes; and (3) when outpulsing ceases, set *S1* to NOR-

MAL. You can do this any number of times.

If for any reason you wish to deactivate Teleguard, simply disconnect its modular plug from the telephone line but leave its ac line cord plugged into the ac receptacle. This way, the telephone number programmed into Teleguard's memory will not be lost and the project will be ready to be instantly returned to service.

Fig. 15.5. Interior view of the assembled Teleguard project shows neat layout.

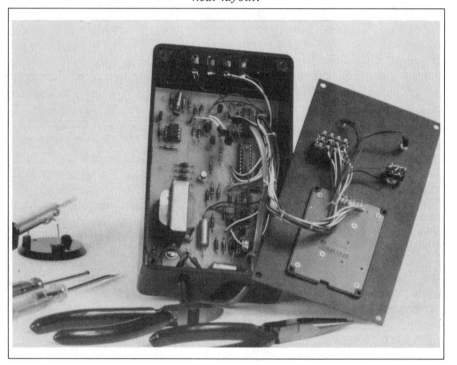

In Closing

With Teleguard at your service, you can have a secure feeling whenever you leave your home or business unattended. With the proper sensors, Teleguard can alert you (or anyone you designate) if an intruder attempts to break into your home or business, a fire starts, water floods a basement, or any other condition that can be indicated by opening or closing a circuit.

Next, we will discuss several types of solid-state sensors you can build at low cost for use with Teleguard. These will monitor such conditions as temperature and pressure and detect the presence of fluids. They will enhance operation of Teleguard and provide state-of-the-art protection.

Solid-State Sensing Modules for Teleguard

ANTHONY J. CARISTI

If you built the Teleguard security system, you will almost certainly want to build and use the solid-state sensing modules described here with it. The modules presented here have been specifically designed to be used with Teleguard to enhance system operation.

The sensing circuits will respond to such parameters as temperature, light and the presence of fluid (specifically water) to detect fire, thieves, water seepage, and heating system and refrigeration failure. Each circuit is low in cost, easy to build from readily available components, and provides state-of-the-art protection.

Teleguard's Sensing Circuit

In Fig. 16.1 is shown a simplified schematic diagram of the sensing circuit and controlling oscillator inside Teleguard that uses the normally open protective circuit connected between terminals A and C of terminal strip *TS1*. With the external sensing switch open, the logic-0 fed to pin 4 of *IC1* holds the voltage at

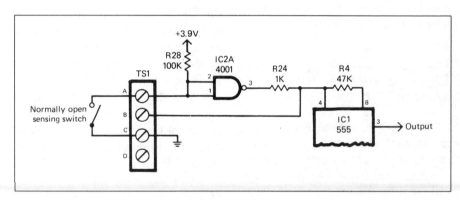

Fig. 16.1. Simplified schematic diagram of sensing circuit and controlling oscillator inside Teleguard, using a normally open protective circuit.

this point to zero by the inverting action of *IC2A*. This prevents *IC1* from oscillating and maintains Teleguard in its standby mode. When the sensing switch closes, 3.9 volts appears at pin 4 of *IC1*, allowing oscillation to occur and Teleguard to dial out its stored telephone number.

Control of Teleguard can be accomplished with ordinary passive switches, thermostats, etc. However, a more reliable—if not more elegant—way to do this is to use solid-state circuitry to control the logic level at terminal A of *TS1*.

When triggering of Teleguard is

to occur, the sensing modules described below will control the logic level by shorting terminal A to ground through a switching transistor. When the circuit is in standby, the transistor will be cut off, allowing terminal A to rise to logic 1 by means of pull-up resistor *R28* in Teleguard's circuitry.

To power the sensing modules, it is necessary to provide a source of dc power. This can be obtained from Teleguard itself, rather than from a separate supply. The Parts List for Teleguard specified a four-contact terminal strip for *TS1*, though in implementing the circuit only three contacts were used (labeled A, B, and C). The fourth contact, which we identify as D, can be used to provide 7.5 volts dc to the sensing modules. Simply connect a wire from the positive end of *C4* to the unused lug on *TS1*. Thereafter, whenever you run wires from Teleguard to the sensor modules, simply include an extra one for the power line.

Since Teleguard's input sensing circuit has a high impedance, you should use two-conductor shielded cable to make connections between it and any sensing modules that are more than about 2 feet away. Connect the shield to terminal C. Also, since Teleguard's ground connection is not isolated from the telephone line, be sure to use an insulated shielded wire so that terminal C does not become accidentally grounded to anything else.

Light-Activated Sensing Modules

A latching-type light-activated sensing module is shown schematically in Fig. 16.2. This module will cause Teleguard to transmit an emergency call to the preprogrammed telephone number when light to photocell *PC1* is interrupted for even a fraction of a second. When this occurs, the logic level fed to terminal A on Teleguard's terminal strip is set to transmit and will remain so even if the light beam to *PC1* is restored.

A practical application of the Fig. 16.2 circuit would be to sense the passage of an intruder through a doorway or a passageway. The sensing module would be located on one side of the doorway or passageway, the light source on the other side and aimed so that it illuminates the sensitive surface of *PC1*. An unauthorized person passing through the protected portal will then break the beam and trigger the circuit.

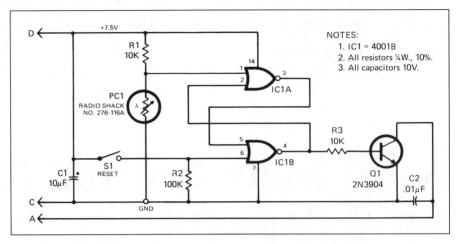

Fig. 16.2. This latching-type light-activated sensing module uses a photocell and light beam to monitor doorways and passageways to detect intruders.

Operation of the circuit in Fig. 16.2 is as follows: *IC1A* and *IC1B* NOR gates are wired in a bistable (latching) multivibrator configuration. This circuit can assume either of two logic states, depending upon the last logic-1 level placed on either of the input terminals at pin 1 of *IC1A* or pin 6 of *IC1B*.

When the circuit is in standby and light is directed onto *PC1*, the voltage at pin 1 of *IC1A* is near zero (logic 0). Similarly, the voltage at pin 6 of *IC1B* is also at logic 0, the result of the open contacts of RESET switch *S1* and *R2*. You preset the logic state of the output terminal at pin 4 of *IC1B* after power is applied to the circuit when you press and release momentary-action switch *S1*. This sets the circuit to its inactive mode. At this point, pin 4 of *IC1B* is at logic 0, cutting off *Q1* and putting Teleguard in its standby mode.

As long as light falls on *PC1*, the circuit will be armed and in standby. Interrupting the light beam causes pin 4 of *IC1B* to go to logic 1, turning on *Q1* and activating Teleguard. Should the light beam be restored, pin 4's logic level will remain high and Teleguard will continue to transmit its emergency call. Only when *S1* is operated will the

circuit return to standby and cancel the call.

A simple modification can reverse the Fig. 16.2 circuit's operation such that it holds Teleguard in standby with no light falling on *PC1* and triggers it when light is detected. To obtain this method of operation, simply connect *R3* to pin 3 of *IC1A* instead of to pin 4 of *IC1B*. This operating scheme is possible because the outputs of the latch circuit at pins 3 and 4 are always at opposite logic states. To put the modified circuit in the standby mode, you simply press and release *S1* as before.

A nonlatching light-activated sensing module is shown schematically in Fig. 16.3. With this circuit, the transmit signal is produced by Teleguard only when light falls on *PC1*. Should *PC1* go dark after some light has been detected, the transmit signal will be canceled and Teleguard will return to standby. With the circuit shown, light must continuously fall on *PC1* for at least 30 seconds for Teleguard to dial out its stored telephone number and the call to be answered.

A practical application of the Fig. 16.3 circuit is protection of a normally closed and dark room. Should a thief break in and turn on a light, the transmit signal wil! trigger Teleguard into making its telephone call.

A common 555 timer, connected as a monostable (one-shot) multivibrator is used in the Fig. 16.3 circuit. The pin-2 trigger input of *IC1* is held to about 7 volts when *PC1* is dark. This inhibits *IC1* from operating and maintains the pin-3 output at 0 volt. It also keeps *Q1* in cutoff and places a logic 1 on terminal A of *TS1*.

When light strikes *PC1, IC1* is triggered into operation with a one-shot period of about 1 second. Since *IC1* is a retriggerable multivibrator, light continuing to fall on *PC1* causes the pin-3 output to remain at about 7 volts. This forward-biases *Q1* and shorts terminal A of *TS1* to ground to initiate the telephone call.

Since the Fig. 16.3 circuit is nonlatching, the emergency call will be made only if light shines on *PC1* long enough for Teleguard to outpulse the number. If desired, you can increase the time constant of the circuit to about 45 seconds by changing the value of *C2* to 47 microfarads. This will assure that at least one telephone call will be made by Teleguard should light strike *PC1*, even if only momentarily.

Temperature-Activated Sensing Modules

Monitoring the temperature of your home or office—or a refrigeration system—is a practical way to alert you that an emergency exists in your absence. With temperature used as the sensing parameter, you can have Teleguard detect fire and heating system, refrigeration, air-conditioning or freezer failure. You could even use such a detector in a greenhouse to warn you when delicate plants might be ruined by a killing frost.

At the heart of the temperature-sensing modules shown schematical-

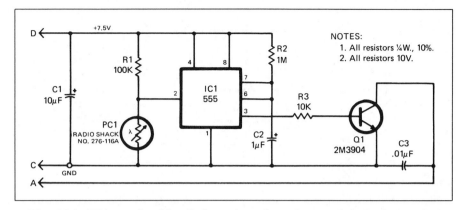

Fig. 16.3. This nonlatching light-activated sensing module is designed to monitor a normally closed and dark room, such as a storeroom or a vault.

ly in Figs. 16.4 and 16.5 is a low-cost specialized IC that reacts to changes in temperature. This precisely calibrated IC can be used to set the desired temperature switching point, using a simple dc voltage measurement between pins 3 and 4 of the LM3911N used for *IC1* in both circuits.

Since a heat emergency, such as a fire, requires opposite logic from a sensor designed for heating system failure, two slightly different circuits are required to monitor the two different conditions. The Fig. 16.4 circuit will cause Teleguard to transmit its emergency call when a rise in temperature is detected and would be used to protect against fire or refrigeration failure. The Fig. 16.5 circuit, on the other hand, detects a fall in temperature and can be used to alert you when a heating system fails or when there is a threat

of frost. Both circuits are provided with potentiometer controls (*R1*) to let you set the switching point to that temperature that is correct for your application.

The circuits in Figs. 16.4 and 16.5 operate in much the same manner. Sensor *IC1* contains a 6.8-volt reference circuit, an operational amplifier and a switching transistor. The last conducts when temperature rises above the trigger point set by *R1*. The temperature at which the on-chip transistor turns on is defined by a simple equation that relates voltage to degrees Celsius.

The output transistor in *IC1* serves as a switching control for terminal A on Teleguard for any application that requires the emergency call to be transmitted when temperature rises in the monitored area. The circuit for this mode of operation is shown in Fig. 16.4. If you

Fig. 16.4. This temperature-sensing module triggers Teleguard when a rise in temperature is detected. Use it as a fire or refrigeration failure monitor.

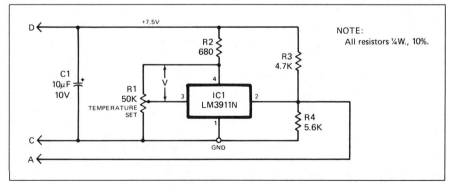

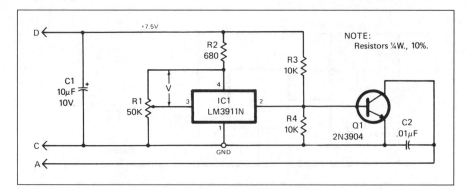

Fig. 16.5. This temperature-sensing circuit detects a fall in temperature. Use it to monitor for heating system failure or danger of frost damage.

wish the system to respond to a fall in temperature, an additional transistor external to *IC1 (Q1)* must be used to invert the output signal.

The voltage between pins 3 and 4 at which *IC1* switches can easily be calculated for the desired temperature in °C as follows: volts = 2.73 + (0.01 × °C). If you do not know the °C equivalent for any temperature expressed in °F, simply convert as follows: °C=[5(°F − 32)/9].

Suppose you wanted to build a sensor that will alert you when a fire breaks out. You would use the Fig. 16.4 circuit. Now assume you want Teleguard to make its call when the temperature in the protected area rises above 105 °F (40.6 °C). Using the voltage formula, you would determine that 3.14 volts would be required between pins 3 and 4 of *IC1*. Should you wish to be alerted in the event of a heating system failure, you would use the Fig. 16.5 circuit and set the circuit to trigger at, say 50 °F (10 °C), which requires a potential between pins 3 and 4 of *IC1* of 2.83 volts.

Connect the temperature-sensing module to Teleguard using terminals A, C, and D of *TS1* (do not use terminal B). Connect a dc voltmeter between terminals 3 (negative) and 4 (positive) of *IC1*. Apply power to Teleguard and adjust *R1* for the desired voltage. Use a fairly accurate (20,000 ohms/volt or greater) voltmeter when making this measurement to

ensure that switchover temperature is as accurate as possible.

Fluid-Activated Sensing Module

Water seepage as the result of a heavy rainfall or spring thaw can cause a lot of damage if it is not caught in time to take remedial action. Using a solid-state fluid detector to trigger Teleguard is an ideal way to guard against water damage. Such a sensor is shown schematically in Fig. 16.6.

At the heart of the Fig. 16.6 circuit is a low-cost LM1830N IC that can detect the presence or absence of a conductive fluid bridging two metallic probes connected to its input. Any *conductive* fluid can be detected with this arrangement.

Inside the LM1830N used for *IC1*

in the Fig. 16.6 circuit is an oscillator, a detector and an on-chip output transistor. This circuitry triggers on when the resistance between the probes is greater than the built-in reference resistor. Since the normal condition for the Fig. 16.6 circuit is an absence of fluid, the on-chip transistor normally conducts. Therefore, pin 12 of *IC1* will be at ground potential and *Q1* will be off.

When a fluid bridges the probes, the potential at pin 12 of *IC1* rises to the 7.5-volt supply level and forward-biases *Q1*, shorting terminal A on Teleguard to ground and causing Teleguard to start the dialing sequence.

Note in Fig. 16.6 that one of the sensing probes is connected to circuit common (ground) and is not isolated from the telephone line. *Under no circumstances should either probe be allowed to contact any conductive object.* To prevent this from happening, mount the probes on an insulated base, such as perforated board, to maintain good isolation between them. Secure the assembly so that the probes touch nothing but the fluid being monitored.

In Summary

Once you have installed your Teleguard security system, you will find that it requires very little attention. Your only real concern will be

Fig. 16.6. Use this fluid-detecting module with Teleguard to alert you to take remedial action when water seepage threatens to damage your home or business.

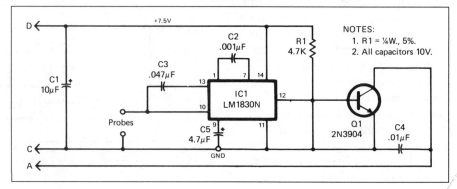

to periodically check to make sure that the OK LED is on. The security provided by the system will give you peace of mind that your home and/or business is protected from intruders, fire, water damage, etc.—even while you are away.

You will also discover that the solid-state sensing modules described here greatly expand upon the type of monitoring provided by the usual switch- and tape-type sensors used in other surveillance systems. In fact, if you wish, you can supplement the solid-state sensors with those passive sensors to achieve both local-area and full-perimeter monitoring with Teleguard.

(Note: The following parts are available from A. Caristi, 69 White Pond Road, Waldwick, NJ 07463: LM3911N, $4.50; LM1830N, $5.75; plus $1.00 postage/handling. NJ residents please add sales tax.)

Part **6**

Computers

chapter **17**

Surge Protection

TJ BYERS

Snap, crackle, and pop may be pleasant breakfast sounds to some people, but to an owner of a computer, amateur radio transceiver, or other expensive electronic gear, they spell trouble. I am referring to the ever-present menace of lightning. Every year, damage done to computers alone by lightning runs into the millions of dollars. And whether you like it or not, your costly equipment could be next.

Protecting your system from the damaging effects of lightning, however, is not as big a chore as you may imagine. I will show you how to do it for $10 or less. But before we get started, let's take a look at lightning and how it gets into a system in the first place.

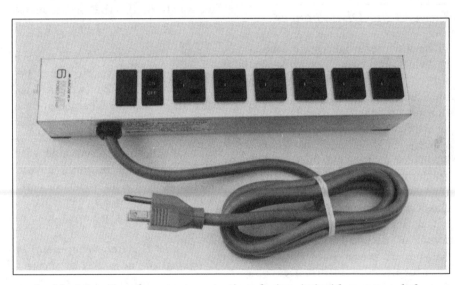

An ideal location for surge-protection devices is inside a grounded ac power-distribution strip like this Archer 6-outlet model from Radio Shack or another manufacturer.

Lightning Spikes

Destructive electrical energy enters your system through the only avenue available to it—your ac power cord. It is ironic that the very lifeline that feeds and sustains your computer and other equipment is also responsible for its demise. The electricity delivered to your home has probably traveled through hundreds of miles of wire and several substations before it reaches you. Herein lies the problem.

A typical lightning flash is composed of many short-duration feeler strikes. A single bolt may contain as many as a hundred individual discharges that, when viewed together, appear as one—much like the scanned dots on a TV screen merge to form a picture.

When lightning strikes, it does so with a force of millions of volts. The rapid succession of feeler strikes produces huge amounts of radio-frequency radiation. In fact, the largest part of it falls below 8 MHz, and you can actually hear lightning (other than the thunder) by listening to an AM radio during

107

a thunderstorm. The high-frequency radio waves are picked up by your antenna and delivered to the speaker as an annoying crackling sound.

In a similar fashion, the sprawling utility grid picks up noise from lightning. When lightning strikes close to a power line, the wires act like a large antenna and absorb part of the radiation. Voltage spikes as high as 6000 volts can easily be injected into the power grid in this manner and be distributed throughout the network. It is not unusual for a lightning strike many miles away to affect you. The voltage spikes travel from the strike down the wires, into your home, and right into your computer.

Power-Line Disturbances

Power-line disturbances are generally divided into two types, *spikes* and *surges*. Although the terms are often used interchangeably, shorter-duration phenomena are usually considered spikes (10 to 500 microseconds), whereas high-voltage disturbances lasting longer than 500 microseconds are looked upon as surges. Therefore, lightning-induced transients are classified as spikes.

But lightning is not the only source of electrical pollution found on your ac power line. Potentially harmful electrical disturbances come from all sorts of places, some of which are closer than you think.

Each time your air conditioner cycles, for instance, the compressor motor places a big high-voltage spike on the line. Likewise, refrigerators, heaters, and other heavy appliances that draw large currents produce momentary power surges when turned on. And believe it or not, the worst offender may be innocently seated right beside your computer—your printer.

Power surges behave differently than spikes, and are normally brought about by the collapse of a magnetic field, such as the motor in your printer. The closer the load is to your computer, the greater its influence. That is why your printer, even though less powerful than, say, a refrigerator or fan, is more influential. And while these surges are not particularly harmful, they can play havoc with a computer system. Video displays come out jumbled, memory is lost or scrambled, and keyboard entries are meaningless.

Metal-Oxide Varistors

The way to solve these problems is to limit the amount of voltage allowed on the line. In other words, clip the spikes and surges. Fortunately, there is an easy and inexpensive way to do this that uses a device called a *metal-oxide varistor* (MOV).

Basically, the MOV (Fig. 17.1) is a voltage-dependent resistor that behaves somewhat like two back-to-back zener diodes. That is, it is a nonlinear device that has a specific breakdown voltage. The MOV is made of zinc oxide combined with small amounts of bismuth, cobalt, and manganese. The zinc oxide combines with the other elements to form an array of p-doped and n-doped semiconductor junctions. The junctions align themselves to form a disoriented array of series and parallel paths that the electrons will ultimately follow. The diversity of this microstructure is what causes its nonlinear semiconductor properties.

When a voltage that is lower than the threshold voltage of the MOV is applied across it, the MOV acts like a nonconducting open circuit. But if the applied voltage exceeds the MOV breakdown voltage, it begins to conduct, effectively clamping the input voltage to a safe level. In other words, the MOV safely absorbs the voltage transient and dissipates the energy as heat.

The physical dimensions of the MOV determine its electrical characteristics. MOVs are available in a wide range of operating voltages and currents, ranging from 5 to 3000 volts and peak currents up to 50,000 amps. Their response time is measured in mere nanoseconds (typically 35 nanoseconds).

As you may have guessed by now, MOVs lie at the heart of our surge protection devices. The amount of protection you need, however, depends upon your system. Therefore, I have devised three protection projects for you to choose from, each with varying degrees of protection.

Fig. 17.1. After wiring them into place, fold the MOV devices flat against the ac socket as shown. The capacitors and r-f chokes wired across the end two sockets make up a noise filter.

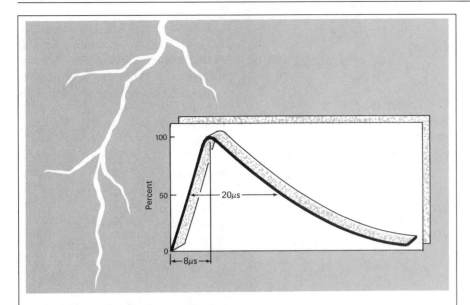

Lightning Bolts

A typical lightning strike is characterized by more than one stroke per flash with peak currents of 20,000 amps or higher. The lightning bolt travels a crooked path to the ground. The path is created by the feeler current as it ionizes its way through the atmosphere, thereby producing the classic zig-zag pattern. Lightning-induced power-line spikes of up to 6000 volts have been recorded with rise times as short as 500 nanoseconds. In an effort to standardize a "typical" stroke, the IEEE has proposed the above waveshape. Based on both RFI (Radio Frequency Interference) and EMI (Electromagnetic Interference) measurements, they developed the so-called 8/20 microsecond-pulse theory. This representative pulse has an 8-microsecond linear rise time to its crest, graduating to an exponential decline to zero. Pulse width, at the 50 percent points, is defined as 20 microseconds. The performance of all surge protecting devices, including MOVs, is gauged according to this standard.

Unfortunately, the Voltage Spike Protector does not protect against all forms of power surge. If the lightning strike is such that a voltage spike of equal proportions is induced into both wires, the MOV cannot sense it. This kind of power-line disturbance is termed *common-mode voltage*. As far as the MOV is concerned, the voltage between the two power legs is just fine, even though they may be riding on a power surge thousands of volts above ground!

Better Protection

To alleviate the foregoing problem, I constructed the second of the surge protectors. It contains three MOV devices. One is wired across the hot and neutral lines of the ac input, just like in the "good" version mentioned. To keep common-mode spikes from creeping into the system, though, two additional MOVs are added, each extending to ground from the power-line legs (Fig. 17.3). With this arrangement, the outlet voltage can never be more than 130 volts in any direction.

Duplicating the surge protector is relatively straightforward and something you can do in a matter of minutes. First, obtain a six-outlet expansion socket, such as Radio Shack's 61-2622, and remove the cardboard back. To do this you must unbolt the four screws located

Good Protection

The first of these devices is also the simplest, because there is nothing to build. It comes already assembled. This product, which is sold by a variety of companies under the name of *Voltage Spike Protector*, contains a single MOV device that is connected across the two prongs of the power line (Fig. 17.2). Any transient in excess of 130 volts is readily suppressed by the MOV and is prevented from entering your equipment.

To use the spike protector, simply plug the computer into the adapter and insert the adapter into the wall outlet. That's it.

Fig. 17.2. Good protection is provided by any number of commercial products with MOV devices.

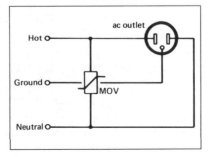

Fig. 17.3. Better protection is afforded when three MOV devices are wired across the prongs as shown.

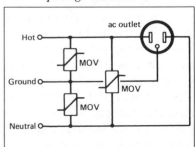

in each of the corners. These screws are actually coarsely threaded rivets that can be backed out with a standard slot screwdriver in a turn or less.

With the cover removed, you are faced with six copper strips that are used to expand a two-outlet socket into six. If you have the misfortune, as I did, of having the metal strips tumble into your hands along with the cardboard back, do not panic. Simply shove them back into their respective slots with a firm thumb.

The next step is to solder the MOV devices in place. There is plenty of room inside the plastic cover to accommodate them; just be sure nothing touches that could short something out. Using the photo as your guide, slip the MOVs into position and solder them in place. Remember, one MOV goes across the lines, another connects between the thin prong and ground (the stripe with the round inserts), and the third is soldered between the remaining prong and ground. It does not make any difference which direction you insert them, because MOVs are bidirectional devices.

Now replace the back. Remove the wall plate from the wall socket and fasten the surge protector in place using the long screw supplied with the adapter. Henceforth, when you plug your computer into this outlet, it will be protected from all forms of voltage surge.

Best Protection

But even this protection is not enough in some cases. Though your computer is protected from the lethal effects of voltage spikes, it is still susceptible to electrical noise. Noise can best be described as unwanted voltage excursions that fall within the limits of the MOV protector. In effect, it is small signals that ride atop the power-line voltage, but are not particularly harm-

Parts List

GOOD
1. Voltage Spike Protector

BETTER
1. 6-Outlet Plug
3. Metal-Oxide Varistor (see sidebar)

BEST
1. 6-Outlet Power Strip (Radio Shack 61-2619A)
3. Metal-Oxide Varistor (see sidebar)
2. 100-μH r-f Choke (Radio Shack 273-102)
2. 0.047-μF, 500 V disc Capacitor

ful to the system. What noise does to a computer, though, is scramble the data contained in the memory chips. Words come out misspelled and, in extreme cases, data is lost altogether.

To remove unwanted noises from an ac line, you need a filter...that brings us to our third design. In addition to being MOV protected, the last option incorporates a filter for the removal of noise from the power line. This is the kind of noise you are likely to experience from your printer.

The entire project is built inside a Radio Shack Power Strip (part number 61-2619A). This power strip has a single, heavy-duty cord that expands to six outlets housed in a sturdy metal case. As added features, the power strip comes equipped with a built-in 15-amp circuit breaker, an off/on switch, and power indicator lamp.

To modify the power strip, the aluminum housing must be split in half. This is accomplished by simply removing the eight screws that secure the two end plates. However, this is easier said than done. For whatever reason (I suspect safety), the retaining screws have recessed square-drive heads that require a special tool to turn them. After sev-

eral false starts, I finally elected to file a groove in the screw heads and twist them out with an ordinary slot screwdriver. Once the screws were removed, I threw them away and replaced them with conventional Phillips-head screws. I strongly suggest you do the same.

With the end plates out of the way, the lower half of the metal case easily slides off, exposing the bottoms of the outlets. Begin the modification by removing a short strip of insulation from each of the three wires connecting the first four sockets together. An X-ACTO® knife works best. Now solder the three MOVs to these wires, bridging one across the black and white wires, one across the black and green wires, and one across the white and green wires. After soldering, bend the leads so the MOVs rest against the back of the outlets, as illustrated.

Next, we will work on the link connecting the last two sockets, numbers 5 and 6 as you count from

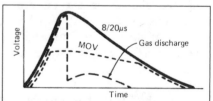

MOV Operation

The Metal Oxide Varistor (MOV) is the most popular of the surge protection devices. Basically, the MOV is fabricated from a ceramic element composed of zinc oxide and several kinds of metal-oxide additives that have been sintered together at relatively high temperatures. The resulting structure produces a disoriented array of semiconductor junctions that behave like two back-to-back zener diodes. Suppression is achieved by clamping the input voltage to a threshold level and dissipating the surge energy as heat.

the breaker end. With a pair of wire cutters, completely remove the section of the black and white wires between sockets 4 and 5, leaving a small pigtail connected to the fourth socket. Strip the insulation from the pigtails. DO NOT cut the green wire!

This last operation divides the power strip into two sections. Into the severed portion of the line will be inserted the filter. Before you can do that, though, you must remove a small piece of insulation from the three wires joining outlets 5 and 6, just like you did when installing the MOV devices.

Solder an r-f choke from the black pigtail of socket 4 to the freshly exposed black wire between sockets 5 and 6. Then do the same for the white wires. Finally, connect a 0.047-microfarad disc capacitor across the green and white leads,

laying the capacitor out of the way after installation. Another 0.047-microfarad capacitor connects across the black and green leads of the last two receptacles.

The power-line filter is unique in that the MOVs serve a dual purpose. First and foremost, they are guardians for spikes and surges on the line. Secondly, the stray capacitance of the MOV, which is about 0.1 microfarad, supplies the input capacitance needed for the pi-section filter.

When using the power strip for a computer system, you should plug the printer and other peripherals into the first four outlets. The computer itself plugs into either of the last two sockets. If your system uses a buffer interface of any sort, plug it into one of the filtered outlets.

And there you have it, three different devices to protect your com-

puter and electronic systems against the ravages of nature. It must be noted, however, that not a one of them is a lightning arrester, so in the rare event that lightning actually strikes your house, damage will result. But when used as intended for everyday power line abuses, they are very effective and cheap insurance.

There are, of course, a host of commercial isolators to prevent high-voltage spikes and power-line hash from damaging or causing your equipment to malfunction. These include high load capacity, high EMI and RFI attenuation, and other refinements. But whether you build or buy, it pays to protect your investment in computers, computer data, and electronic equipment with such protective devices.

chapter **18**

A Computer System Power Controller

PAUL M. SPANNBAUER

Are you tired of reaching around or to the back of your computer, the side of your printer, and the back of your modem to turn each on or off? Or wonder if you should add more surge and spike protection devices? You can overcome these irritants by buying a bunch of commercially available devices, of course, but at considerable cost. My solution to this problem was to build my own ac-line power controller with built in surge/spike suppressors. Cost was about $62, including a fancy cabinet for the project.

Everything fits inside a handsome shielded metal box. The ac outlets, into which the system equipment plugs, are located on the rear panel, while all switches and their status indicators mount on the front panel. If you examine the photos, you can see that my Controller was designed to have four outlet/switch/indicator combinations to suit the needs of my computer system, plus a master POWER switch and panel lamp. You can add more outlet/switch/indicator sections as needed to customize your Control-

ler for the needs of your system. You can also use this device for other electronic systems, such as stereo and video setups, of course.

About the Circuit

The complete schematic diagram of the Controller is shown in Fig. 18.1. The circuit is really quite simple in design. Note that throughout the circuit the standard white/black/green three-conductor wiring scheme is used. It is highly recommended that you maintain this scheme exactly and do not attempt to change it to a two-conductor system. All computer products use this wiring scheme for ac line operation, though most consumer video and

audio products don't. Even if you want to control power to only two-conductor wired products, you'll find that they are compatible with this Controller.

Items in your system you want to control plug into ac receptacles *SO1* through *SO*$_n$. (The subscript *n* simply indicates that you can have four or more of each component in your Controller.) Power to these receptacles is individually controlled by switches *S2* through *S*$_n$, while the neon lamps in *I2* through *I*$_n$, respectively, will light whenever the switch in a given circuit is closed and power is being delivered from the ac line. You can add receptacle/switch/lamp combinations as needed by your system, the only limit being the amount of

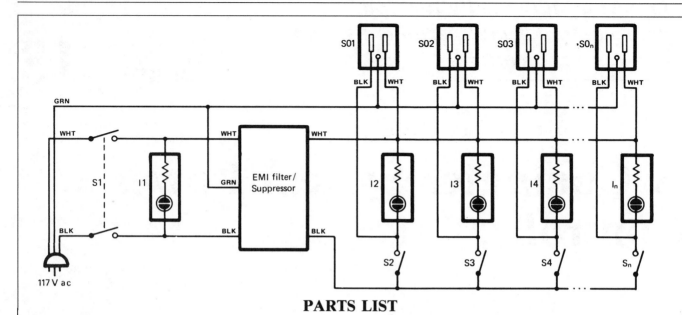

PARTS LIST

Miscellaneous
S1—Dpdt miniature toggle switch
S2 thru S$_n$—Spst miniature toggle switch
SO1 thru SO$_n$—Chassis-mount, three-conductor ac receptacle
EMI filter/suppressor module
I1 thru I$_n$—Panel-mount neon-lamp assembly
Corcom Model 8109 (or similar);

suitable metal enclosure (5⅞″ (149 mm) W by 5¼″ (133 mm) D by 3″ (76.2 mm) H Radio Shack No. 270-253 accommodates a four-receptacle system; adjust size accordingly for more than this); heavy-duty, three conductor ac line cord with plug and strain relief; 12- or 14 gauge stranded

white, black and green wire; wire nuts (5); spade lugs (optional); rubber feet (4); dry transfer lettering kit; clear acrylic spray; etc.
Note: You can substitute illuminated push-on/push-off switches (Radio Shack No. 275-676) for 12/ S2 through I$_n$/S$_n$ combinations.

Fig. 18.1. Overall schematic of a minimum controller system.

power the EMI filter/suppressor can handle.

Main power switch *S1* determines whether or not ac line power is available for switching to the individual ac receptacles. With *S1* closed this power is available and can be selectively fed to the receptacles. With *S1* open, no power is available, regardless of the status of the other switches in the Controller.

The circuit shown in Fig. 18.1 is a minimum Controller system. There are, of course, a few modifications you can make to it to further customize and enhance it. For example, in hi-fi and video systems, there are items you never want the power removed from. These include timers, turntables, videocassette recorders and the like. Therefore, you can incorporate into your Control-

ler one or more ac receptacles that are nonswitchable. Connect these directly across the ac line where the line cord enters the Controller box, ahead of *S1* (see Fig. 18.2A).

Another modification you might wish to make is the addition of a circuit breaker. You can obtain pushbutton-reset circuit breakers in a wide variety of load ratings. Determine what the maximum load would normally be for your system and select an appropriately rated breaker. Install the breaker in the line between the point where the ac line cord enters the Controller box and *S1* (Fig. 18.2B).

Putting It Together

The most difficult step in building this project is making the cutouts in

which the receptacles mount on the rear panel (Fig. 18.3). These must be cut square and uniform in size and location. Depending on the tools you have, there are several ways to make these cutouts. The easiest, of course, is with a chassis punch. Second best is to use a nibbling tool. If neither tool is available, you're stuck with drilling holes and working with a file or metal saw to make the cutouts the proper size and shape. Be careful to make the cutouts just the right size.

Once you've finished making the receptacle cutouts, drill the entry hole for the ac line cord at one end of the rear panel. If you plan on using a circuit breaker, drill its mounting and reset button holes in the rear panel, too. Then work on the front panel. Here, you need two

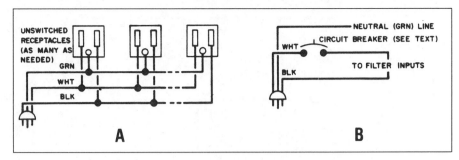

Fig. 18.2. Options that can be added to a basic controller system include series of nonswitchable receptacles (A) and circuit-breaker protection (B).

holes for each lamp/switch combination, unless you opt for the more expensive lighted push/push switches mentioned in the Note at the end of the Parts List, in which case you need only one hole for each $S2/I2$ through S_n/I_n combination.

Determine where to mount the EMI filter/suppressor module. Make sure that it is completely isolated from all other components. Then drill its mounting holes. This done, deburr all holes.

Label all switch/lamp pairs on the front panel and all ac receptacles on the rear panel with their appropriate legends, using a dry-transfer lettering kit. Then spray two or more light coats of clear acrylic over all exterior surfaces of the front and rear panels. Allow each coat to dry before spraying on the next.

When the acrylic has completely dried, mount the components in their respective locations. Then, referring back to Fig. 18.1, wire the circuit exactly as shown. Use only heavy-duty (12- or 14-gauge) stranded wire throughout, and maintain the white (WHT), black (BLK) and green (GRN) color-code scheme throughout. Connections to all filter/suppressor module leads are made with wire nuts; all other connections are soldered.

Double check all your wiring. Then plug the Controller's line cord into an ac outlet. Flip master POWER switch *S1* to on and note that *I1* lights. Leave *S1* set to on and toggle on then off and then on the other switches on the front panel, observing that their respective neon lamps come on then go off and then come on again. Flip the POWER switch to off; *all* neon lamps should extinguish, indicating that all is well.

Disconnect the ac line cord from the wall outlet and finish assembling the enclosure. Your Power Controller is now ready to be put into service.

Fig. 18.3. Photo shows details of controller's rear panel. Ac power cord enters through and ac receptacles mount on panel. So, too, does a circuit breaker.

Part **7**

Test Equipment

Designed to provide all the voltages required by modern IC circuits, it may be all the power supply you ever need on your workbench

chapter **19**

An Experimenter's Multivoltage Power Supply

WILLIAM R. HOFFMAN

Most power supplies for the experimenter's workbench are inadequate for modern circuit designs. The problem is not that they do not provide sufficient current for complex circuits or that voltage regulation is not adequate. Rather, it is that even relatively simple circuits nowadays are likely to contain a mix of analog and digital IC devices that can require up to four different voltages and polarities. Few low-cost power supplies are capable of delivering what these circuits need. The solution to the dilemma is to build a power supply that can, such as the multivoltage supply described here.

The Experimenter's Multivoltage Power Supply may be the ultimate low-cost solution to your breadboarding powering problem. It offers simultaneous outputs at +15, −15, +12 (or −12), +5 and −5 volts. Full regulation is supplied on all output lines, and current delivery is sufficient for the great majority of experimenter projects. This article discusses the design concept, provides the formulas

and procedures to design and build your own supply designs, and lists an assortment of popular three-terminal voltage regulators along with their important specifications.

Designing the Supply

Designing a power supply for a particular set of needs requires that you give careful consideration to the transformer/rectifier and regulator

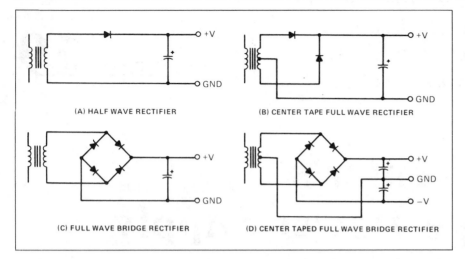

Fig. 19.1. In these drawings are illustrated the four basic transformer/ rectifier configurations commonly used in electronic circuit designs.

circuits. Figure 19.1 illustrates four common transformer/rectifier circuits. Keeping in mind that the regulator requires an input that is 2 to 10 volts greater than its output voltage, select the circuit that most nearly supplies the correct voltage with the transformer you plan to use.

You can determine rectifier output voltage relative to transformer output voltage using the appropriate formulas as follows:

$$(A) \ V_o = T_o \times 0.7$$
$$(B) \ V_o = (T_o/2) \times 1.4$$
$$(C) \ V_o = T_o \times 1.4$$
$$(D) \ V_o = (T_o/2) \times 1.4$$

The letters in the parentheses preceding each formula are keyed to the lettered configurations shown in Fig. 19.1. In these equations, V_o is a transformer/rectifier output voltage and T_o is total voltage at the secondary of the transformer. These are approximate voltages that will be delivered to the input of the regulator. Keep in mind, too, that the result obtained with equation (D) is for *total* voltage from + to −; the voltage from + to ground and from −to ground will be half the calculated value.

The best way to understand how to design a power supply (or any circuit, for that matter) is to run through an illustrative example. Let us assume for the moment that you want to build a 12-volt dc supply using a 24-volt center-tapped transformer. Using the formula for this particular circuit, you obtain (24/2) × 1.4 = 16.8 volts output from the circuit, which is about the minimum voltage required by the regulator for this circuit.

The next step is to select the filter capacitor. This is a fairly simple task. Just keep in mind that the voltage rating of the capacitor should always be at least 50% greater than the calculated rectifier output voltage and that you should figure about 1000 to 2000 microfarads of capacitance for each ampere the supply is to deliver.

Selecting the appropriate regulator is your final task. Shown in Fig. 19.2A is a typical regulator circuit, which consists simply of the regulator IC itself and a 0.1-microfarad bypass capacitor. Choose your regulator according to the desired output voltage and current levels and polarity of output voltage. The IC Voltage Regulator specifications table shown elsewhere will be a good reference for this step. The table lists most popular types of three-terminal regulators in IC packages.

Designing Your Own Supply

Designing a power supply is a relatively easy task. Here are steps to follow:

1. Determine what voltage(s) and maximum current your supply will have to deliver for your breadboarded projects.

2. Next, Using Fig. 19.1 and the equations presented in the main article, determine what transformer/rectifier configuration will suit the parts you have on hand or can obtain.

3. Choose rectifiers that have an equal or greater current rating than your circuits will require, preferably the latter, and with a voltage rating at least twice that of the transformer's output voltage.

4. Determine the value of the filter capacitor, figuring 1000 to 2000 microfarads for each ampere the supply is to deliver.

5. Select the appropriate regulator(s) from the table.

6. Make sure to adequately heat sink all regulators; no regulator should ever become so hot that it is uncomfortable to the touch.

7. Select a fuse for the incoming ac line, figuring about ½ ampere for each ampere of current drawn by 5-to-6-volt sections and ³/₈ ampere for each ampere drawn by 10-to-15-volt sections. A fast-blow fuse is best here.

Choose a positive supply regulator for a positive regulated output voltage or a negative supply regulator for a negative output voltage. Should your application require both positive and negative output voltages, use both types of regulators. If you already have a pair of same-polarity regulators (or cannot obtain both polarity devices), you can use these to fill your needs, as shown in Fig. 19.2B. It is extremely important that both transistor/rectifier circuits be *completely* isolated from each other when using same-polarity regulators. A center-tapped transformer will not do. You *must* use either a transformer with two separate and isolated secondaries or two separate transformers.

About the Circuit

Now that you know how to design a power supply, let us take a quick look at the Multivoltage Power Supply that is the subject of this article. It is shown schematically in Fig. 19.3. Note that this supply actually consists of four different power supplies on the same chassis, each with its own transformer, rectifier, filter capacitor, and voltage regulator. Each of these supplies can be individually turned on and off, if desired, simply by putting a spst switch and appropriate size fuse in one transformer primary line and then wiring all to the main ac line cord. However, it is more convenient to use just one switch and fuse, as shown, to control power to all supply sections simultaneously.

In this power supply, the topmost section delivers +15 and −15 volts, the second +12 (or −12) volts and the third and fourth sections +5 and −5 volts, respectively. Note in the last two sections that same-polarity (+5-volt) voltage regulators are used to provide the positive and negative outputs. Consequently, these sections each have their own separate transformer/rectifier and regulator circuits, as described previously and that each polarity of the 5-volt output is referenced to the terminal between the +5- and −5-volt outputs.

Within the supply itself, no portion is referenced to chassis ground. This being the case, you can select the grounding desired in the circuit to which the supply is connected and thereafter use the 12-volt supply as either a positive or a negative source, depending on your circuit's needs.

Though the schematic in Fig. 19.3 does not show one, you can have a power-on indicator, too. Simply connect a panel-type neon lamp across the primary circuits of the transformer, after fuse *F1*. Before installing this pilot lamp, check to see if it has a current limiting resistor built in. If it does not, install a 100,000-ohm resistor in series with the lamp.

Construction

With the components specified in the Parts List, the power supply can

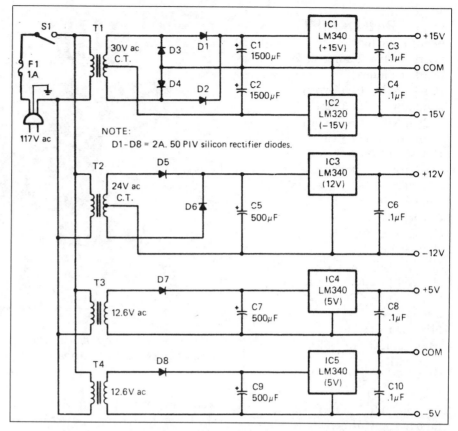

Fig. 19.3. Overall schematic of the multivoltage power supply. Note use of separate transformer/rectifier/regulator arrangements for each output.

Fig. 19.2. In (A) is shown the arrangement to use for single-ended output; (B) shows how you can use two same-polarity regulators to obtain both positive and negative output voltages.

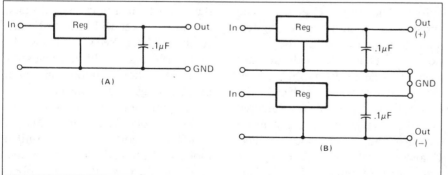

PARTS LIST

Semiconductors

D1 thru D8—2-ampere, 50 PIV rectifier diodes
IC1—LM340 (+15-volt) regulator in TO-3 case
IC2—LM320 (−15-volt) regulator in TO-3 case
IC3—LM340 (+12-volt) regulator in TO-220 case
IC4, IC5—LM340 (+5-volt) regulator in TO-220 case

Capacitors

C1, C2—1500-μF, 25-volt electrolytic
C3, C4, C6, C8, C10—0.1-μF, 100-volt plastic
C5, C7, C9—500-μF, 25-volt electrolytic

Miscellaneous

F1—1-ampere fast-blow fuse (see text)
S1—1-ampere, 125-volt spst toggle switch
T1—30-volt, 1-ampere center-tapped transformer
T2—24-volt, 0.5 ampere center-tapped transformer
T3, T4—6.3-volt, 0.5-ampere transformer
Metal chassis (8″ by 4½″ by 1½″ (203 by 114 by 38 mm)); eight-lug screw-type terminal block; assorted standard solder-lug terminal strips; holder for F1 (optional); heat sinks; transistor sockets; panel-type neon lamp and 100,000-ohm limiting resistor (optional); semiconductor insulators; perforated metal for transformer cover; line cord with plug; plastic line cord strain relief; rubber grommets; labeling kit; heavy-duty stranded hookup wire; machine hardware; solder; etc.

Fig. 19.4. All components mount on terminal strips; incoming/outgoing wires pass through rubber-grommet-lined holes to guard against short circuits.

be built on a standard 8 by 4½ by 1½ inch (203 by 114 by 38 mm) aluminum chassis (Fig. 19.4). The transformers and the 8-contact screw-type terminal block that serves as the supply's output con-

nector mount on top of the chassis. The power switch (and power-on indicator and fuse holder, if you use these items) mount on one short wall, which should also be drilled to provide access for the ac line cord. On one of the two long walls, you should mount the 5-volt and 12-volt regulators, using standard insulators and silicone or other thermal paste and appropriate hardware. The other long wall accommodates the 15-volt regulators, each mounted on pc-board type heat sinks with insulators, thermal paste, and appropriate hardware.

Because of the simplicity of the power supply's circuit, no printed-circuit board construction is required. The entire circuit can be wired using standard solder-lug terminal strips mounted on the underside of the chassis and held in place with the same hardware that secures the transformers in place. The photo shows a pig-tail fuse soldered into the circuit, but you can use a bayonet-type fuse and holder. Chances of the fuse blowing are small; so a soldered-in fuse is fully

practical. The regulators are all internally current limited so that a shorted load on any of the supplies will not be reflected back as an overload. The only time the fuse would blow is if one of the diodes or a filter capacitor shorted.

With regard to heat sinking the regulators, the heat sinks shown in the photo for the +15- and −15-volt supplies were chosen for compactness and radiating ability. Other types can be used, including many of those available from surplus parts dealers. The actual need for a heat sink is determined by the load the regulators are to feed. Keep in mind that the greater the input voltage to the regulators from the transformer/rectifier circuits, the more power will have to be dissipated as heat. Because of this, the input voltages should be as close as possible to the regulators' minimum input voltage (see Table 19.1).

As you build the Multivoltage Power Supply, keep in mind that all conductors going to the terminal block and all leads from the transformers must go through rubber-grommet-lined holes for connection to the terminal strips on the underside of the chassis. Failure to do this might result in insulation wearing away and causing a short circuit to the chassis.

Checkout

There is only one check to be made once the circuit is fully assembled. That is to measure the voltages available at each of the supply's outputs. Just plug in the line cord, flip *S1* to on, and measure with a voltmeter, noting polarities as you go. If you have installed a power-on indicator, the lamp should light when the power switch is flipped to on.

If everything checks out okay, turn off the power and disconnect the line cord from the ac line. Install the bottom plate on the chassis, check it to make sure that all electrically "live" points of the circuit do not come into contact with either the chassis or the plate. Then fabricate a "cage" out of perforated metal to fit over all transformers and bolt this into place. Finally, label each of the supply's terminal block positions with the appropriate output voltage and polarity.

Table 19.1. IC Voltage Regulator Specifications

IC type	Case	Current	Output Voltages
LM-309	TO-5	200 mA	+5 volts only
	TO-3	1 A	(negative regulator)
LM-320	TO-3	1.5 A	−5, −6, −8, −9, −12,
	TO-5	0.5 A	−15, −18, −24 volts
	TO-220	1.5 A	(negative regulators)
LM-340	TO-3	1.5 A	5, 6, 8, 10, 12, 15,
	TO-220	1.5 A	18, 24, volts (positive regulators)
MC-7800	TO-3	1.5 A	5, 6, 8, 10, 12, 15,
	TO-39	100 mA	18, 24 volts (positive
	TO-92	100 mA	regulators)
	TO-220		
MC-7900	TO-3	1.5 A	−5, −6, −8, −9, −12,
	TO-39	100 mA	−15, −18, −24
	TO-92	100 mA	(negative regulators)
	TO-220	0.5 A	

The Looker

J. DANIEL GIFFORD

Though everyone regularly acknowledges that a digital logic probe is a very useful tool to have around any electronics bench, many people still don't own one. This is surprising since a logic probe offers a fast, powerful way to check out digital circuits and devices with easy-to-use go/no-go indicators.

If you don't yet have a logic probe, here is a low-cost project that will give you a good idea of what it can do for you in tracing digital circuits and isolating defects. I call this probe the "Looker" because it lets you "look into" a circuit.

When completed, this probe offers good, professional performance. It uses the universal 30 percent/70 percent thresholds, has a high 2-megohm input impedance, has a 3.5-to-16-volt supply range, and low standby current of about 1.5 mA at 15 volts. It easily handles multifamily logic, such as CMOS and TTL devices. If the probe has any shortcomings it is in its limited input-frequency response, which is up to 800 kHz. Also, the shortest pulse handled is 300 nanoseconds.

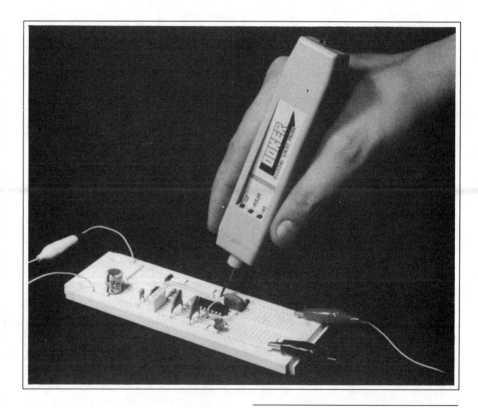

However, a simple design option extends these specifications, though trading away other advantages.

The finished probe shouldn't cost you more than $20 and could cost much less. At the higher price there's a probe case kit available.

Circuit Description

At the heart of the Looker (Fig. 20.1) are two ICs, a TLC274 quad CMOS operational amplifier (*IC1*) and a CD4001B quad CMOS NOR gate (*IC2*). Though the TLC274 is a

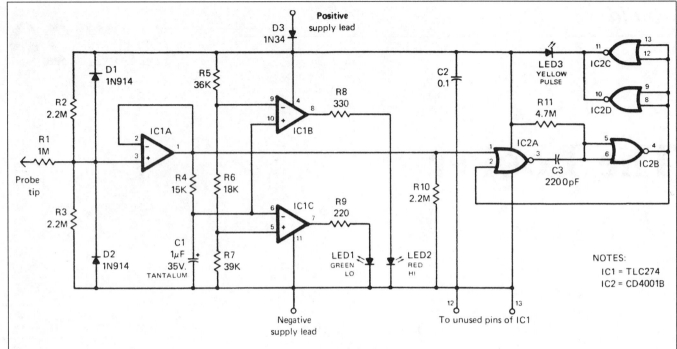

PARTS LIST

Semiconductors
D1, D2—1N914 or 1N4148 signal diode
D3—1N34A germanium signal diode
IC1—TLC274 quad CMOS op amp (Radio Shack No. 276-1750) or TL084
IC2—CD4001B quad CMOS NOR gate
LED1 thru LED3—T-1 light-emitting diode (one each red, green, yellow/amber)
Capacitors
C1—1-μF, 35-volt dipped tantalum
C2—p.1-μF, 50-volt Mylar

C3—2200-pF, 50-volt Mylar
Resistors ($\frac{1}{4}$-watt, 5% carbon-film)
R1—1 megohm (or 100,000 ohms; see text)
R2, R3, R10—2.2 megohms
R4—15,000 ohms
R5—36,000 ohms
R6—18,000 ohms (or 47,000 ohms; see text)
R7—39,000 ohms
R8—220 ohms
R9—330 ohms
R11-4.7 megohms
Miscellaneous
quad JFET op amp (Radio Shack No. 276-1714) or LM324 quad op

amp (Radio Shack No. 276-1711) (see text)
Global Specialties No. CTP-1 probe case kit with perforated board and test leads/clips (available from Global dealers locally or from some mail-order houses); printed-circuit or perforated board and solder posts; gold-contact, low-profile 14 pin DIP IC sockets (2); one red, one black alligator test clips with attached leads; rubber cement; $\frac{3}{4}$" (19 mm)-wide clear tape or clear spray acrylic; hookup wire; solder; etc.

Fig. 20.1. Note in this overall schematic diagram of the Looker digital logic probe that only three of the four operational amplifiers in IC1 are used. The fourth op amp is disabled by having its inputs grounded. Also, IC2C and IC2D are tied together in parallel to form a high-current buffer/driver for LED 3.

pin for-pin replacement for the common LM324 quad op amp, it offers vastly improved performance, most notably very low supply current and very high input impedance (10^{12} ohms).

Only three of the four op amps in the TLC274 are used. The fourth must be disabled by tying its inputs

to ground. The first op amp, *IC1A*, is used as a voltage follower to decouple the input from the rest of the probe circuit. The output of *IC1A* is always equal, within a few millivolts, to the input voltage. Resistors *R2* and *R3* bias the input at about 50 percent of the supply voltage when no signal is applied to the

probe tip. Diodes *D1* and *D2* protect the input against over- and under-voltages, and resistor *R1* limits input current to a safe level.

The other two op amps in *IC1* are used as an offset comparator string, with the inverting (−) inputs of *IC1B* connected to the junctions between *R5* and *R6* and of *IC1C* to the junction between *R6* and *R7*. The values of *R5, R6,* and *R7* were chosen so that comparator *IC1B* switches on when input voltage rises past 70 percent of supply voltage, and comparator *IC1C* switches on when input voltage drops below 30 percent of the supply. HI/LO visual indication is provided by *LED2* (red), driven by *IC1B,* and *LED1* (green), driven by *IC1C.*

A low-pass filter, composed of *R4* and *C1,* deliver the switching signal from the output of *IC1A* to the noninverting and inverting inputs of *IC1B* and *IC1C,* respectively. The filter keeps the HI and LO LEDs from flashing or lighting up at input frequencies beyond about 15 Hz.

To detect fast pulses that might not otherwise be captured by the Looker, the circuit also contains a pulse stretcher consisting of *IC2* and PULSE indicator *LED3* (yellow). Two of the NOR gates (*IC2A* and *IC2B*) are used as a positive edge-triggered monostable multivibrator with an output period of about 0.01 second. The other two gates are wired together as a high current buffer/driver, with their inputs connected to the monostable's output and their outputs driving *LED3.* The input of the monostable is connected directly to the output of *IC1A.* A brief positive or negative pulse at the probe tip will cause *LED3* to flash, while a pulse train at the input will continually retrigger the monostable and hold *LED3* on at a steady brightness.

Like all logic probes, the Looker is powered by the circuit it is testing via a cable terminated in a pair of alligator clips. Diode *D3* is inserted into the positive supply lead to protect the probe against damage from reversed connections. A germanium diode is used here, rather than a silicon diode, because of its lower voltage drop—0.3 versus 0.7 volt for silicon. The lower voltage drop means less interference with the

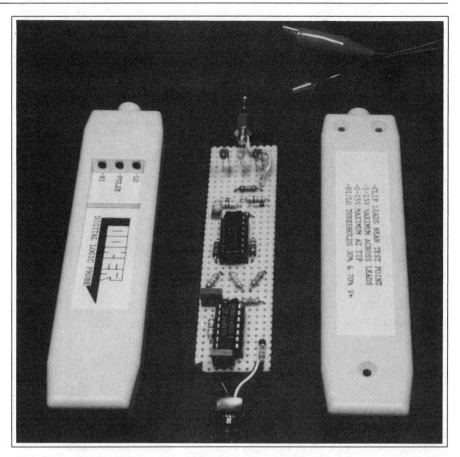

Fig. 20.2. Shown here is the probe case kit described in the text. Note the threaded removable tip; replacement and specialty tips are available.

probe's thresholds at lower supply voltages. (The *R5/R6/R7* resistor divider string is also offset upwards slightly to compensate for the unavoidable drop across *D3* and to give true 30 percent/70 percent thresholds.) Capacitor *C2* filters out transients and stray frequencies that may interfere with the Looker's operation.

Construction

For a professional appearance, as well as comfortable handling, the Looker is best built into a molded-plastic housing designed specifically for probes. In this case, the No. CTP-1, logic probe kit from Global Specialties is ideal (Fig. 20.2). The kit is composed of the two shell halves, perf board, tip holder and tip (replacement tips are available),

LED support and lead set with preattached clips and molded strain relief. If you make your own case, follow the general layout shown in the photos.

As mentioned earlier, with only one design change you can extend the Looker's frequency range to about 3.5 MHz, pulse sensing to about 100 nanoseconds, and voltage range to 18 volts. You do this by replacing the CMOS TLC274 with a pin-for-pin compatible JFET-input TL084. However, there's a penalty to be paid. The TL084 will cause the Looker to draw more standby current (about 10 mA at 15 volts). More importantly, it will not permit full operation when connected to a power source that delivers less than 6 volts.

The TL084 version will indicate HI logic levels as well as frequencies and pulses at the 5-volt level, but because the JFET voltage follower cannot swing its output below the LO threshold at 5 volts, it cannot indicate LO logic levels correctly. If you're willing to accept these shortcomings to obtain a greatly extended frequency range, the TL084 version may be the better choice.

A second design option, suitable only for very-low performance use, is to use the original LM324 quad op amp in place of the TLC274. The LM324 will operate from 5 to 18 volts, but has a very-low input impedance and a maximum frequency response under 50 kHz.

If either the TL084 or LM324 are used, the values of *R1* and *R6* must be changed to 100,000 and 47,000 ohms respectively. No other changes are necessary, and all three devices have identical pinouts.

Since space on the kit's perf board is limited, it's necessary that you carefully follow the layout shown in Fig. 20.3. Use low-profile gold-contact sockets for the two ICs. Sockets will allow you to exchange ICs easily in the event you change your mind about the op amp you wish to use.

All resistors are ¼-watt, 5 percent tolerance carbon film types—avoid carbon-composition devices here. Tantalum and Mylar are specified for the capacitors, as much for their small size as for their performance characteristics. Other types can be substituted for *C1* and *C2*, space permitting, but only a Mylar or polystyrene capacitor should be used for timing capacitor *C3*.

Connections from the probe tip holder to *R1, R1* to the voltage follower input, and the voltage follower output to the input of *IC2A* at pin 1 should be at least 22-gauge wire to ensure a low-impedance path for high frequencies. The supply bus wires should also be at least 22 gauge, but the rest of the connections are not critical and may even be made with wire wrap.

One tricky part of building the

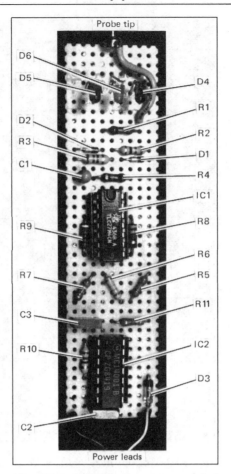

Fig. 20.3. *This is the recommended layout for the parts on the perforated board supplied with the probe case kit. Note the unusual mounting of the LEDs. Use sockets for the ICs.*

Looker is properly positioning the three LEDs. They must be raised above the perf board and angled to fit into the three holes in the top half of the case. The kit includes a support that was useful for aligning the LEDs but was discarded from the prototype as it tended to interfere with assembly of the two case halves.

The only other tricky part of building the Looker is properly applying the two case labels shown in Fig. 20.4. These can be cut from the page or photocopied on a good-quality plain paper copier and cut from the copier sheet. (The copier method is recommended, since there will be no bleed-through from

backside images, lets you use color bond paper, and allows room for mistakes.)

Use either rubber cement or a artist's stick adhesive (Glue Stic, UHU etc.) to fix the labels in place. Also, to protect the labels from smearing and/or wearing away, it's a very good idea to cover them with a strip of ¾ inch (19 mm) *clear* tape or spray several thin coats of clear acrylic over them.

Using the Probe

The Looker can be used to test any circuit or device with a minimum supply of 3.5 volts (6 volts for the TL084; 5 volts with the LM324) and a maximum supply of 16 volts (18 volts with the other two ICs). Since the Looker is partly or wholly CMOS, performance varies with the supply voltage (one of CMOS's quirks). For this reason, the Looker will respond to a maximum frequency of 800 kHz at 15 volts, 500 kHz at 10 volts, and 150 kHz at 5 volts. Pulse sensing is correspondingly voltage related, but the HI and LO indicators operate the same regardless of supply voltage.

The Looker can be used to test almost any logic family, including regular and LS TTL, CMOS, NMOS, and even PMOS and ECL, if the supply voltage is within range of the probe. With regard to the last, it is important that you first use a voltmeter to measure the supply voltage of the circuit to be tested to make certain that it is within the supply range of the probe. Be especially alert for negative voltages; application of a voltage that is lower than the probe's supply ground can damage the instrument.

Once the supply voltage is determined to be safe, connect the probe's power leads to the most positive and most negative supply rails in the circuit being tested. Unless unavoidable, the power leads

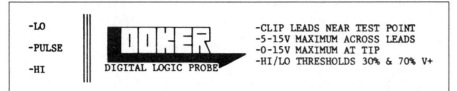

-LO

-PULSE

-HI

DIGITAL LOGIC PROBE

-CLIP LEADS NEAR TEST POINT
-5-15V MAXIMUM ACROSS LEADS
-0-15V MAXIMUM AT TIP
-HI/LO THRESHOLDS 30% & 70% V+

Fig. 20.4. These are actual-size labels for the Looker's case. The left label goes on the top of the case, with the LO, PULSE and HI legends aligned with the LEDs. The right label goes on the bottom of the case. Photocopy both labels and protect them with clear tape or several coats of acrylic.

should not be more than about 6 inches (152 mm) from the test area. If necessary, a pair of minihooks, such as Radio Shack's No. 270-334, can be added to the alligator clips to facilitate hookup on crowded circuit boards.

Before touching the probe tip to any test point, touch it briefly to the two supply clips to confirm proper operation. You should obtain a HI indication from the positive clip, a LO from the negative clip. If you obtain neither indication, you have a bad or reversed connection. This test should always be repeated each time the clips are moved; it takes only a moment and it may save you from damaging the probe, the circuit, or both.

Once the probe is connected and tested, all you need do is touch the tip to any point in the circuit to see what's happening there. Be careful to avoid shorting together IC pins and other closely spaced component leads. Most probes, like the Looker, have very high input impedance and will disturb the circuit under test only minimally, if at all.

Although you can't determine frequency with a logic probe, you can trace a waveform through a cir-

cuit to see where it goes, disappears, or goes awry. A common indication is to have the probe indicate all HI or all LO conditions for every point in a circuit or pins on an IC. This means that the circuit or IC is lacking a ground or positive supply voltage.

There are seven basic responses a probe can give. With a schematic diagram or other documentation and a little practice, you'll soon learn to interpret them:

1. *No indication at all*—the point being tested is dead or is at a voltage level between the two thresholds (see 7 below).
2. Steady HI *indication*—the point under test is at a voltage level greater than 70 percent of the supply (logic-1 for most circuits).
3. *Steady* LO *indication*—the point under test is at a voltage level less than 30 percent of the supply (logic-0 for most circuits).
4. *Steady* HI *with flashing* PULSE *indication*—the presence of a negative pulse or pulses at that point.
5. *Steady* LO *with flashing* PULSE *indication*—the presence of a positive pulse or pulses at that point. [Note: The probe point must

be held firmly against the test point to eliminate the chance of false pulse indications. Many probes—including the Looker—may flash the PULSE indicator when the tip is touched to or removed from the test point.]

6. *Steady* PULSE *indication*—the presence of a frequency between 0 Hz and maximum range of the probe at that point. The presence of a steady HI or LO simultaneously may mean a frequency that's slightly out of range for the probe, a frequency with a strong dc component, a very high or very low duty cycle, or a waveform with its amplitude biased toward one end of the supply.

7. *Flickering* PULSE *indication*—may indicate a frequency that's out of range of a voltage that's between the thresholds. This shouldn't be interpreted as a valid state. Use a voltmeter or frequency counter to check.

Conclusions

If you've never used a logic probe before, you will be surprised how quickly and easily it can give a comprehensive look at the operation of a digital circuit. With a schematic diagram or a timing chart of a circuit and a logic pulser for signal injection, you will find that a logic probe is particularly useful in design/experiment work as well as for troubleshooting.

A Universal Coil Tester

TJ BYERS

Earphone is modified and glued to back of front panel. Circuit board and panel are joined with adhesive and clamped until adhesive sets.

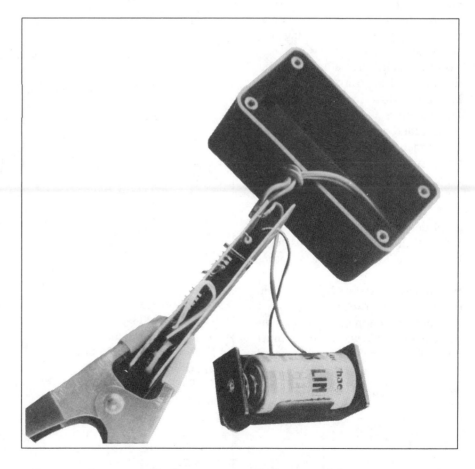

Trying to determine the integrity of a low-resistance, high-impedance coil can be a frustrating experience. The kind I'm talking about are those used in TV receivers, such as CRT yokes, filters, and flybacks.

The internal resistance of these devices is so low it is virtually impossible to measure the coil-winding with an ohmmeter. In fact, many such coils have a wire resistance of less than one ohm! Therefore, the difference a shorted turn or two makes in the overall resistance pattern is too minuscule to detect. Many items, it seems, your only recourse is to replace the suspected part with a new one—a costly and time-consuming chore.

There is, however, a simple, inexpensive alternative: The universal coil-tester presented here that is built around low-cost integrated circuits and should cost you less than $20 in parts.

It not only tests coils for opens and shorts, it can even reveal parallel resistance paths such as the kind you might encounter when dealing with carbon tracks or leakage.

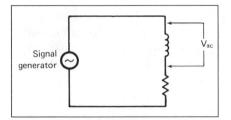

Fig. 21.1. Typical reactance test setup.

As you might know, there's more than one way to test an inductor. For example, you could measure its resistance to an ac signal, the coil's inductive reactance. A simple test setup to do this can be seen in Fig. 21.1.

Notice that the coil has a resistor in series with it. When an ac voltage is applied across the combination, a voltage is generated across each device that's proportional to its effective resistance and the current passing through it. By knowing the frequency and the voltages, you can easily calculate the value of the inductor. In fact, this is how most laboratory instruments are used to test inductors.

A second method is to test the coil under actual operating conditions, such as placing it in an oscillating circuit. Such an oscillator is represented by the drawing in Fig. 21.2. Basically, an oscillator is an amplifier that has part of its output fed back into an input. This feedback produces oscillation. In order to sustain the oscillation, though, the signals must be shifted to 180 degrees of each other.

Phase inversion can be accomplished in many ways. In its most basic form, the signal is passed

Fig. 21.2. Typical oscillator setup.

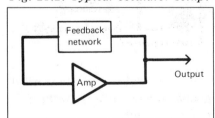

through a phase-shifting network. The network is frequency sensitive, so phase inversion occurs at only one frequency. This is the frequency at which the amplifier will oscillate. The network can contain capacitors, resistors, or inductors—or any combination thereof. The universal coil tester described here uses this test method.

By replacing the inductor in the feedback loop with the inductor being examined, we can determine its quality. A good inductor will oscillate; a bad one won't.

How It Works

The coil tester here is designed around a pair of LM3909 integrated circuits. The LM3909 is a special integrated circuit that operates directly from a 1.5-volt battery. It was originally designed as a low-power LED flasher, but it can do

much more. The LM3909 can also function as an amplifier, an alarm, a trigger, or an oscillator element.

In the circuit shown in Fig. 21.3, the first LM3909 is configured as an oscillator—but with one notable difference. Its feedback path is not complete. Part of the feedback loop consists of capacitor C1 and timing resistor R1. These two components set the basic oscillator frequency.

The missing link is the inductor. When a coil is connected from B+ to pin 2 of IC1, the feedback loop is completed and the chip oscillates. The tone of the oscillator's output is directly proportional to the quality of the coil. An analysis of the circuit's operation runs as follows.

When a good inductor is connected from B+ to pin 2, it supplies an out-of-phase feedback pulse to the chip that initiates the charging of C1. As C1 charges, the LM3909 monitors its voltage. When the voltage across C1 exceeds 1.3 volts, the

Fig. 21.3. Schematic diagram of Universal Coil Tester.

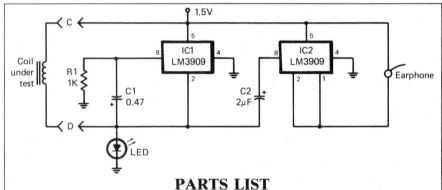

PARTS LIST

Semiconductors
IC1, IC2—LM3909 Radio Shack 276-1705 or equivalent
LED—T-1¾ red (276-041A)
Capacitors
C1—0.47-µf, 35 V tantalum C2—2-µf, 16 V electrolytic
Resistors
R1—1k, ¼-watt resistor
Miscellaneous
Battery—C cell
Battery holder—Radio Shack 270-402 or equivalent

Earphone—Radio Shack 33-174 or equivalent
Project case—Radio Shack 270-231 or equivalent
Note: The following are available from Danocinths Inc., P. O. Box 261, Westland, MI 48185: Model RW-1 etched and drilled printed-circuit board, $7.50 ppd. Michigan residents add 4% sales tax. Allow 4 to 6 weeks for delivery.

IC discharges the capacitor through the LED. This causes the LED to flash.

If you're wondering how an LED will light from a 1.5-V source, it's simple. During the discharge phase of C1, the 1.3-V charge stored in the capacitor is added to the 1.5-V battery to create a total charge of 2.8 volts. This is enough potential to light the LED.

A portion of the discharge current is also bypassed through the inductor, causing it to initiate another cycle. If the inductor is completely shorted (zero inductance), B+ is applied directly to pin 2 of IC1 with no inductive relief. Constant application of voltage on pin 2 (which is the negative feedback path for timing-capacitor C1) squelches oscillation.

The oscillator is also very sensitive to the inductance of a coil. A shift of just a few millihenries will produce a significant change in the frequency. Such a change can be brought about by shorted turns. Shunt resistance, created by a carbon path or leakage, also has a pronounced effect on the output.

In many cases, a shorted turn or leakage path prevents oscillation from occurring. It is often the case, too, that a defective coil will add a "strained" sound to the audio output.

The oscillator's output signal is fed into IC2 through coupling capacitor C2. IC2 is biased to operate as an amplifier. Its purpose is to isolate the oscillator from the audio output. The sound is heard through an earphone.

Construction

The complete tester is built right inside a 4 by 2½ by 2¼ inch (102 by 63.5 by 57.2 mm) plastic utility box. The box is large enough to accommodate all parts, including the battery.

Begin by drilling two ¼-inch (6.35 mm) holes in the front aluminum panel, using the accompanying photo as your guide. One hole is for the LED, the other is for the earphone.

Before you can use the earphone, though, it must be modified. With an X-ACTO® knife, carefully remove the protruding earplug. Take care not to damage the fragile speaker diaphragm inside. Some earphones have removable, clear plastic earplugs, which makes your job that much easier. Cut the leads to about 2 inches (50.8 mm) and strip the ends. An actual size etching-and-drilling guide is shown in Fig. 21.4.

Now solder the components to the printed-circuit board, observing polarity and IC orientation (Fig. 21.5). Note that capacitors C1 and C2 are positioned on their sides rather than standing upright. *Don't* install the LED at this time, though.

Using a silicon adhesive such as RTV, now cement the modified earphones to the aluminum front panel directly under one of the ¼ inch (6.35 mm) holes. Make sure the diaphragm is pointing outwards, facing the outside world.

The LED can be installed in the circuit board as soon as the glue has set. First, push the dome of the LED through the front panel and glue it in place. Now adjust the length of the leads so that one end of the PC board rests against the earphone, all the while keeping the board parallel to the front panel. Solder the LED in place and then attach the PC board to the back of the earphone with a dab of glue.

While the assembly is drying, drill a hole in one end of the plastic case large enough to accommodate a pair of wires (Fig. 21.6). These wires will serve as the test leads for the coil tester. You may make a nifty pair of test leads by cutting a jumper clip lead in half and pushing the cut ends through the hole. Tie a knot in the wires and solder them to the PC board so that they can't be pulled back through the hole.

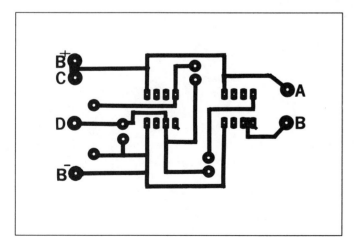

Fig. 21.4. Actual-size etching-and-drilling guide.

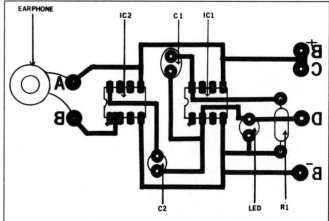

Fig. 21.5. Components-placement guide for printed-circuit board assembly.

Fig. 21.6. Photo shows author's prototype housed inside typical Bakelite project box with aluminum cover. Test leads exit box through hole in side of box.

Using the Tester

Your instrument is now ready for use. All you need do is insert the battery into its holder. No provision has been made for an on/off switch; it really isn't necessary. The circuit draws very little power, so a fresh battery will provide many months of service.

Here are some helpful hints that will make your coil-tester even more useful. Your coil-tester is extremely frequency sensitive, so you must make a good connection to the inductor. Just a couple of ohms of series resistance makes a big difference in how audio sounds.

Shunt resistance also plays an important role in the quality of the sound. If the coil has a short—even if it's just a couple of turns—there is a noticeable change in the tone. It may sound very strained or not be audible at all. The LED will probably light under these conditions, however, indicating that you are making proper connection to the coil. In this manner, leakage resistance as large as 100 ohms is easily detected with this tester. Try that with your ohmmeter!

If you happen to have an identical coil on hand, you can even be more critical in your testing. Test the good coil first, then the suspect coil. Listen for a difference in the sound. The questionable coil must produce an identical sound or it isn't good. This same technique can be used to identify unmarked coils in your junk box.

Other uses include the testing of induction motors, auto ignition coils, and power transformers. Although this is not the most sophisticated coil-tester around, it is extremely versatile, portable for field work, and costs very little when compared to commercial models.

A Degrees Celsius/Fahrenheit Thermometer Accessory

BILL OWEN

An accurate electronic thermometer can be a very useful item, both on your workbench and for general use around your home. It can be used to monitor heat build-up in and around all types of powered equipment and to track down heat-related problems in malfunctioning circuits and systems. Around the home, it can be used to monitor ambient room and outdoor temperatures; keep tabs on air-conditioning and heating systems; monitor refrigerators and freezers; and much more. In fact, once you use an easy-to-read and accurate electronic thermometer, you are likely to find all sorts of uses for it you never considered before.

Our electronic thermometer accessory starts off with the premise that you have on hand an accurate dc voltmeter. A garden-variety DMM will do nicely. Actually, this accessory can be used with any digital or analog multimeter, basic voltmeter, or panel meter. The accessory is built around special solid-state circuitry, including the temperature sensor, that provides a lin-

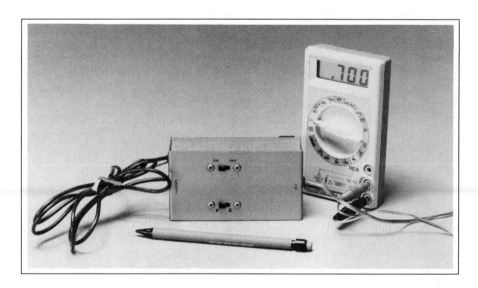

ear 10 millivolts/degree output. It is switch-selectable to allow you to measure temperatures in both °C and °F. Furthermore, its active-circuit design allows the temperature sensor to be located literally thousands of feet away without the attendant problem of noise pickup.

About the Circuit

Though the temperature accessory circuit (Fig. 22.1) appears to be very

simple, it is really quite sophisticated in terms of performance and the technology it uses. The AD590 temperature sensor integrated circuit used for *IC2* produces an output current that is proportional to temperature. The output current produced when the device is connected to a voltage source is equal to 1 µA per degree on the Kelvin temperature scale. The Kelvin degree is equal to the Celsius degree, but the °K temperature scale has its zero at −273.2 °C, or absolute zero. The relationship between Kelvin, Celsius, and Fahrenheit temperature scales is as follows:

$$°C = °K - 273.2$$
$$°F = [(9 \times °C)/5] + 32$$
$$°F = [9(°K - 273.2)/5] + 32.$$

It should also be noted that there is a little-used Rankine temperature scale that starts at absolute zero and has Fahrenheit-scaled degrees. Ran-

kine degrees are offset 459.7 higher than Fahrenheit degrees. Rankine to Fahrenheit conversion is as follows:

$$°F = °R - 459.7.$$

Connecting the sensor's output to a microammeter makes a °K thermometer. The next step, then, is to remove the 273.2 °C or 459.7 °F offset to obtain the more useful °C

and °F outputs. To achieve this, sensor output current is converted to a voltage when passed through a scaling resistor. A voltmeter is then used to measure the difference between the scaled temperature output and an appropriate voltage reference.

The °C scaling resistance is formed by the series network made up of resistor R8 and trimmer potentiometer R9, while °F scaling is accomplished with R10 and trimmer R11. Switch S1A routes sensor output current through the appropriate scaling network to select either °C or °F. Switch S1B selects either the 2.732- or the 4.594-volt reference so that the differential output is 10 mA per °C or °F.

The two reference voltages are tapped from resistive dividers connected to precision 6.9-volt reference VR1. Resistors R2 and R4 and trimmer control R3 make up the °C divider, and resistors R5 and R7 and trimmer R6 make up the °F divider.

Precision reference VR1 is an LM329DZ, which is biased by the LM334Z current source used for IC1. Resistor R1 sets the current source's output to 2 mA. The combination LM334/LM329 reference is very stable over wide temperature and voltage changes and uses very little current, assuring long battery life.

Fig. 22.1. This overall schematic of the thermometer accessory is deceptively simple. The circuit is actually quite sophisticated. Almost any analog or digital voltmeter or multimeter can be used as the temperature display device. Power for the accessory is provided by a 9-volt transistor battery.

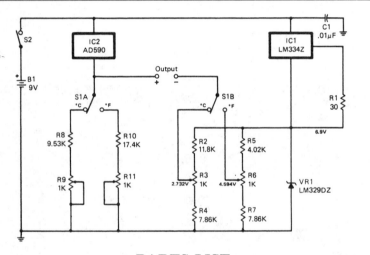

PARTS LIST

Semiconductors
IC1—LM334Z current source
IC2—AD590 sensor
Resistors
R1—30 ohms (2%)
R2—11,800 ohms
R4, R7—7860 ohms
R5—4020 ohms
R8—9530 ohms
R10—17,400 ohms
R3, R6, R9, R11—1000-ohm pc-mount trimmer potentiometers
Miscellaneous
B1—9-volt transistor battery
S1, S2—Dpdt switch
VR1—LM329DZ voltage reference
Printed-circuit board; one each

red and black banana jacks and plugs; 4″ × 2¼″ × 1¼″ (102 × 57.2 × 31.8 mm) aluminum cabinet; 9 volt battery connector; 4-ft. RG174 coaxial cable; 2-ft. miniature zip cord; dry-transfer lettering kit; clear spray acrylic; ¼″(6.35 mm) rubber grommets (2); 4 40 × ⅛″ (3.18 mm) machine screws (6); solder; etc.
Note: The following is available from NRG Electronics, P. O. Box 24138, Ft. Lauderdale, FL 33307: Complete Model T-100 kit, less battery, for $29.95 + $2.50 P&H + 5% sales tax for Florida residents.

Construction

To make the thermometer accessory as compact as possible and to facilitate easy assembly, it is suggested that you assemble the circuit on a printed-circuit board. You can purchase a ready-to-go pc board from the source given in the Parts List. Alternatively, you can fabricate your own pc board, using the actual-size etching guide given in Fig. 22.2.

Wire the circuit board as shown

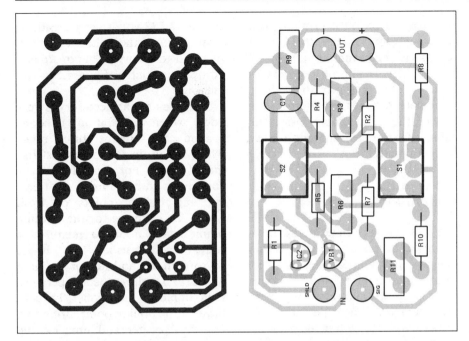

Fig. 22.2. Fabricate the printed-circuit board for the project using the actual-size etching-and-drilling guide at left. Install the components on the board exactly as shown in the placement/orientation diagram shown at right.

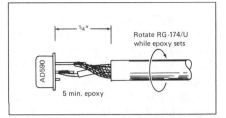

Fig. 22.3. After tack-soldering a 4-foot length of coaxial cable to the shortened leads of the AD590 sensor, flow epoxy cement over connections, sensor and cable as shown and slowly rotate the assembly as the cement sets to obtain an air-tight, symmetrical seal.

in the components-placement/orientation diagram in Fig. 22.2. Note that all components except sensor IC2 and battery B1 mount directly on the pc board and that controls R3, R6, R9, and R11 mount on the foil side of the board. When you have finished wiring the pc board, temporarily set it aside and proceed to machining the small metal utility or project, in which the project, with battery, is to be housed. You must drill a hole through each side wall of the box to provide the means for the meter and sensor cables to enter the box.

The only other holes that must be drilled or cut will be in the top of the box, which will serve as the project's front panel. You must cut two rectangular slots, one for each switch's toggle and drill two mounting holes for each switch. When you are finished machining the box, temporarily install the circuit board assembly to make sure all parts fit as they should. Make whatever adjustments are needed. Then disassemble the box, remove the pc as-

sembly, and clean all exterior surfaces of the metal box with fine steel wool. Using a dry-transfer lettering kit, label (on top of the box) the legends PROBE and METER just above the entry holes on the left and right sides of the box, respectively. Then label the two switches with the legends °C and °F for the alternate positions of S1 and ON and OFF for the appropriate positions of S2. If you wish, you can also label the legend THERMOMETER ACCESSORY on top of the box for future identification.

When all lettering is completed, spray two or more *light* coats of clear acrylic on all exterior surfaces on the box to give the project a professional finished appearance and to protect the lettering. Allow each coat to dry before spraying on the next.

Referring to Fig. 22.3, prepare the probe/cable assembly. Trim the leads of the AD590 so that they are just long enough to permit good electrical and mechanical connection of the coaxial cable. To pre-

pare the ends of the 4-foot length of coax, first trim away ¼ inch (6.35 mm) and ¾ inch (19 mm) of outer insulation from opposite ends. Separate the shield from the inner conductor at both ends back to the outer insulation. Then, making sure not to cut any of the inner conductor wires, trim ⅛ inch (3.18 mm) of insulation at the ¼ inch (6.35 mm) prepared end and ¼ inch (6.35 mm) of insulation from the ¾ inch (19 mm) prepared end. Tightly twist together the shields and inner conductors and lightly tin with solder. Connect and solder the conductors at the ¼ inch (6.35 mm) prepared end of the cable to the shortened pins of the AD590 sensor as shown in Fig. 22.3. Use heat and solder sparingly and make certain you do not create any solder bridges. When the solder cools, gently separate the connections to obviate any possibility that the two can short together. Then apply 5-minute epoxy cement to the connection, flowing it over only the skirt of the AD590 and about ¼ inch (6.35 mm) beyond the point where the outer insulation was removed from the coax. As the cement sets, slowly rotate the cable assembly to allow it to assume a symmetrical form. Then allow the cement to set solidly for a couple of hours.

Now prepare the meter cable. For

this, you will need a 3-foot length of miniature zip cord and a pair of red and black color-coded banana jacks. Split the cord apart for a distance of about 5 inches (127 mm) at one end and 1 inch (25.4 mm) at the other end. Trim away ¼ inch (6.35 mm) of insulation from all conductors at both ends, taking care to avoid cutting through any fine wires. Tightly twist the wires into neat bundles and sparingly tin with solder. Install a banana jack on each conductor at the long split end.

When the acrylic spray paint on the box has completely dried, place small rubber grommets in the holes in the box's sides (Fig. 22.4). Then feed the free ends of the prepared cables into the box through the grommets and tie a knot in each cable about 3 inches (76.2 mm) from the free ends on the *inside* of the box. Connect and solder these to the appropriate pads on the pc board. Do the same with the battery connector wires.

Position the pc board assembly in the box and secure it in place with four 4-40 by ¼ inch (6.35 mm) screws via the mounting tabs on *S1* and *S2*. Gently pull on both cables until the knots touch the rubber grommets. Mount the battery at one end of the pc assembly inside the cabinet (see photo) and clip on the battery connector.

Calibration

The voltage reference in the thermometer accessory is very stable and will assure linear measurement results in both the °C and °F modes when properly calibrated. It is very important for you to perform calibration with the voltmeter or other readout device that will be used to display temperature.

Connect the negative (COM) lead of the preferably digital voltmeter to the negative (black) battery connector pad and the positive (red) meter lead to the wiper (center) lug of trimmer control *R3*. Turn on the power and adjust the setting of *R3*

for a 2.732-volt meter reading. Then connect the voltmeter's positive lead to the wiper lug of *R6* and adjust this control for a 4.594-volt reading.

Accuracy of the accessory is very good when calibration is done around the temperature range where the project is to be most frequently used. For general use, it is convenient to calibrate at the freezing and boiling points of fresh water. To calibrate for the freezing point, place a 50/50 mixture of water and crushed ice in a Styrofoam cup and stir for a minute or so to stabilize the temperature then immerse the probe. To calibrate at the boiling point, bring to a boil fresh water and immerse the sensor probe in this.

Fresh water freezes at 0 °C and boils at 100 °C. So, setting the mode switch to °C, first immerse the sensor probe in the ice/water mixture and adjust *R9* to obtain a 0 °C reading on the meter when the latter is connected to the METER cable on the accessory. Then immerse the sensor probe in the boiling water and readjust *R9* to obtain a 100 °C reading. Repeat this calibration procedure several times to determine which end of the scale is the most accurate. (Note: Water's boiling point drops to 1 °F for each 550 feet above sea level or 1 °C for each 990 feet. Thus, in Laramie, WY *R9* should be adjusted for 93 °C instead of 100 °C.)

Once the thermometer accessory is properly calibrated for the °C mode, switch to the °F range and use *R11* to calibrate the scale for the freezing (32 °F) and boiling (212 °F) points of water. This completes calibration of the accessory. Set the power switch to OFF and assemble the case.

Fig. 22.4. All components except the battery and sensor mount on the pc board.

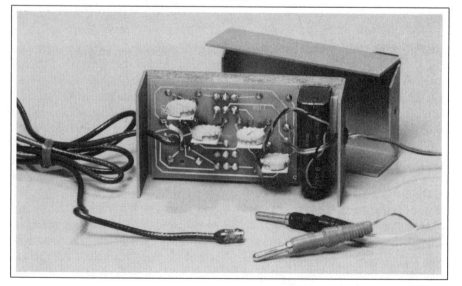

Offers digital-circuit experimenters a source of reliable clock pulses to 10 kHz

chapter 23

Low-Frequency Dual-Pulse Generator

DUANE M. PERKINS

If you intend to do serious experimenting with digital circuits, you will soon discover that you need a source of reliable clock pulses. You can, of course, buy an expensive pulse generator to meet your needs. However, for less than $100 you can build the Dual-Pulse Generator described here, using only readily available parts.

Each of the two pulse outputs is independently adjustable in phase, pulse width and amplitude. Though both are driven by the same oscillator, which provides for clocking a circuit that requires a two-phase clock, one output can be set up to provide a frequency that is a subharmonic of the other.

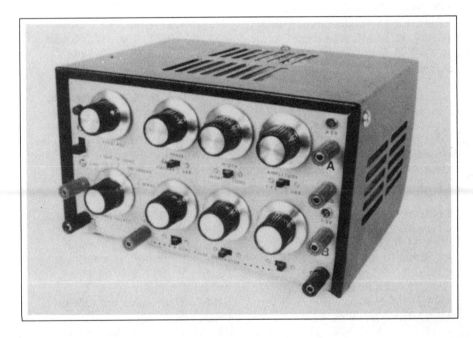

Circuit Description

Though the pulse generator provides two independently controllable outputs, it has a single oscillator from which the pulses are derived, as shown in Fig. 23.1. Therefore, the frequency of the pulses is established by the relaxation oscillator designed around unijunction tran-

sistor *Q1*. In addition to providing four frequency ranges for the internal oscillator, the generator's RANGE switch (*S2*) has a position for a 60-Hz pulse, derived from the ac line at the center tap of the power supply transformer (see Fig. 23.3), plus an input at *BP4* for an external signal source.

There are four internal oscillator frequency ranges. These are 1 to 10

Hz, 10 to 100 Hz, 100 to 1000 Hz and 1 to 10 kHz. These limits are only approximate. Exact range limits will depend on the intrinsic standoff ratio of the unijunction transistor used for *Q1*.

Because the pulse generator contains a ÷ 2 circuit, its output will be half the frequency of the oscillator. The 60-Hz output is generated from the 120-Hz pulses taken from the

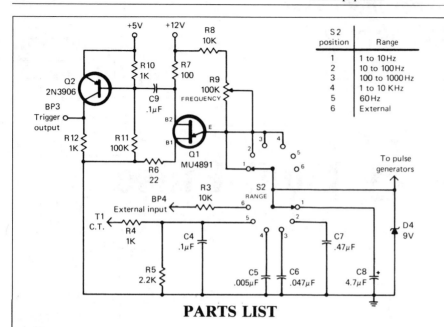

PARTS LIST

S 2 position	Range
1	1 to 10 Hz
2	10 to 100 Hz
3	100 to 1000 Hz
4	1 to 10 KHz
5	60 Hz
6	External

Semiconductors

D1, D4—9-volt zener diode (1N4739 or similar)
D2, D3—1N914 switching diode
LED1, LED2—Light-emitting diode
IC1—7812 12-volt regulator
IC2—7805 5-volt regulator
IC3—LM339 voltage comparator
IC4—4013 flip-flop
IC5, IC7—556 dual time
IC6, IC8—LM317 voltage regulator
Q1—MU4891 unijunction transistor
Q2, Q3, Q5, Q6, Q8—2N3906 transistor
Q4, Q7—2N3904 transistor
RECT1—VM08 or similar 50-PIV bridge rectifier

Capacitors

C1—3300-μF, 35-volt electrolytic
C2, C3—0.22-μF disc
C4, C9, C10, C17, C18, C19, C26, C27, C28—0.1-μF disc
C5, C13, C22—0.005-μF disc
C6—0.046-μF disc
C7—0.47-μF tantalum
C8, C16, C25—4.7-μF, 35-volt electrolytic
C11, C20—0.001-μF disc
C12, C21—1-μF tantalum
C14, C23—0.1-μF disc
C15, C24—22-μF, 35-volt electrolytic

Resistors ($\frac{1}{2}$-watt, 10% tolerance)

R1, R5—2200 ohms
R2, R4, R10, R12, R18, R28, R32, R42—1000 ohms
R3, R8, R16, R17, R26, R30, R31, R40—10,000 ohms
R6—22 ohms
R7—100 ohms
R11, R13, R14, R27, R41—100,000 ohms
R20, R21, R34, R35—470 ohms
R23, R24, R37, R38—15,000 ohms
R25, R39—100 ohms, 2 watts
R9—100,000-ohm linear-taper potentiometer
R15, R19, R29, R33—1-megohm, linear-taper potentiometer
R22, R36—5000-ohm, linear-taper potentiometer

Miscellaneous

BP1 thru BP7—Five-way binding posts (five red, four black)
I1—Panel-mount neon lamp assembly with current-limiting resistor
S1—Spst slide or toggle switch
S2—6pdt nonshorting rotary switch
S3, S5, S6, S8—Spdt miniature slide or toggle switch
S4, S7—Dpdt miniature slide or toggle switch
T1—12.6-volt, 1.2-ampere, center tapped power transformer
Printed circuit board; 14-pin DIP IC sockets (4); metal cabinet (see text); four-lug (none grounded) terminal strip; panel clips for LEDs (2); pointer-type control knobs (8); line cord with plug; plastic strain relief or rubber grommet; plastic cable ties or lacing cord; lettering kit or tape labeler; aerosol clear lacquer; stranded hookup wire; machine hardware; solder; etc.

center tap of the power transformer.

Any waveform with an amplitude between 0.5 and more than 9 volts can be applied to the EXTERNAL INPUT at *BP4*. Output pulse frequency will be half the input frequency and can go as high as 15 kHz. For maximum phase control range, a sawtooth dc waveform with a peak amplitude of about 9 volts works best. However, an ac sine wave will permit some degree of control. A square wave or pulse input will drive the pulse generator but will not permit phase control.

Referring to Fig. 23.1, the TRIGGER OUTPUT at *BP3* is taken from the base-2 (B2) terminal of *Q1*, after being amplified by *Q2* to a peak amplitude of about 5 volts. This amplitude is sufficient to assure positive triggering of an oscilloscope. Trigger frequency will be twice that of the output pulses from the generator circuits. PHASE control *R15* in Fig. 23.2 sets the amount of delay between the trigger pulse and the following output pulse. This delay permits events just prior to the output pulse to be viewed on an oscilloscope's screen.

Both pulse generator circuits are identical. Hence, when you refer to Fig. 23.2, you will note two sets of component numbers and IC and transistor lead designations. Numbers in parentheses refer to components and connections for generator B, while those not in parentheses refer to generator A. Resistors *R13* and *R14* are common to both generators and are not repeated.

An input signal to the noninverting input of *IC3A* (taken from the output of the Fig. 23.1. circuit) is converted to pulses with fast rise and fall times by the LM339 voltage comparator. The reference voltage for *IC4A* is taken from the wiper of

Fig. 23.1. Generator uses this single oscillator for both pulse channels.

PHASE control *R15*, which determines the timing of the output pulse relative to the input signal cycle.

The pulse that appears at the comparator's output is used to clock ÷ 2 flip-flop *IC4A*. The symmetrically square pulse at the output of *IC4A* then goes to SQUARE/VARIABLE switch *S3*, which directs it to the output amplifier made up of *Q3* and *Qr*.

With *S3* set to SQUARE, the output of *IC4A* goes directly to the input of output amplifier *Q3/Q4*. Setting *S3* to VARIABLE diverts the output from *IC4A* to the trigger input of *IC5A* at pin 6. Before arriving at *IC5A*, however, the square pulses from *IC4A* are differentiated by the RC value of the network composed of *C11* and *R17*. From the output of *IC5A* at pin 5, the signal is routed to *S3*'s VARIABLE contacts and then on to the input of the *Q3/Q4* output amplifier.

The brief negative-going pulses are fed to the trigger input of *IC5A* to generate positive output pulses whose duration is determined by the RC value of the timing network connected to the discharge (pin 2) and threshold (pin 1) terminals of *IC5A*. Potentiometer *R19* provides a means for setting the timer's pulse duration, while SHORT/LONG switch *S4* selects the range by switching in either *C12* for a short duration or *C13* for a long-duration pulse.

Because output amplifier *Q3/Q4* uses complementary transistors in a totem-pole configuration, one transistor will be saturated while the other is cut off. Hence, the output

Fig. 23.2. Because both generator channels are identical, only one channel's circuitry is shown here. Items in parentheses are components/connectors for channel B; those not in parentheses are for channel A. Only R13 and R14 are common to both channels.

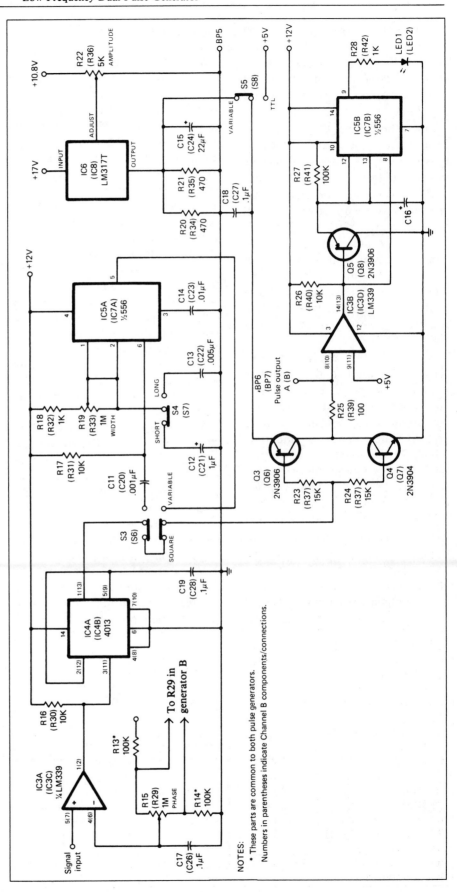

NOTES:
* These parts are common to both pulse generators.
Numbers in parentheses indicate Channel B components/connections.

is alternately switched between ground and the supply voltage. This enables the amplifier to sink or source a large current with equal ease and results in very fast rise and fall times.

Since the output amplifier is an inverter, it is the intervals between pulses from the timer that become positive output pulses. The pulse WIDTH control, *R19*, has the direct effect of varying the interval between output pulses, which indirectly varies pulse width. This becomes apparent if the control is set for a certain pulse width and the frequency is then changed. Pulse width varies with frequency, but the interval between pulses remains fixed.

By varying the supply voltage to the output amplifier, the amplitude of the output pulses is also varied. Adjustable voltage regulator *IC6* permits a range of from 1.2 to 12 volts. Alternatively, amplitude switch *S5* can be set to TTL to supply the output amplifier from the fixed 5-volt supply. This arrangement maintains a constant output impedance regardless of amplitude. Resistor *R25* prevents damage to the transistors in the event that the output is short-circuited to ground or a positive supply voltage. Since output impedance at the collectors is very low, output terminals is es-

sentially equal to the 100-ohm resistance.

The voltage-sensing circuit connected to the output consists of voltage comparator *IC3B* with a 5-volt reference and missing-pulse detector *IC5B* and *Q5* with a timing cycle of about 0.5 second. If the amplitude of the output signal exceeds 5 volts, the pulse will be inverted by the comparator. The negative-going pulse causes *Q5* to conduct, discharging timing capacitor *C16*, and trigger the timing circuit to begin a 0.5-second positive output pulse that causes *LED1* to turn on. The timing cycle will be continually retriggered as long as output pulse amplitude exceeds 5 volts, and *LED1* will glow continuously if the frequency exceeds about 1 to 2 Hz, depending on pulse width. At lower frequencies, *LED1* will turn on and off in time with the pulses.

The power supply, shown in Fig. 23.3, is a straightforward circuit consisting of bridge rectifier *RECT1* across the 12.6-volt secondary of *T1* and fixed 12- and 5-volt regulators *IC1* and *IC2*. Zener diode *D1* provides the 9-volt low-current supply for the phase control circuits. Silicon diodes *D2* and *D3* in series drop the 12-volt supply to 10.8 volts to limit maximum supply voltage to the output amplifiers to 12 volts. (The output of the LM317

regulators is 1.2 volts above the voltage at the ADJ terminals of *IC6* and *IC8*).

Construction

Due to the relatively complex nature of the circuitry and the need for low-impedance ground and positive-voltage supply buses, a printed-circuit board is almost mandatory for this project. You can fabricate your own pc board, using the actual size etching-and-drilling guide in Fig. 23.4 and wire it according to the accompanying components-placement diagram.

Wire the pc board exactly as shown in Fig. 23.4. Take care to orient the components as shown so that electrolytic capacitors, diodes, and LEDs are properly polarized and the bridge rectifier, ICs, and transistors have their pins go into the proper holes in the board. Incidentally, it is an excellent idea to use sockets for all dual in-line package (DIP) ICs and reserve installation of these ICs for last, after voltage checks have been made.

When making connections to the pc board, use heat and solder judiciously. Use only enough to assure good electrical and mechanical connections. Take particular care to avoid creating solder bridges be-

Fig. 23.3. This is the power supply schematic for the Dual Pulse Generator.

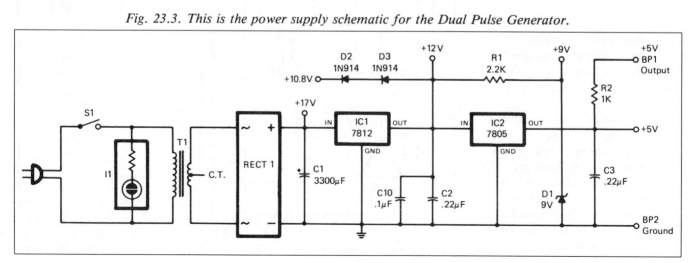

Fig. 23.4. Above is the actual size etching-and-drilling guide; page 144 shows components-placement diagram.

tween the closely spaced pads be-tween IC pins and transistor leads.

Note in Fig. 23.4 that, because of the large number of wires that inter-connect the board with the compo-nents on the front panel, all but two of the connection pads are arranged along two edges of the pc board. This makes it possible to neatly bundle the wires into a cable, using plastic cable ties or lacing cord. It also makes it easy to flip up the board assembly for circuit tracing should this become necessary. To

this latter end, it is recommended that you use stranded hookup wire throughout project assembly.

Your next task is to machine the metal cabinet in which the pulse generator is to be housed. The cabi-net will have to be fairly large in or-der to accommodate the large pc board and power transformer and all the various controls, switches, indicators, and binding posts on the front panel, along with their identi-fying legends. The author chose Ra-dio Shack's No. 270-270 cabinet for

his prototype. This cabinet mea-sures 9¼ inches (235 mm) W by 6¾ inches (171 mm) D by 5⅜ inches (137 mm) H and easily accommo-dates all components, as shown in the photos.

In his prototype, the author used miniature slide-type switches for *S1* and *S3* through *S8*, which require three holes each for mounting (two round for securing it to the panel with machine screws and one rec-tangular for the toggles). If you wish to simplify the machining op-

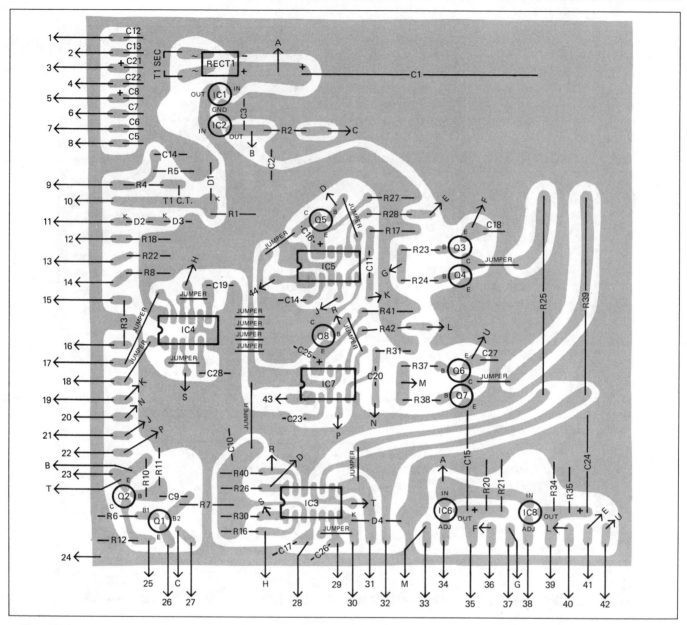

Fig. 23.4. cont.—When installing polarized components, make certain you properly index their leads and pins.

eration, you can substitute miniature toggle switches, which require a single round hole. Bear in mind, however, that toggle switches normally operate exactly opposite the manner in which slide-type switches operate. That is, if you flip a horizontally mounted toggle-type switch to the left, the *right* contacts will close. Therefore, you will have to either reverse the front-panel legends for these switches or wire the switches backward from the directions shown in Fig. 23.5.

If you use slide-type switches, you will have to drill and cut a total of 46 holes in the cabinet, one in the rear wall for the cord, six in the bottom for mounting the pc board and power transformer (Fig. 23.6), and the remainder in the front panel for the switches, controls, indicators, and binding posts. By substituting toggle-type switches, you can reduce the number of holes to 33 (one for mounting the terminal strip for *R13* and *R14*), all of them round, though of different diameters.

After machining the cabinet and deburring all holes, test fit the switches, controls, indicators, and binding posts on the front panel. The only component that must be securely mounted at this time is RANGE switch *S2*, since you will have to place its pointer knob on its shaft and rotate it through each position to mark off the range locations on the panel. This done, remove the components and set them aside.

Carefully label the front panel

with the appropriate legends, using a dry-transfer lettering kit or a tape labeler. If you use a lettering kit, spray two or more *light* coats of clear lacquer over the entire surface of the front panel to protect the lettering. Allow each coat to dry before applying the next. Do *not* try to get by with only one or two heavy coats; if you do, the lettering will almost certainly lift and dissolve.

When the final coat of lacquer has completely dried, mount the front-panel controls in their respective locations, with *LED1* and *LED2* set into panel clips. Place the knobs on the shafts of the potentiometers and *S2* and check that they point straight up at mid-rotation for the pots and properly index to the marked locations on the panel for *S2*. Then mount the power transformer to the floor of the cabinet with machine screws, lock washers, and nuts.

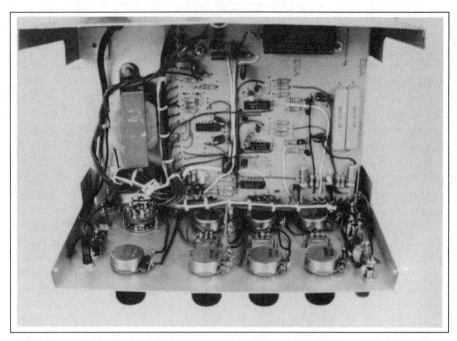

Fig. 23.6. Pc board and T1 go on floor of enclosure, everything else on front panel.

Next, split apart the conductors at the free end of the line cord for a distance of about 8 inches (203 mm) and cut off 5 inches (127 mm) from one conductor. Trim ¼ inch (6.35 mm) of insulation from each con-

Fig. 23.5. Details for wiring front-panel-mounted components into rest of generator's circuitry.

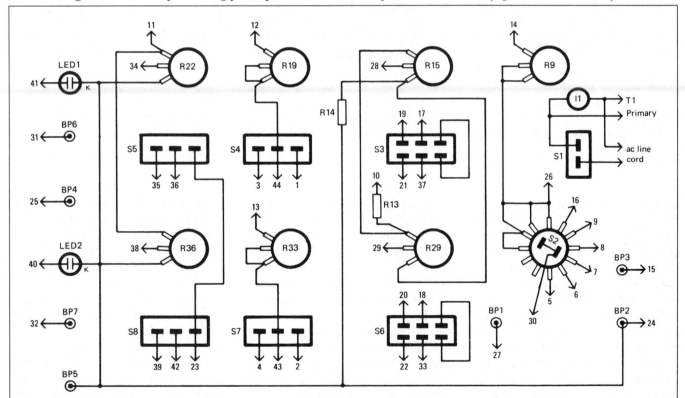

Applications

Different families of digital integrated circuits have different input voltage requirements. As a rule, though, the input voltage should not exceed the circuit's positive supply voltage nor go below the circuit's reference ground. However, the nearer the input voltage's excursion comes to the circuit's positive supply and ground, the more reliable will the IC change state when it should.

TTL devices, for example, operate with a positive supply of +5 volts ±0.5 volt. When driving a TTL device with the pulse generator presented here, output amplitude switch *S5 (S8)* should be set to TTL to assure that the maximum allowable voltage will not be exceeded.

The input of a TTL device is a current source. When the input voltage is low (logical 0), the pulse generator must sink enough current to pull the voltage below 0.8 volt. A regular TTL device requires a current of 1.6 mA per input. Low-power and low-power Schottky devices require considerably less current.

Since the pulse generator's output resistance is 100 ohms, the maximum current it can sink without exceeding the 0.8-volt limit is 8 mA. Accordingly, it can drive four regular TTL inputs, or any combination of inputs that requires less than 8 mA.

When the input voltage of a TTL device is high (logical 1), there is very little current and the output of the pulse generator will be nearly 5 volts. It is not possible to obtain more drive by increasing the voltage. This would cause the supply voltage of the TTL circuit to be exceeded, and damage the IC.

The CMOS family can be operated with a wide range of supply voltages, from a minimum of about 3 to a maximum of 16 volts. Split suppliers are often used so that V_{ss} is below ground level. When driving CMOS with a split supply, the pulse generator's ground should be connected to V_{ss} rather than the ground of the circuit.

When driving CMOS, the output voltage should be adjusted to a level that is well above the midpoint between V_{ss} and V_{dd}, but sufficiently below V_{dd} to assure that the input voltage does not exceed V_{dd}. A voltage of 80% to 90% of the difference between V_{ss} and V_{dd} will assure positive operation.

The voltage level of the output pulse can be set by using a dc voltmeter. Simply obtain a square output and measure the voltage. The peak voltage will be twice the measured voltage. When pulse width is varied, peak voltage will remain the same even though there will be a change in average voltage.

CMOS inputs require very little current. Therefore, any reasonable number of CMOS inputs can be driven without concern for the power required.

The +5-volt output can be used to calibrate a voltmeter or dc scope. This output has a 1000-ohm series resistor (*R2*) to prevent short-circuit damage. It is *not* intended for use as a power supply for other circuits.

An ac or dc scope can be voltage calibrated by setting the output pulse amplitude to 5 volts. Rotate the AMPLITUDE control to the point where the LEDs turn on. Peak voltage will be 5 volts, regardless of pulse width. If there is no load on the output, the TTL amplitude will also be 5 volts.

One of the two outputs can be adjusted to a frequency that is a submultiple of the other. Rotate the WIDTH control counterclockwise until the timer locks in on the submultiple desired, then continue counterclockwise rotation slightly to obtain the desired pulse width.

ductor, tightly twist together the fine wire conductors in each and lightly tin with solder. Pass the free end of the cord through the hole in the rear wall of the cabinet and secure it in place with a plastic strain relief, about 4 inches (102 mm) from the split point. Alternatively, line the hole with a rubber grommet, pass through the cord, and knot it about 4 inches (102 mm) from the split point, thereby eliminating the need for a strain relief.

Front-panel wiring in Fig. 23.5 is keyed to the components-placement diagram in Fig. 23.4. That is, numbered points in both figures mate with each other. Note in Fig. 23.4 that there are also several lettered points. These do not connect to similar points on the front panel but to the same lettered points on the circuit board itself. In essence, they are long jumpers but are treated as part of the cable wiring.

Study Figs. 23.4 and 23.5 before actually wiring the board to the front panel. Once you are satisfied you know what goes where, place the circuit board on the floor of the cabinet with one row of pads facing toward the front panel and the other row facing the power transformer.

Make the stranded wires that connect the board to the front panel 3 inches (76.2 mm) to 4 inches (102 mm) longer than really necessary to allow the board to be removed from the cabinet should troubleshooting ever be needed. Make the wire jumpers only as long as needed to route them through the cable harness.

As you proceed with wiring, make sure to isolate the common ground from the cabinet. If you do not and connect the generator to the negative supply of a circuit being driven, you may create a short circuit.

Once wiring is complete, mount the circuit board on ½ inch (12.7 mm) spacers to the floor of the cabinet. Then gather the wires together into a bundle and secure it every 1½ inches (38 mm) or so with plastic cable ties (or lace with cord) to form a neat cable harness.

Checkout

With *IC3, IC4, IC5,* and *IC7* still not installed on the board, plug the generator's line cord into an ac outlet and flip the POWER switch to on. The neon lamp should light. Now, referring to Figs. 23.3 and 23.2, measure the voltage at the points indicated in the power supply and at the supply pins of IC sockets. When you are satisfied that all is okay, turn off the power and unplug the line cord. Wait a minute or so for the capacitors to discharge. Then install the DIP ICs in their respective sockets, taking care to properly orient them and practicing safe handling procedures for CMOS *IC2.*

Plug the line cord back into the ac outlet and flip the POWER switch to ON. Set the RANGE switch to any of the generator's internal oscillator ranges and use an oscilloscope to check for the presence of a sawtooth waveform at the emitter of *Q1.*

Next, check each pulse generator as follows:

Set the PHASE controls to about the middle of their ranges. Using

the scope, check the outputs of the comparators in *IC3.* All should be delivering positive dc pulses. Rotate the PHASE controls while observing on the screen that the widths of the pulses vary as you do this.

A square-wave pulse should be observed at the outputs of *IC4* at pins 1 and 13. Set *S3 (S6)* to SQUARE and *S5 (S8)* to TTL. The output pulses at A and B OUTPUT terminals *BP6* and *BP7* should be square and have an amplitude of 5 volts. (This part of checkout will be easier to perform with a two-channel scope that can simultaneously display the outputs from generators A and B.) Set *S5 (S8)* to VARIABLE and rotate AMPLITUDE control *R22 (R36).* Observe that the amplitude of the displayed pulses varies between 1.2 and 12 volts and that *LED1 (LED2)* lights when the control is rotated past the 5-volt position. If this does not occur, measure the supply voltage at the output of *IC6 (IC8)* as the control is rotated.

Check for output pulses from both generators with all four frequency ranges and over the full range of the FREQUENCY control. Set the RANGE switch to LINE and check for 60 Hz output pulses. It may be necessary to rotate the PHASE control to a point below mid-position to obtain an output pulse. Set the RANGE switch to EXTERNAL and apply an appropriate signal to EXTERNAL input *BP4.* Rotate the PHASE control to a position that results in an output pulse.

Return the RANGE switch to the LINE position and rotate the PHASE controls as necessary to obtain output pulses. Set *S3 (S6)* to VARIABLE and *S4 (S7)* to SHORT. Slowly rotate WIDTH control *R19 (R33)* counterclockwise from its fully clockwise position. Observe

that the pulse, which will be almost equal to the period of the fully clockwise position, becomes shorter as the control is rotated counterclockwise.

Set the RANGE switch to its highest range and the FREQUENCY control to about the middle of its rotation. Set *S3 (S6)* to SQUARE and observe the square pulse output. Set *S3 (S6)* to VARIABLE and *S4 (S7) to* LONG. Rotate WIDTH control *R19 (R33)* fully clockwise and then slowly counterclockwise. As you do this, the pulse width will become narrower and continue to narrow until it suddenly becomes wide again and drops to half the original frequency. Further counterclockwise rotation will cause the pulse to narrow again until the frequency drops to a third of the original, and so on.

Feed the TRIGGER pulse output at *BP3* into the scope. You should observe a very narrow positive pulse with an amplitude of 5 volts. Because this pulse is very brief, it may be difficult to observe on the CRT screen. If your scope has a triggered-sweep capability, use this pulse to trigger the sweep while observing one of the output pulses. Note that the PHASE control varies the position of the pulse on the CRT screen.

For details on how to use the Dual Pulse Generator, refer to "Applications."

In Closing

From the foregoing, it should be obvious that this is no ordinary "experimenter's" instrument. With its two independently adjustable generators, it offers a flexibility not usually expected in an instrument that costs as little as this one does to build.

Part **8**

Electronic Designing

A hands-on approach to creating new circuits, using a water-pump controller as a design example

chapter 24

Circuit Design From Scratch

JULES H. GILDER

As an electronics hobbyist, you've probably assembled a few kits, put together some projects that have appeared in magazines, and maybe even "designed" your own projects from ideas borrowed from magazines and books. But have you ever wondered just how you go about designing a circuit from scratch? Where do you begin? How do you know what components to choose? How do you know how to interconnect the components?

If you've ever asked yourself these and similar questions, you're ready to take a big step. You can start with this chapter, which will show you how things are done, take you from the concept, through the intermediate design, and onto the final circuit-building stages.

The objective in designing a project comes from a specific need. Once you know *what* you want a project to do, you can map out the circuits that will accomplish the objective. So, let's assume that you need a controller that will turn on and off a pump to remove the water resulting from minor flooding in

your basement. This defines your need. Now you can proceed with the actual design stage.

Let's take the concept phase just a step further. Designing a control-

ler to turn on a pump when the water reaches a certain level isn't difficult. But having the pump continue operating when the water level drops below the high water level is another matter altogether. So, it would be wise to design into the controller the ability to turn on the pump when a certain high water level is reached and continue to operate until the water falls to some predetermined lower level. It should then turn off and remain off until the water once again rises to the high level. In addition, it would be nice if the two water levels at which the pump turns on and off could be easily adjusted.

Let's take things a step at a time:

Define the Task

Now that you know roughly what you want your project to do, you can flesh out things a little more. The first design step, then, is to define *exactly* what is to occur and in what sequence. To detect the water level electronically, you'll need some sort of sensor. For the time being, however, let's assume you have a device that will give an electrical signal when the required water level is reached.

Next, write down exactly what's going to happen when the pump is used. A handy way to do this is in tabular format, such as in Table 24.1. The first six entries define basic operation. In line 1, when no water is present or the water level is too low (no sensors covered with water), the pump should be off and the controller should keep it off. When water starts to rise and covers the low-water sensor, nothing should happen (line 2). Only when the water has risen to the high water mark and covers the second sensor (line 3) should the controller turn on the pump. Once the pump is on, it should remain on as long as both sensors are activated (line 4). As the pump drains the water and the level drops below the high-water mark (and sensor) but is still above the low-water mark, it should continue pumping (line 5). Finally, when the

pump reduces the level of the water to below the low-water mark, the pump should turn off (line 6).

Table 24.1. Make up a list of your needs.

	(A) Low Sensor	(B) High Sensor	(C) Pump Is on	(D) Turn or Keep on Pump
1.	Dry	Dry	No	No
2.	Wet	Dry	No	No
3.	Wet	Wet	No	Yes
4.	Wet	Wet	Yes	Yes
5.	Wet	Dry	Yes	Yes
6.	Dry	Dry	Yes	No
7.	Dry	Wet	No	Yes
8.	Dry	Wet	Yes	Yes

Lines 7 and 8 in Table 24.1 have been added as a safety measure that deals with the problem of a sensor failure. This feature tells the pump to turn on when rising water triggers the high-level sensor even if the low-level sensor fails and tells the system that conditions are dry.

Summarizing your needs in the tabular format shown in Table 24.1 completes the most important design phase. Knowing exactly what the circuit should do and when it should do it helps later on in determining if the circuit is working properly because it sets a standard against which to measure performance.

Design Approach

In addition to clarifying the function of the pump controller and summarizing its operation, Table 24.1 also helps you decide what approach should be taken for the design of the system. There are eight distinct conditions the controller circuit must meet. Looking at Columns A and B and then at columns C and D you can readily see that in each case only one of two possible conditions can exist—wet or dry in

columns A and B and yes or no in columns C and D. Since there are only two conditions with which the circuit must cope, you have a binary situation that suggests a *digital* approach to circuit design. On the other hand, if your definition of the task required continuous operation, such as generation of a voltage that varied in level with changing water level, an analog approach would have been more appropriate.

In digital circuits, only one of two conditions exist. Something is either on or off. To make the design rules universal, digital designers use easily recognizable symbols to define the on and off states. These symbols are the digits 1 and 0 for on and off, respectively. Hence, in Table 24.1, "wet" could be replaced by a 1 and "dry" by a 0. Rewriting Table 24.1 in binary yields Table 24.2.

Table 24.2. Truth table of your needs list.

	(A) Low Sensor	(B) High Sensor	(C) Pump Is on	(D) Turn or Keep on Pump
1.	0	0	0	0
2.	1	0	0	0
3.	1	1	0	1
4.	1	1	1	1
5.	1	0	1	1
6.	0	0	1	0
7.	0	1	0	1
8.	0	1	1	1

Rules of Logic. Before proceeding, it's important that you know something about digital logic and the digital elements that will perform the functions you wish to implement. So here's a short course on the subject.

Digital devices can perform several different types of operations called logical functions. The three most basic functions, upon which all the others are built, are known as the AND, OR, and NOT functions.

Understanding the principles of each of these operations will give you a firm foundation upon which to develop your digital design skills.

Let's look at the simplest first— the NOT function. This is simply a device that takes a single input and outputs the opposite of it. The diagram for the digital logic element that performs this function is shown in Fig. 24.1. If you feed a 0 into the NOT element, the output would be 0, as shown, and vice-versa. Hence, the output is *not* the same as the input, and thus the name for this logic element. Another name for the NOT element is "inverter."

In examining the symbol for the NOT element in Fig. 24.1, you will note that there is a small circle at the apex of the triangle. This circle is universally used in digital electronics to indicate a not or invert function. If there were no small circle at the apex of the triangle, the input and output would be identical and the device would be called a buffer. The purpose of the buffer is to isolate signals sent to it from other circuits.

In addition to assigning special symbols to each of the various logic operations, digital designers have devised a shorthand method of defining the logical operations that can be performed. As we did in Table 24.2, the summaries are in tabular format, using 1s and 0s to represent the two logic states. These summaries are called "truth tables." The NOT truth table is shown to the right in Fig. 24.1.

The next logic function we'll examine is the OR function, whose symbol is shown in Fig. 24.2, along with its truth table. An OR device must have two or more inputs and one output. When examining the symbol for the OR device (also known as the OR "gate"), note that there is no small circle at its output, indicating that no signal inversion takes place.

The rules of operation for the OR gate state that an output signal will occur if there is an input signal on any one or more input lines. Thus, examining the truth table for this device, if input A is 1 *or* input B is 1 *or* both inputs A and B are 1, the output (C) will also be 1. The only time there will be no output signal is when both input A and input B have no signal applied to them. In Fig. 24.2 only two inputs are shown to the OR gate. Actually an OR gate can have any number of inputs, though there is a practical limit to the number you'll find in available IC gate packages. Additional inputs would be added to the truth table as columns between input 2 and output. The same rules apply in any case. More than two inputs can be given to any of the logic elements discussed here *except* for the inverter and the buffer elements.

The last of the basic logic operations is the AND function. The symbol for this gate and its truth table are shown in Fig. 24.3. Like the OR gate, the AND gate must have two or more inputs and one output. The rules for operation of the AND gate state that an output signal will occur only if there are signals on *all* input lines simultaneously. If any one or more input lines doesn't have a signal on it, there will be *no* output.

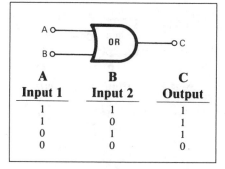

A Input 1	B Input 2	C Output
1	1	1
1	0	1
0	1	1
0	0	0

Fig. 24.2. The schematic/logic symbol and truth table for the OR gate.

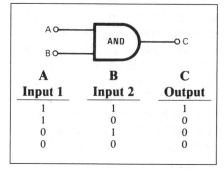

A Input 1	B Input 2	C Output
1	1	1
1	0	0
0	1	0
0	0	0

Fig. 24.3. The schematic/logic symbol and truth table for the AND gate.

Now that you're familiar with the basic building blocks used in digital circuit design, you must take your knowledge one small step further. That is, you should also be aware that there are complementary devices to the OR and AND devices, known as the NOR and NAND functions. Technically, these are the NOT OR and NOT AND functions and, as you may already have surmised, are implemented by combining NOT gates (inverters) with the standard OR and AND gates. The symbols for these two types of gates are given in Fig. 24.4. Note in the truth tables for each of these gates how the outputs differ from those in the truth tables in Figs. 24.2 and 24.3 with the same output conditions.

Reading a Truth Table. When you read a truth table, such as that for the NAND gate, you say that output C is equal to 1 when input A equals 1 and input B is not equal to 1, or when input A is not equal to 1

Fig. 24.1. The NOT gate is so named because its output is the opposite of its input. Hence, the NOT gate is also commonly referred to as an "inverter."

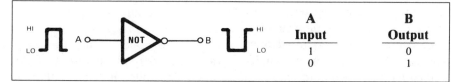

A Input	B Output
1	0
0	1

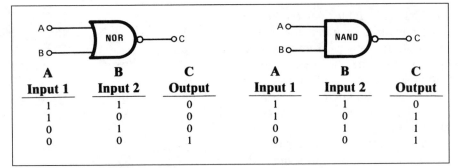

A Input 1	B Input 2	C Output
1	1	0
1	0	0
0	1	0
0	0	1

A Input 1	B Input 2	C Output
1	1	0
1	0	1
0	1	1
0	0	1

Fig. 24.4. Shown here are the schematic/logic symbol for the NOR *(left) and* NAND *(right) gates, along with the truth tables that define their operation.*

and input B is equal to 1, or when input A is not equal to 1 and input B is not equal to 1. This description of what's happening is awkward and doesn't lend itself to easy analysis or manipulation. To overcome this problem, English mathematician and logician George Boole in 1847 published a *Mathematical Analysis of Logic* pamphlet in which he stated a mathematical way of expressing the relationships between logical statements. Thus was born Boolean algebra.

In Boolean algebra, the AND function is represented by multiplication and the OR function by addition. The NOT function is represented by placing a bar over the variable that represents the input to the circuit. Thus, AB is read as A and B; A + B is read as A or B; and $\overline{A}$ is read as not $-A$, or the inverse of A.

Returning to the NAND truth table in Fig. 24.4, you begin writing the Boolean equation by first marking off only those rows that have a 1 in the output column, since all you're interested in are the conditions that generate an output. Now, working one row at a time, construct the equation. Since there are three rows that have a 1 in the output column, your equation will have three terms.

For the first term, C equals 1 if A equals 1 and B is not equal to 1:

$$C = A\overline{B}.$$

This is only part of the equation. Note that C also equals 1 if the condition in the next row is true or the condition in the last row is true. Since C = 1 for row 2 or row 3, a plus sign will be used to connect the terms in your equation. The next term comes from row 3 in the truth table. Here, C = 1 if A is not equal to 1 and B is equal to 1. Similarly, for row 4, C = 1 if A is not equal to 1 and B is not equal to 1. Therefore, the equation becomes

$$C = A\overline{B} + \overline{A}B + \overline{A}\,\overline{B}.$$

By writing the Boolean equation for your circuit, you have taken a major step in synthesizing digital circuits. From the previous equation, you can now use AND, OR, and NOT gates to construct the equation of a NAND gate, as shown in Fig. 24.5.

If you connect all As together and all Bs together in the Fig. 24.5 circuit and apply 1s and 0s to the circuit according to the truth table, you'll find that the output corresponds exactly with that in the truth table. Obviously, this is a rather complex, although functional, circuit. If you could simplify the equation so that it had fewer terms in it, your circuit would become simpler. Since you already know in advance that this function can be implemented with a NAND gate, you also

know that your equation can be reduced to only one term.

To simplify your equation, you'll have to use some rules of Boolean algebra. The ones you'll be using are:

1. $\overline{X} + X\overline{Y} = \overline{X} + \overline{Y}$
2. $\overline{XY} = \overline{X} + \overline{Y}$
3. $X(Y + Z) = XY + XZ$
4. $X + \overline{X} = 1$
5. $X + \overline{X}Y = X + Y$
6. $X + Y = \overline{\overline{X}\,\overline{Y}}$

Using these relationships, you can now simplify your equation, starting with:

$$C = A\overline{B} + \overline{A}B + \overline{A}\,\overline{B}.$$

Using rule 3, you get

$$C = A\overline{B} + \overline{A}(B + \overline{B}).$$

Then, from rule 4, you get:

$$C = A\overline{B} + \overline{A}.$$

And from rule 1, you get:

$$C = \overline{A} + \overline{B}.$$

Finally, from rule 2, you get:

$$C = \overline{AB}.$$

From the foregoing, you can see that the original equation for a NAND gate that was composed of AND, OR, and NOT gates has been reduced to an equation of one term, which represents the equation for a NAND gate. Similarly, the circuit in Fig. 24.5 reduces to the simplified NAND gate in Fig. 24.4.

Developing an Equation

Now that you know how to convert a truth table into an equation, you can proceed to the next step in your circuit design-converting the truth table that defines operation of the pump controller into an equation.

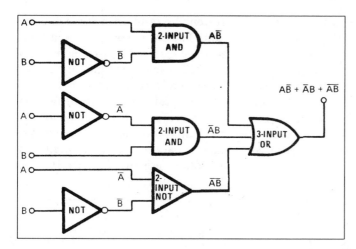

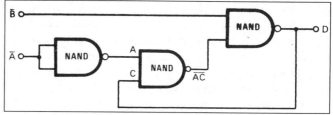

Fig. 24.6. The basic circuit of the water-pump controller has only three NAND *gates.*

Fig. 24.5. By using a combination of AND *and* OR *gates and inverters, you can construct a 2-input* NAND *gate, as shown here. Note the complexity of the circuit.*

You do this in the same way as you did for the NAND truth table.

Referring back to Table 24.2, you can see that the output column (D) has five rows in which 1s appear. This means that your equation will initially have five terms in it and that you're probably going to want to simplify it later. Using the same technique as before, you write out the equation as

$$D = AB\overline{C} + ABC + A\overline{B}C$$
$$+\overline{A}B\overline{C} + \overline{A}BC.$$

Next, using rule 3, you get

$$D = B(A\overline{C} + AC + \overline{A}\overline{C} + \overline{A}C)$$
$$+A\overline{B}C.$$
$$D = B[A(\overline{C} + C) + \overline{A}(\overline{C}+ C)] +$$
$$A\overline{B}C.$$

Now, using rule 4, you get

$$D = B(A + \overline{A}) + A\overline{B}C$$
$$D = B + A\overline{B}C.$$

Optimizing the Equation and Circuit

Although the last equation represents a considerable simplification of the original, implementation would require you to use a 3-input AND gate, an OR gate, and an inverter. Digital logic devices are typically sold with several gates per chip, and buying three chips to im-plement this function, while inexpensive, would be wasteful. Therefore, you should try to simplify your equation further.

To do this, you'll use rule 5, setting X = B and Y = AC. By substituting these values in the equation, you get

$$D = B + A\overline{B}C = B + AC.$$

Using rule 6 and again setting X = B and Y = AC, you get

$$D = \overline{\overline{B}\,\overline{AC}}$$

Now you have only one term, and only two NAND gates and a NOT gate are needed if the inputs from the water sensors supply inverted signals. This is great, because 2-input NAND gates come packaged four to an integrated circuit. Plus, if the two inputs to a NAND gate are shorted together, the gate operates like an inverter (see lines 1 and 4 in the NAND gate truth table in Fig. 24.4). Hence, you can construct the controller from a single integrated circuit and still have one NAND gate left over. The basic circuit is shown in Fig. 24.6.

Choosing an IC

Having decided on the design of the logic portion of the controller, you must now decide on what IC you're going to use to build the circuit. Unless you have specified reasons to do otherwise, I suggest you use a CMOS IC, because it requires very little power and is fairly insensitive to variations in supply voltage. (Any source that delivers up to +16 volts dc can be used to power a circuit built around a CMOS digital IC.)

The ideal choice of a CMOS IC for your controller is the 4011 quad 2-input NAND gate. If you prefer, however, you can substitute a 7400 TTL device for the 4011, but if you do, make certain that the voltage delivered to it from the power supply doesn't exceed 5.25 volts.

Interfacing to the Pump

You've completed the difficult part of designing your controller. Now all that's left to do is interface the controller to the real world. The first thing you must do is connect the controller to your pump. But you can't do this directly, since the controller can't deliver enough power to directly drive the pump, nor can it handle the ac power that the pump requires. Instead, you're going to design an "interface" circuit to accomplish your goal. In this case, the interface circuit consists of a driving transistor that takes the low current output from the logic circuit and amplifies it to operate a relay. In turn, the relay delivers ac line power to the pump.

The design of the interface circuit hinges upon your selection of a relay. Since it's assumed that you want low-power operation to permit use of a battery or perhaps an ac adapter from a tape recorder, a 5-volt relay with a 72-mA coil current (see Parts List) neatly fills the bill. The contacts of the specified relay are rated to handle 125 volts ac at 3 amperes, which is sufficient to handle most pumps. If your pump draws more than 3 amperes, choose a relay whose contacts will handle the higher load.

Choosing a transistor is your next step. Since the controller is going to output a positive voltage level (logic 1) when the pump should turn on, you need a transistor that will turn on when a voltage is applied to its base. Npn transistors operate this way. Your choice of transistor isn't critical; virtually any npn silicon device will do. The only thing you have to be careful about is to make sure that the maximum deliverable current from the transistor isn't lower than the current required to energize the relay's coil. Because the specified relay requires only 72 mA, a commonly available and low-cost 2N2222 transistor, with a maximum collector current rating of 800 mA, is a good choice here.

Since the relay's coil is an inductive device, on turn-on, it can generate a high-voltage spike that can damage the rest of the circuit. To obviate this possibility, you'll want to connect a diode across the coil. Again, your choice of diode isn't critical. In fact, just about any general-purpose rectifier diode will serve. A typical example is the 1N4148 diode specified in the Parts List.

Finally, a current-limiting resistor should be connected to the base of the transistor. Any resistor whose value is between 220 and 1000 ohms will do. A 470-ohm resistor is speci-fied because that's what I had on hand when I built my circuit.

Once you have the relay connected to the controller and operating properly, you must connect it to the pump. You can do this by simply placing the switching contacts of the relay between the "hot" side of the ac power line and the pump, as shown in Fig. 24.7.

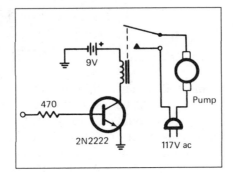

Fig. 24.7. Pump controller drive circuit.

The Water Sensor

You're now coming into the home stretch. There's just one more thing to do—design the water sensor—and the project will be complete.

There are lots of ways of determining when water reaches a certain level. Most of them rely on some sort of mechanical movement to turn on a switch. The preferable approach, however, is to use the simple, direct approach of electrical detection.

To detect the level of the water, you'll use two electrodes and take advantage of the fact that most of the water around isn't pure. Unless it's distilled, water almost always contains some impurities that convert it from a nonconductor to a modest conductor of electricity. When two probes (metal wires, bars, etc.) are placed in water and a battery is connected to them, a current will flow through the water.

A sensor requires two probes. One goes to the positive (+) side of the circuit's power supply, the other to some device that can use a low current to produce a switching action. The switching device is a transistor. Once again, you can use a 2N2222 transistor, since by design it's a switching device.

The circuit for the sensor portion of the project is the same as for the relay driver in the interface circuit, except that the relay is replaced by a 470-ohm resistor (Fig. 24.8). The

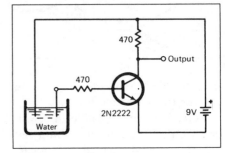

Fig. 24.8. Water sensor circuit.

output is taken from the point where the resistor joins the collector lead of the transistor ... identical to that for the NOT gate. Hence, the sensor circuit fulfills the inverted-output requirement for the controller's logic section.

Because your circuit is going to be detecting two water levels, it will need two identical sensors. The level adjustment is made by simply spacing the sensor wires at different levels. Since both sensors are to connect to the same circuit, it isn't necessary to have two separate wires from the positive side of the power supply. Once is sufficient. A convenient way to arrange the three probes is to fasten them to a piece of plastic (see Fig. 24.9), with the power lead and low-level sensor placed at the same level and the high-level sensor placed higher up.

Putting It All Together

Now that you've designed all the bits and pieces, you must construct the circuit. A complete schematic of the entire controller is shown in Fig. 24.10. Shown are all sensors, the

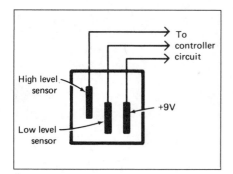

Fig. 24.9. Details of water sensor.

controller logic circuit, and pump interface. In fact, everything but the pump itself is shown. The reason for this is that, strictly speaking, the pump isn't part of the project. It's a device all its own, with its own ac power cord. This being the case, all you need to use the controller with the pump is a convenient way to plug it in, which is provided by the chassis-mount ac receptacle, *SO1*.

Construction of the project is simple and straightforward. The very few components that make up the circuit obviate the need for a printed-circuit board (though you can use one of your own design if you wish). The whole system can be hand-wired in about one-half hour on a piece of breadboard or a solderless socket.

The only thing you must be a bit cautious about during construction is the CMOS IC. This device can be permanently damaged by mishandling. But if you don't walk across a carpet on a dry day just before

handling the IC, you should have no problem—you can use an IC socket and keep the IC aside until everything is wired and ready to go.

Fig. 24.10. This is the overall schematic diagram of the water-pump controller. The only element not shown is the pump itself, which plugs into socket SO1.

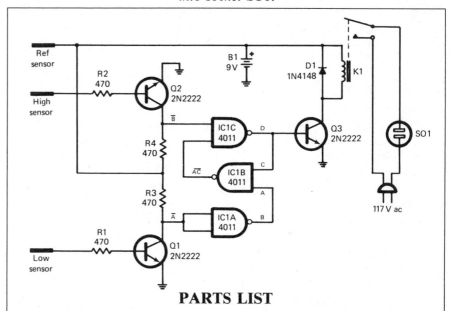

PARTS LIST

Semiconductors
D1—Rectifier diode (1N4148 or similar)
IC1—4001 CMOS NAND gate
Q1 thru Q3—2N2222 npn transistor
Resistors (¼-watt, 10%)
R1 thru R4—470-ohm
Miscellaneous
B1—9-volt battery
K1—5-volt dc spst relay (Radio Shack No. 275-246 or similar)

SO1—Chassis-mount ac receptacle
Printed circuit board (or perforated board and solder clips); socket for IC1; holder and connector for B1; suitable enclosure; ac line cord; rubber grommet (or line-cord strain relief); hookup wire; solder; machine hardware; etc.

How to use the popular LM386 IC in a variety of applications

chapter **25**

A Versatile Audio Amplifier Chip

MICHAEL A. COVINGTON

National Semiconductor's LM386 integrated circuit is an easy-to-use audio amplifier that delivers as much as 0.4 watt into an 8-ohm speaker load. You can use this 8-pin chip in such projects as receivers, intercoms, alarms, and all types of battery-operated audio equipment. In this chapter we'll explore how to use the LM386 effectively.

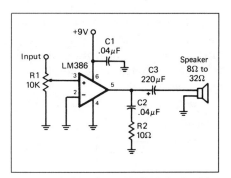

Fig. 25.1. Basic LM386 amplifier circuit. Place C1 as close as possible to the LM386 integrated circuit.

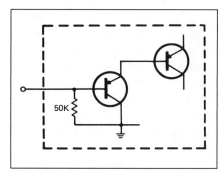

Fig. 25.2. An LM386 input's upside-down emitter-follower stage allows input voltage to swing below ground.

Low-Gain Amplifier

Figure 25.1 shows the simplest LM386 circuit, an amplifier with a voltage gain of 20. Its input can come from a tuner, a tape deck, or a crystal phono cartridge. (If you wish to drive this circuit from a magnetic cartridge, the LM386 circuit will have to be preceded by a preamplifier.) An output signal of about 400 millivolts peak-to-peak is sufficient to drive the speaker to full volume. This circuit is exactly what you need to use a speaker with a Sony Walkman or the like. Stereo sound, of course, requires two such amplifiers, one for each channel.

Harmonic distortion in this circuit is well below 0.5% almost up to maximum volume.

In the circuit shown, potentiometer *R1* serves as a volume control. Its value determines the input impedance, which can be anything from 500 to 20,000 ohms. The value of *C3* can range from about 50 microfarads (which gives rather poor bass response) up to 1000 microfarads or more. Capacitors *C1* and *C2* and resistor *R2* are needed to prevent high-frequency oscillation that would result in garbled sound. Although the manufac-

turer's literature states that these last three components are optional, I've found that trying to do without them is a very risky proposition. During assembly, be sure to keep all leads short and adequately isolate the input from the output.

If you use a 16-ohm or greater impedance speaker, supply voltage can be anywhere between 4 and 14 volts. With an 8-ohm speaker, however, keep supply voltage to less than 10 volts to prevent overheating the LM386. With a 4-ohm speaker, the supply should not exceed 7 volts.

It usually isn't practical to drive more than one speaker from a single LM386. However, if you must do so, connect the speakers in series rather than in parallel with each other to maintain a relatively high total impedance. The LM386 consumes very little power. The only significant power drawn by the circuit is what is actually delivered to the speaker. With no input, current consumption is typically 2 mA. At moderate volume this increases to 15 mA and can go as high as 70 mA at high volume or when driving a large speaker.

The LM386 looks a lot like an operational amplifier, but there are some important differences to keep in mind. For example, unlike an op amp, the LM386 requires only a single positive supply voltage. Also, the output at pin 5 is automatically biased to a dc level halfway between the supply voltage and ground, with C3 preventing dc from flowing through the speaker.

In an operational amplifier, the inputs would normally be at the same dc level as the output. But the inputs of the LM386 operate at ground level, and the input signal can swing to either side of ground. Figure 25.2 shows how this is achieved—the input stage is an emitter-follower whose "ground" is actually the positive supply voltage. The internal 50,000-ohm resistor sets maximum input impedance.

Like an op amp, the LM386 has both inverting and noninverting inputs (Fig. 25.3). In the low-gain circuit shown in Fig. 25.1, you can apply the signal to either input, depending on whether or not you want it to come out inverted. Inversion has no effect on sound quality, and there is little reason to prefer one configuration over the other. For other applications, such as higher-gain amplifiers and oscillators, only the noninverting configuration will work.

The LM386 performs best if the

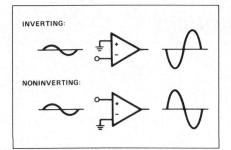

Fig. 25.3. In low-gain mode, LM386 can be used as inverter (upper) or noninverter (lower); high gain requires operation in noninverting mode.

dc resistance to ground from both inputs is roughly the same ("roughly" here means within 10,000 ohms or so). If you ground one input, you should provide a path from the other one to ground through a resistor (Fig. 25.4). If the input signal is coupled to the LM386 through a capacitor, so that there is no dc path to ground, the other input should be grounded through a capacitor or simply left unconnected.

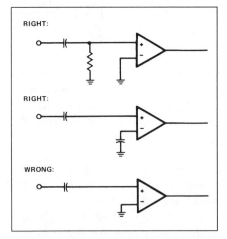

Fig. 25.4. For best results, provide a dc path from both inputs or neither.

High-Gain Amplifier

Figure 25.5 shows the LM386 configured as a high-gain amplifier, with a voltage gain of 200. The main change here is that C4 has been added to bypass an internal

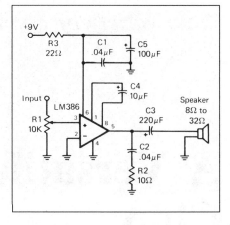

Fig. 25.5. In the high-gain mode, be sure to place C1 as close as possible to the IC, isolate input from output.

feedback resistor. Resistor R3 and capacitor C5 change the dynamic characteristics of the power supply.

Figure 25.6 shows why R3 and C5 are necessary. Without them, the LM386 suffers from noticeable distortion when driving a low-impedance (8- or 16-ohm) load. The distortion isn't affected by the signal level or the impedance of the signal source, nor by bypassing pin 7 to ground through a capacitor as suggested in the manufacturer's literature. In fact, the distortion surprised me so much that I tried two LM386s from different manufacturing lots, just to make sure I wasn't dealing with a defective IC.

Apparently, the explanation is that the LM386 is designed to be battery powered, and the internal resistance of the battery is figured into its feedback network. The internal resistance of a 9-volt battery is between 10 and 100 ohms, whereas the resistance of a well-regulated power supply is nearly zero. So R3 takes the place of the resistance of the battery, and C5 is the bypass capacitor that would normally be used with battery-powered equipment. If the power supply is in fact a battery, or if the load impedance is more than 32 ohms, R3 can be omitted.

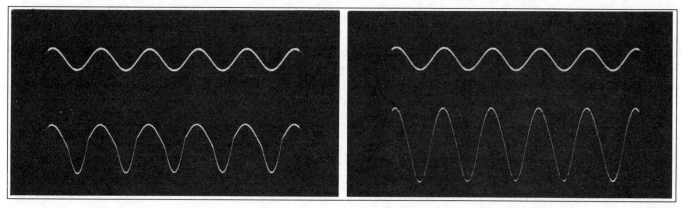

Fig. 25.6. Distortion in high-gain mode (left) is cured (right) by using R3 and C5 in Fig. 25.5. Top traces are input.

Even a gain of 200 isn't quite enough to drive a speaker with the signal from a microphone, tape head, or magnetic phono cartridge. As mentioned earlier for the Fig. 25.1 circuit, an extra stage of preamplification is required. If the LM286 and the preamplifier are connected to the same power supply, feedback may cause oscillation—usually an audio-frequency squeal or a low putt-putt sound ("motorboating"). Figure 25.7 shows how to prevent this. The resistors and capacitors send the incoming power down two paths that are isolated from each other.

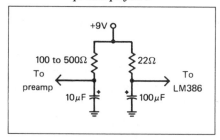

Fig. 25.7. Split power supply prevents feedback when using a preamplifier.

Figure 25.8 shows a complete amplifier for microphone-level input. Total voltage gain is about 4000. The transistor is the first stage can be any small-signal npn transistor with a beta (h$_{fe}$) of at least 50. For experiments, you can use a second 8-ohm speaker as a microphone; by

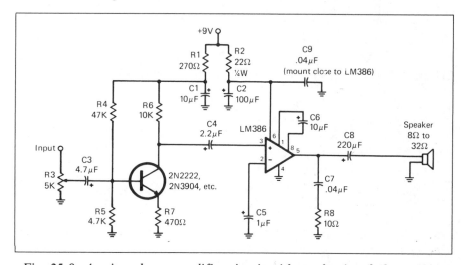

Fig. 25.8. A microphone amplifier circuit with total gain of about 4000.

doing this and adding a switch to interchange the two speakers, you have an intercom. In a high-gain circuit like this, it is doubly important to keep leads short and isolate the input from the output.

Oscillator Configuration

Finally, Fig. 25.9 shows how to use the LM386 as an oscillator. The output is a square wave with a frequency (in hertz) of $2.5/(R_t C_t)$ where R_t is between 10,000 and 100,000 ohms. Because the circuit is designed to oscillate, the anti-oscillation measures used in the amplifier circuits aren't needed here, and the power supply voltage isn't critical. Also, since linear amplification isn't required, pins 1 and 8 can be

Fig. 25.9. This is an LM386 square-wave generator. A speaker can replace R3.

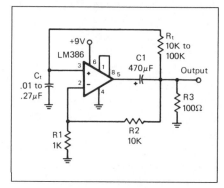

joined by a direct connection, rather than through a capacitor.

If you connect a speaker in place of R3 in this circuit, the output is no longer a square wave. Instead, what you hear will be a loud, piercing squeal that makes a good alarm sounder. The LM386 is an efficient noisemaker. It delivers a lot of sound for a small amount of battery power. To reduce the volume of the sound, connect a 10- to 300-ohm resistor in series with the speaker.

Going Further

Once you've mastered the LM386, you'll want to look at several of its relatives in the National Semiconductor line. the LM389 consists of an LM386 plus three individual npn transistors, all on one chip. This IC is often used to save space in radio receivers. The popular LM380 is a 2.5-watt power amplifier that requires a 12-to-15-volt supply and delivers a voltage gain of 50. Stepping up to the LM380's big brother, you come to the LM384, which delivers a hefty 5 watts of output from a 20-volt supply. You can begin immediately experimenting with the LM380 and LM384, since their external circuitry differs only in minor details from that of the LM386.

This simple op-amp circuit gives frequently overlooked attention to the outputs of your projects.

chapter 26

A Universal Rear End

JOSEPH J. CARR

One of the major failings of hobbyist-designed projects, and not a few supposedly professionally designed instruments, is inadequate attention to the rear-end circuitry. In most instruments, the really neat circuits are in the front end. So by the time you get to the rear end, you think of it as just the output section and, thus, don't give it much consideration. But proper design of the back end of an electronic instrument/control circuit can spell the difference between ho-hum operation and a really useful project.

In this chapter, we'll explore how to build a "Universal Rear End" you can actually use in your designs.

Terminology

Before we begin, let's get a little terminology straight by defining what is meant by the terms "front end" and "rear end." In electronics parlance, the front end of an instrument or other device is the section where input signals are received.

Typical examples of front ends are the r-f amplifier in a communications receiver, a transducer amplifier in a temperature monitor, and the differential amplifier in an ECG (electrocardiogram) amplifier or Wheatstone bridge transducer circuit. Almost all signal processing and shaping are performed in the so-called front end.

Though less glamorous than the front end, the rear end is nevertheless very important in overall instrument and project design. By definition, the rear end is the section that contains the output stage(s).

About the Circuit

Shown in the schematic diagram in Fig. 26.1 is a semi-universal rear-end circuit I've used professionally in numerous cases. I've built this circuit into physiological (biopotential) amplifiers, transducer amplifiers, and numerous other projects. The circuit has several very useful features: it has (1) gain when $R2$ is greater than 10,000 ohms (otherwise gain is unity); (2) a gain control with a range of 0 to 1 or 0 to A_v; (3) a dc balance control/offset null; and (4) a position control.

The circuit is built around two 1458 operational amplifiers, each of which contains a pair of 741-family op amps in an 8-pin miniDIP package. Any other standard op amp will also work here, though use of the 1458 has the advantage of reducing parts count and wiring times.

Power for this circuit must be from a bipolar source that delivers both positive-to-ground (V+) and negative-to-ground (V−) dc. Potentials between ±4.5 and +15 volts dc will serve nicely.

The circuit in the schematic diagram consists of four inverting followers in cascade. As arranged, it serves overall as a noninverting follower. Removing any one stage (IC1B recommended) will make the circuit into an inverting follower, since there would be an odd number of inverting stages.

The gain of an inverting follower operational amplifier stage is set by the ratio of the feedback and input resistors. For example, the gain of stage *IC1A* is *−R2/R1,* where the negative sign indicates that inversion (180-degree phase reversal) is taking place. Similarly, the gain of *IC1B* is *−R6/R5;* of *IC2A,* *−R8/R7* and of *IC2B,* *−R10/R9.* Overall gain for the entire circuit is simply the product of all the individual gains, or $A_{vt} = A_{V1} \times A_{V2} \times A_{V3} \times A_{V4}$.

Since all gains in the circuit shown are unity, overall gain is one. However, you can increase or decrease the overall gain by varying individual stage gains. The recommended procedure is to vary the gain of fixed stage *IC1B*. In this case, you can assume that the gain of the overall circuit will be *−R6/R5*. Leave *R5*'s value at 10,000 ohms in most cases, unless it's impossible to find a value for *R6* that will result in the correct gain without modifying the value of *R5*. In any event, don't let the value of *R5* become less than 100 ohms. The rules for changing the gain are: (1) unity gain: leave as is (*R5=R6*=10,000 ohms); (2) for less than unity gain, *R5* is greater than *R6* (e.g., if *R5*=10,000 ohms and *R6*=2000 ohms, gain is 2,000/10,000 or 0.20); (3) for greater than

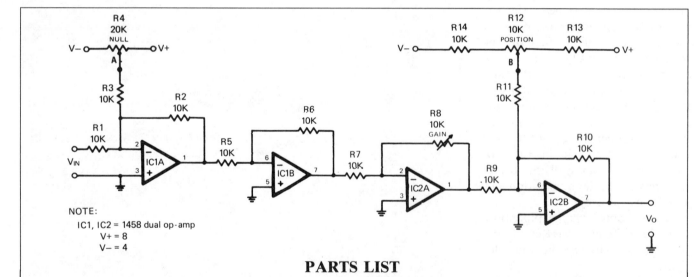

PARTS LIST

Semiconductors
IC1, IC2—1458 dual op amp (see text)
Resistors 1/4-watt, 10%
R1, R2, R3, R5, R6, R7, R9, R10, R11—10,000-ohm
R4—20,000-ohm, linear-taper potentiometer

R6, R12—10,000-ohm, linear-taper potentiometer
R13, R14—See text
Miscellaneous
Printed-circuit board or perforated board with solder posts; 8

pin DIP sockets (2); control knobs (3); input, output, and power connectors; suitable enclosure; machine hardware; hookup wire; solder; etc.

Fig. 26.1. The schematic diagram of A Universal Rear End.

unity gain, $R5$ is less than $R6$ (e.g., if $R5 = 10,000$ ohms and $R6 = 100,000$ ohms, gain is $100/10=10$).

Gain control $R8$ is used to vary overall gain of the circuit from zero to full. If the values are as shown in the schematic, $R8$ varies the gain from 0 to 1. This potentiometer is usually a front panel control and is accessible to the user of the project.

Null control $R4$ is used to cancel the effects of dc offsets created both in this circuit and in previous stages. It also provides the dc balance effect noted earlier. The dc balance controls on some instruments are used to cancel the change of output baseline as the sensitivity control is varied—a most disturbing effect to someone making a measurement! Potentiometer $R4$ is adjusted using a dc output meter at V_o, and is adjusted until there's no shift in dc output when $R8$ is varied through its full range. If there are dc offsets present in the input signal (V_{in}), there will be such a shift noted in output.

The function of $R4$ is to provide an equal but opposite polarity offset signal to cancel the offset from all other sources. In some cases, there might be 10,000-ohm resistors (similar to $R13$ and $R14$ near $R12$) between the end of the potentiometer and the power supply potentials. These resistors reduce the offset range, while increasing the resolution of the adjustment. Use these resistors only if there's a problem in homing in on the correct value.

Position control $R12$ is optional. It's normally used when the output signal is to be displayed on an analog paper chart recorder or dc CRT oscilloscope. Potentiometer $R12$ provides an international offset to final stage $IC2B$ independent of the input signal. It's used to position the output waveform anywhere on the scope's or chart recorder's vertical axis.

In some cases, the range of $R12$ may be too great. Only a small adjustment of the potentiometer will send the trace off the screen. You can counteract this problem with the simple expedient selecting of values for $R13$ and $R14$ (note that $R13=R14$) that allow the trace to just disappear off the top when the $R12$ reaches the limit of its upward travel and off the bottom when the potentiometer reaches its lower limit.

Adjustment

Adjustment of this circuit requires either a dc voltmeter or a dc-coupled oscilloscope that has a scale grid on the screen or graticule to permit potentials to be read. If an oscilloscope is used for that purpose (set the switch to GND in AC/GND/DC arrangements), and set the trace to exactly the center of the vertical lines on the grid. Select a sweep speed that yields a nonflickering line. Next, place the switch into the DC position. The vertical deflection factor should be around 0.5 volt/division.

Now, follow this procedure:

1. Disconnect V_{in} from the front-end circuit and short this input to ground.

2. Using a dc voltmeter, set the potential at point "A" to 0.00 volt.

3. Similarly, set the potential at point "B" to 0.00 volt.

4. Set $R8$ to maximum resistance (highest gain).

5. Make all adjustments to the front-end circuits as needed and then return to the rear-end circuit.

6. Adjust $R8$ through its range from 0 to 10,000 ohms several times while monitoring scope or meter connected to the output. If the output potential shifts, adjust $R4$ until the shift is cancelled. You'll have to continually run $R8$ through its range while adjusting $R4$. Because this adjustment is somewhat interactive, try it several times, or until no further improvement is attainable.

7. Check the range of the position control.

In Closing

The universal rear-end circuit is a simple project that can give your instrument and control projects that final "professional" touch that makes them more useful to you and anyone else who uses them.

MORE
FROM
SAMS

☐ **The Howard W. Sams Crash Course in Digital Technology**   *Louis E. Frenzel, Jr.*
Back by popular demand, the "crash course" format is applied to digital technology. This concise volume provides a solid foundation in digital fundamentals, state of the art components, circuits, and techniques in the shortest possible time. It builds the specific knowledge and skills necessary to understand, build, test, and troubleshoot digital circuitry. No previous experience with digitals is necessary.
ISBN: 0-672-21845-3, $19.95

☐ **IC Timer Cookbook (2nd Edition)**
Walter C. Jung
You can learn lots of ways to use the IC timer in this second edition which includes many new IC devices. Ready to use applications are presented in practical working circuits. All circuits and component relationships are clearly defined and documented.
ISBN: 0-672-21932-8, $17.95

☐ **Design of Op-Amp Circuits with Experiments**   *Howard M. Berlin*
An experimental approach to the understanding of op amp circuits. Thirty-five experiments illustrate the design and operation of linear amplifiers, differentiators and converters, voltage and current converters, and active filters.
ISBN: 0-672-21537-3, $12.95

☐ **Design of Phase-Locked Loop Circuits with Experiments**   *Howard M. Berlin*
Learn more about TTL and CMOS devices. This book contains a wide range of lab-type experiments which reinforce the textual introduction to the theory, design, and implementation of phase-locked loop circuits using these technologies.
ISBN: 0-672-21545-4, $12.95

☐ **Electronic Prototype Construction**
Stephen D. Kasten
Breadboarding can be fun. Learn contemporary construction and design methods for building your working prototypes. Discusses IC-based and microcomputer-related schematics and ideas for evaluation and testing. Techniques include wirewrapping, designing, making, and using double-sided PC boards; fabricating enclosures, connectors, and wiring; and screen printing the panels, chassis, and PC boards.
ISBN: 0-672-21895-X, $17.95

☐ **IC Op-Amp Cookbook (3rd Edition)**
Walter G. Jung
Hobbyists and design engineers will be especially pleased at this new edition of the industry reference standard on the practical use of IC op amps. This book has earned respect in the industry by its comprehensive coverage of the practical uses of IC op amps, including design approaches and hundreds of working examples. The third edition has been updated to include the latest IC devices, such as chopper stabilized, drift-trimmed BIFETS. The section on instrumentation amps reflects the most recent advances in the field.
ISBN: 0-672-22453-4, $21.95

☐ **Electronic Instruments: Instrumentation Training Course (3rd Edition)**   *Dale R. Patrick*
Technicians will learn to understand and use electronic instruments, including the latest digital instruments and computer-based systems used in industry today. Geared toward those in industrial training programs and technical schools, this book can also be used as an introduction for those with no prior electronics or math background. Beginning with a general introduction to electricity, the text moves on to real instruments, covering each piece of equipment's operation, circuitry, and uses. Topics covered include measurement circuits and primary devices, power supplies, amplifiers, digital electronics, transmitters, electronic controllers, converters, and computer-based systems.
ISBN: 0-672-22482-8, $21.95

☐ **How to Build Speaker Enclosures**
Alexis Badmaieff and Don Davis
A practical guide to the whys and hows of constructing high quality, top performance speaker enclosures. A wooden box alone is not a speaker enclosure — size, baffling, sound insulation, speaker characteristics, and crossover points must all be carefully considered.
ISBN: 0-672-20520-3, $6.95

☐ **Modern Recording Techniques (2nd Edition)**
Robert E. Runstein and David Miles Huber
Engineers and students alike will find this a valuable guide to state-of-the-art developments and practices in the recording industry. This revised edition reflects all the latest equipment, controls, acoustics, and digital effect devices being used in modern recording studios. It explores the marriage of video and audio multi-track studios and illustrates sound and studio capabilities and limitations.
ISBN: 0-672-22451-8, $18.95

☐ **Principles of Digital Audio**
Ken C. Pohlmann
Here's the one source that covers the entire spectrum of audio technology. Includes the compact disk, how it works, and how data is encoded on it. Illustrates how digital audio improves recording fidelity. Starting with the fundamentals of numbers, sampling, and quantizing, you'll get a look at a complete audio digitization system and its components. Gives a concise overview of storage mediums, digital data processing, digital/audio conversion, and output filtering. Filled with diagrams and formulas, this book explains digital audio thoroughly, yet in an easy-to-understand style.
ISBN: 0-672-22388-0, $19.95

☐ **Fiber Optics Communications, Experiments, and Projects**   *Waldo T. Boyd*
Another Blacksburg tutorial teaching new technology through experimentation. This book teaches light beam communication fundamentals, introduces the simple electronic devices used, and shows how to participate in transmitting and receiving voice and music by means of light traveling along slender glass fibers.
ISBN: 0-672-21834-8, $15.95

☐ **Digital Logic Circuits: Tests and Analysis**   *Robert G. Middleton*
No experience is necessary to learn digital circuitry with this book by performing basic digital tests and measurements as efficiently as possible.
ISBN: 0-672-21799-6, $16.95

☐ **Fun Way Into Electronics**   *Dick Smith*
This three volume series features 50 introductory projects for beginning electronics enthusiasts. Beginning with Volume 1 and continuing through the series, each project is designed as an instructional building block allowing the beginner to progress to more sophisticated projects. Each book features easy-to-understand, concise construction methods and descriptions, providing a rewarding learning program.

Volume 1: Includes 20 introductory projects including basic materials and tools, component descriptions, component codes, guide to successful projects, component listing, and other projects.
ISBN: 0-672-22548-4, $9.95